The cooperative housekeeping movement of the nineteenth and early twentieth centuries set out to improve women's lives through domestic revolution. The cooperative home, with private rooms centred on a core of communal facilities, was to take the place of the private house. The movement was at its peak in the early years of the twentieth century when connected with the Garden City and arts and crafts movements. Several cooperative homes, including some designed by women, survive today and are popular because they combine the qualities of privacy and community. This book traces the social and architectural history of the movement, which, in spite of government opposition, marked the start of a domestic revolution which is not yet complete.

Lynn F. Pearson is an architectural historian. She has degrees in physics, physical education and sociology, and has held posts at the Hull School of Architecture and the Centre for Urban and Regional Studies, University of Birmingham. She is the author of *The Organization of the Energy Industry*.

THE ARCHITECTURAL AND SOCIAL HISTORY OF COOPERATIVE LIVING

The Architectural and Social
History of Cooperative Living

Lynn F. Pearson

St. Martin's Press   New York

First Published in the United States of America in 1988

Printed in Hong Kong

ISBN 0-312-01293-4

Library of Congress Cataloging-in-Publication Data
Pearson, Lynn F.
The architectural and social history of cooperative living.
Bibliography: p.
Includes index.
1. Communal living—Great Britain—History.
I. Title.
HQ972.G7P43   1988   307.7'74   87-26409

ISBN 0-312-01293-4

Contents

List of Figures

List of Plates

All photographs copyright the author unless otherwise stated.

Acknowledgements

I would first of all like to thank the Economic and Social Research Council, who provided the funding for the research fellowship at the Centre for Urban and Regional Studies (CURS), University of Birmingham in 1983–4 which enabled this book to be written. Professor Gordon E. Cherry of CURS provided support, ideas and encouragement during my work on the book, and with Christopher Watson of CURS was instrumental in guiding the project through its initial stages. I am indebted to them both for their interest in this book. I would also like to thank the staff of CURS Library and the University of Birmingham Library, particularly the Inter-library Loans section, without whose efficient service this research would have been severely impaired.

I want to thank some long-suffering friends who saw this work from its very early stages, especially Jenny Brennan who was first to encourage me to pursue this line of research. Frances Anderson added constructive criticisms which helped change my initial ideas into a research proposal, Helene Hogg bought me endless lunches and Janet Smith endured several long conversations. Throughout the research and writing of the book, Caroline Moseley offered constant support, ideas and willingness to discuss even its smallest details, for which I am deeply grateful. Lastly, Sam the dog succeeded in preventing me from becoming totally immersed in cooperative housekeeping.

I have an academic debt to Dolores Hayden for her work on *The Grand Domestic Revolution* (referred to in the text), as this was one of the inspirations behind my investigation of the English cooperative housekeeping movement. I would finally like to thank the large number of people and institutions who contributed to this work in one or more ways, by allowing me to inspect and/ or to reproduce material in their collections, or by giving their time and information. The study relied enormously on access to a wide variety of archives and personal reminiscence, and I am very grateful to the following: Ian Allan Group Ltd, Ambleside Tourist Information Office, County of Avon Planning Department, BAAS, Borough of Barnet Engineer and Surveyor's Department, Mr A. H. Beatty, Bell and Hymans Ltd, City of Birmingham

Reference Library, Mr and Mrs Hugh Bidwell, University of Birmingham Library, Bournville Village Trust, David Brightwell, British Architectural Library, BAL Drawings Collection, Building Societies Association, Miss Bury, Doreen Cadwallader, Jane V. Dansie and the Essex County Council, Roy Evans and the Letchworth Settlement, Miss V. G. Exton, Fabian Society, Fawcett Library, Neville Fay, First Garden City Museum, Mrs Stella Goldman of the Hummingbird Housing Association, Brigid Grafton Green, Guildford Museum, Guildhall Library, Hampshire County Libraries, Hampstead Garden Suburb Archives Trust, Philip Henslowe, Hertfordshire County Council, Hertfordshire County Council Record Office, Housing Corporation (all regions), Howard Cottage Society, M. R. Hughes, Imperial War Museum Department of Printed Books, Kenneth Johnson, George F. D. Jones, Miss K. M. Kaye, the Labour Party Library, Paul Larkin and Runnymede Borough Council, Helen Lloyd, London City and Westcliff Properties Ltd, Valerie Marett, Mr McBride, Rosemary Melvin, Mervyn Miller, T. E. Morgan, Mount Provincial Developments Ltd, Stella Mary Newton, Nuffield College Library, Onslow Village Ltd, Mr and Mrs K. Pegg, Mrs Petherick, Margaret Pooley, Public Record Office, Alison Ravetz, Registry of Friendly Societies, David N. Robinson, Mr J. Rogers, Philip Sharp, Mrs G. Shaw, Kathleen Slack, Ken Spinks, Jane Sutton, Miss L. Tetley, Elaine Tickel, Town and Country Planning Association, Kathleen Vinall, the Venerable Geoffrey Walton, Welwyn Hatfield District Council, Nina West, Mr and Mrs Woollons, Miss Wright. Transcripts of Crown-copyright records in the Public Record Office appear by permission of the Controller of HM Stationery Office.

Lynn F. Pearson
Whitley Bay

1 The Nineteenth-century Home and its Alternatives

Cooperative housekeeping was a system for improving the quality of home life, in which several households of one or more people combined to share the costs and labour involved in providing themselves with services such as cooking, laundry and cleaning. Households retained their individual homes and privacy, but ate some meals in a communal dining room and shared other communal facilities. Ideally, cooperative homes would be situated close together, and centred on a specially-built complex of buildings containing the dining room, central kitchen and common room. Cooperative housekeeping was possible for households with or without servants, but if servants were involved they would live in the central building rather than in their employers' homes. The aim of the system was to allow households to combine resources to achieve economic and other domestic improvements, but it could be portrayed as the first step towards communal living and socialism, or as a purely economic measure.

Its popularity as an idea widely discussed in England in the nineteenth and early twentieth centuries reflects the difficulties of conventional domestic life in those years, and the broad spectrum of political views which cooperative housekeeping could be adapted to serve. Fifteen cooperative housekeeping developments were begun between 1874 and 1925, but this small number belies their importance. These exemplary developments showed that domestic life was not immutable, their existence acting as a focus for women's consideration of the possibilities opened up by change in their lifestyles and immediate environments.

Urban and rural working-class housing in the early nineteenth century was generally of a very low standard. In towns, families might live in cellar rooms or in tenement houses, renting a single room or floor; at best, a 'one down, one up' or 'two down, two up' back-to-back could be rented.[1] Cooking was normally carried out over an open fire or, towards the middle of the century, a

1

small iron range, but there was no piped water supply and houses were tightly packed together around unpaved courts.[2] Water had to be carried from pumps or taps, private pumps being kept locked and used only by those who paid to do so. Fetching and carrying water from public pumps took a considerable amount of time and effort:

> A man had to fetch water from one of the public pumps in Bath, the distance from his house being about a quarter of a mile, – 'It is as valuable', he said, 'as strong beer. We can't use it for cooking, or anything of that sort, but only for drinking and tea.' 'Then where do you get water for cooking and washing?' – 'Why, from the river. But it is muddy, and often stinks bad, because all the filth is carried there.'[3]

This quotation from the Chadwick Report of 1842 was typical of its descriptions of appalling housing conditions. The report was intended to shock the public and therefore concentrated upon the worst examples of overcrowding and the effects of the general lack of sewers and sinks.[4] Medical officers and other officials reported on the extreme overcrowding of small rooms, which was a problem in both town and country. In one Bedfordshire village,

> Very few of the cottages were furnished with privies that could be used . . . Scarcely any cottage was provided with a pantry, and I found the provisions generally kept in the bed-rooms. In several instances I found whole families, comprising adult and infant children with their parents, sleeping in one room.[5]

Reports of 12 to 14 people sharing a single bedroom were frequent.

A wide variety of housing was occupied by the working class in the first half of the nineteenth century, ranging in quality from the worst of the slums to the growing number of through terrace houses built for skilled artisans.[6] House plans differed in detail throughout the country, but the general pattern of domestic life for many working-class people in the early part of the century was that of existence in one room.[7] Facilities for cooking and washing were totally inadequate and space was severely restricted. Outside the dwelling, the network of courts and alleys formed a semi-public space in which certain facilities such as the privy, water supply and washhouse were shared.[8] Meals were still a communal activity in many areas in the early nineteenth century; in 1832, workers at Manchester cotton factories ate from a communal dish, while in the middle of the century in Yorkshire, soup was eaten from plate-sized depressions cut into the dining table.[9]

In the early part of the century, married women often combined paid work with their domestic responsibilities, but by the 1840s the number of women working solely in the home on domestic tasks had begun to increase. Women came to be seen primarily as mothers rather than paid workers, and employment outside the home was viewed as detrimental to the family.[10] Whether or not women worked outside the home, the responsibility for the performance of domestic work lay with them. Only in rare instances, such as the young, single farmworkers of Northumberland, were women relieved of all duties in the home.[11] By the end of the nineteenth century the doctrine of feminine domesticity had become widespread amongst working-class families, and housing standards were improving.[12] As working-class standards of living rose, households could afford to rent larger homes, often a four- or five-roomed through terrace house.[13] As the amount of space available to each household expanded, rooms were allotted particular functions; instead of an all-purpose living room, a household might have a parlour, living room and scullery. Improved sanitation, gas and piped water were introduced into the working-class home towards the end of the century, decreasing the drudgery involved in domestic work and permitting higher standards of cleanliness.[14]

An alternative to the increasingly domesticated lifestyle of the nineteenth-century working-class woman was provided in the communities set up by various political and religious groups.[15] Their philosophies varied widely, but many of the communities aimed to reform the performance of domestic work and encourage communal life.[16] The Owenite socialists concentrated particularly on collectivising living arrangements and socialising domestic work, thus breaking down the isolation of the individual family.[17] The Owenites established seven communities in England, Scotland and Ireland between 1821 and 1845, as well as conducting several less formal experiments in communal living.[18] The first of the communities to be set up was that of the Cooperative and Economical Society in Clerkenwell, London, in 1821. The aim was to create a community for 250 families, and although only 21 families joined, the experiment lasted until 1824.[19] A year after its foundation, the community was reported to be making good progress. Families contributed to a common fund for most expenses, and

> The domestic duties of the females are performed under a system of combination, which greatly lessens the labour, and enables the females either to be profitably employed, or to command a considerable portion of leisure for rational pursuits and innocent recreations.[20]

The women's communal performance of domestic tasks enabled them to gain enough time to look after the community's children during the whole of the day; men took no part in domestic work.

The largest Owenite community was founded at Orbiston, near Glasgow, in 1825. It lasted until 1827, during which time one wing of the building, originally planned for 200 families, with a central kitchen and bakehouse, was erected. Over 300 people lived in the community at its height and the communal eating arrangements, which had begun rather chaotically, eventually improved although those families eating separately profited from the sytem. The overall organisation of the community was poor, and the original ideal of improved domestic life was never attained.[21] Orbiston's originator suggested that the community's building should be equipped with labour-saving devices such as a lift from the kitchen to the dining room and shoe-cleaning machinery. The communities at Manea Fen and Harmony Hall also emphasised this technological approach to labour saving; prospective members of the community at Manea Fen in the Isle of Ely (1838–41) were told that

> The food will be cooked by a scientific apparatus; thus saving an immense labour to the females; . . . Machinery, which has hitherto been for the benefit of the rich, will be adopted in the colony for lessening labour.[22]

Harmony Hall (1839–45) near Salisbury was the official Owenite community project, and was equipped by Robert Owen himself with an extravagant building which included an expensively fitted kitchen connected to the dining room by a small railway.[23] The women's workload at Harmony Hall was heavy, particularly before the new hall was built. A male observer commented that:

'The women, too, are untiring in their exertions, and most kind to each other; in fact, a complete sisterly feeling prevails . . .'[24] Women in several of the Owenite communities, including Harmony Hall, became discontented with their burden of domestic duties, but this did not lessen their commitment to the communities themselves.[25] The working-class women who joined the communities were ultimately disappointed in their search for a new method of organising domestic work; although domestic duties were performed communally, they were performed by the women alone. Women were sometimes able to take part in other work for the community after domestic work was finished, but women's responsibility for domestic work was never challenged.

Urban working-class families who were dissatisfied with their housing conditions, but who did not want to replace the forced communality of the city by communal living on a voluntary basis, were offered a means of escape to the country by the Chartist Land Company, which existed from 1845 to 1851. The company was launched by Feargus O'Connor, a leader of the Chartist movement which advocated universal male suffrage; to mainstream Chartists, the Land Company appeared peripheral, but in retrospect it seems that the company was important to the continued unity of the movement.[26] The idea behind the company was that it would sell a large number of cheap shares, using the capital raised to purchase land and build cottages. Subscribers would then be eligible to enter a lottery through which the plots of land would be allocated. Colonists would pay rent on their two to four acres of land and their cottage, and it was hoped that the tenants would be able to support themselves by farming.[27] The scheme was very popular, attracting over 70 000 subscriptions, and eventually five communities were set up, mainly in the south midlands, and ranging in size from 25 to 73 plots of land. In 1847, a single share cost only £1 6s 0d and could be paid for in weekly instalments of 3d, thus enabling artisan families to participate in the scheme, as well as a small number of women.[28] Three tenants at the last settlement to be established, Great Dodford in Worcestershire (1848), were single women.

O'Connor designed a cottage for the colonists, a three-room bungalow well provided with outbuildings for farm work. The central kitchen was flanked by a sitting room and bedroom, and a door led from the rear of the kitchen to the washhouse and another door from there to the small yard at the rear.[29] The cottages were well designed for their purpose, and many are still in use today.[30] Women colonists had to combine their domestic duties with extra farm work; at O'Connorville, the first community established in 1846, a quarter of the original settlers left within a year, partly because the women were not used to dairy work and could not bake bread.[31] Some of the settlers were successful, however, and the improvement in living conditions was appreciated.[32]

The voluntary communalism of the Owenite communities and the individualism of the Chartist settlements provided alternatives to town life for the working-class household, which normally had to endure the forced sharing of facilities, uncomfortable housing conditions and industrial surroundings. Both types of settlement offered an opportunity to escape from authority and to attempt to become self-sufficient.[33] Although the actual number of settlers and communalists was small, there was great interest in the Owenite and Chartist movements themselves. The Land Company presented householders with a chance to improve their housing conditions without changing their lifestyle from individual to communal living, and this may have appealed to many town-dwellers who had seen the practical difficulties of sharing facilities. As working-class housing standards slowly rose towards the end of the nineteenth century, more households could obtain decent housing within the towns. Industrial villages, such as Egerton (1829), Akroydon (1859) and later Port Sunlight (1888) and Bournville (1895) were erected by philanthropic industrialists to house their workers and ensure the availability of a healthy workforce.[34] Neither the participants in alternative communities nor the conventional town-dwellers made any consistent attempt to reorganise domestic work on a more equitable basis between men and women. The first priority for working-class households was a decent home; ultimately facilities might be shared out of choice, but after many years of cramped living conditions, with minimal private outdoor space, any suggestion of cooperation in housekeeping might be felt to have implications of poverty and lack of control.

Middle-class housing of the nineteenth century was characterised by its multitude of rooms with specific functions, designed to separate servants from household members and males from females.[35] Houses were normally rented, whether a detached or semi-detached house in the increasingly popular suburbs or a terrace house near the centre of the city. A family would require at least three bedrooms, for parents, male and female children, and also servants' bedrooms and perhaps a guest room. Reception rooms might comprise a drawing room, dining room and parlour or family room, and a large house might include a study, conservatory, billiard room, library or nursery. The kitchen and scullery would be situated in the servants' area with the servants' hall and housekeeper's room, and possibly a butler's pantry and wine cellar.[36] The exact size of the house occupied by a family depended upon the amount of rent they could afford, some smaller middle-class homes being similar in size to the largest terrace houses built for working-class families, the four up, four down. The change from terrace housing to suburban villas enabled the privacy of the home to be increased, by siting houses in spacious gardens and increasing the segregation of areas of middle-class and working-class housing.[37] The external emphasis of the middle-class home was on privacy and confirmation of the occupier's social status, while inside, comfort was ensured by high standards of servicing. Towards the end of the century the complex internal divisions of the home were replaced by greater openness in planning; the kitchen began to be sited on the ground floor rather than in the basement, thus creating an increased floor area.[38] By the end of the century, the burden of domestic work was being eased by the introduction of gas and electricity into the home.

The nineteenth-century middle-class home, as portrayed in the many domestic manuals of the time, was a model of 'domestic bliss', where 'health and happiness, joy and sorrow' depended upon the qualities of the mistress of the house. It was her task to 'raise housekeeping to the level of the fine arts', and certainly by the middle of the century, being a middle-class wife had become a full-time occupation.[39] The leisured image of the mistress or housekeeper contrasted with the drudgery of reality in all but the most wealthy households which could afford to employ several servants. In general, a middle-class home would probably have only one servant, leaving the wife to do much of the domestic work herself.[40] Towards the end of the century, as good servants became harder to find, the burden on the wife became even greater. The segregation of tasks implicit in the design of the Victorian home ensured that cooking became the province of the servants; although the mistress was advised to spend time in the kitchen overseeing her staff, both the quality of the food and economy in preparation were felt to suffer from this arrangement. Mrs Pedley, in her *Practical Housekeeping*, published in 1867, concluded that: 'If cooking could be done in the drawing-room, I have no doubt the culinary art would be carried to as great perfection as many other accomplishments that are seriously cultivated there.'[41] The gulf between the reality of the hard domestic work performed by the wife and the need to appear in leisurely control of the household was summed up by Mrs Caddy in her *Household Organization* of 1877: 'It seems to be only in England that [women] dread to be seen doing anything useful.'[42]

The frustrations and imperfections of Victorian domestic life ensured that any feasible alternative methods of organising the home would be seriously considered, provided that the conventional middle-class lifestyle was not threatened; overworked servants might also have welcomed changes in the organisation of their duties.

Three alternative building types were suggested during the middle and late nineteenth century which were intended to provide a more economic home for middle-class families than the villa or terrace house. The first of these was the luxury flat; a speculative block of flats for the middle class was erected in 1853 in Victoria Street, west London, but the flats were not a commercial success, partly because of their high rent.[43] Initially flats tended to be used as second homes by those with country houses, but by the 1870s they had become more popular and several more blocks were built in London in the 1880s.[44] Flats were more economic to run than houses with three or four floors, and towards the end of the century particular social groups, such as single people, young couples and poorer families, began to take flats because of their convenience.[45] However, flats never found great popularity within the middle class, dislike of their architectural style and urban situation being reflected in the growth of interest in the two other alternative building types, the country cottage and the bungalow, towards the end of the century.[46]

The country cottage, which could cost more than a large villa, was intended to be run by one resident servant with a daily help.[47] Bungalows, which were at first built on the coast and then on inland sites from the late 1880s onward, became popular with the middle class because they were economic and easy to run.[48] Although these three alternatives to the town house or suburban villa were less demanding in terms of domestic drudgery, their introduction did not indicate any change in attitude to the performance of domestic work; domestic duties were still the responsibility of the middle-class wife. Residents of the Bedford Park estate, built from 1876 onwards in west London, did consider one innovation in household organisation, the communal kitchen. Bedford Park was a middle-class estate of red-brick and tile-hung houses standing in large gardens along tree-lined avenues. A club, a church and an inn were included in the estate, and residents took part in a range of communal activities.[49] Bedford Park was intended to attract artistic and 'progressive' tenants, and in 1883 a plan to set up a communal kitchen to cook hot meals and deliver them to individual homes was under discussion.[50] The kitchen was to have been run on a cooperative or subscription basis, but in the end the idea came to nothing. The communal kitchen would have reduced the amount of domestic work necessary within each house, but neither decreased privacy nor changed the nature of household organisation.

Some members of the middle class were attracted to small colonies such as Whiteway, near Stroud, which had been set up on anarchist principles. Whiteway was founded in 1898, and at first members lived and worked communally; it was the intention that women and men should be treated equally.[51] Women shared the farm labour; Nellie Shaw, who joined the community in 1899, felt it was 'real work', 'better than making dresses, anyhow. Heaps!'[52] Men did not, however, share the domestic work, newcomers to the colony in particular considering themselves to be above 'women's work'.[53] Eventually communal eating and finally the communal laundry ceased, but the colony's collectively-built community hall and some houses remain in existence.[54]

Thus even the dramatic change in lifestyle from individual to communal had left the basic sexual division of labour unaltered. For those middle-class households who were searching for a means of improving the quality of their home lives, neither communal living nor advances in the design of the home appeared to provide the answer. On the other hand, the idea of cooperative housekeeping implied that households could retain their conventional lifetyles while benefiting from efficient domestic organisation, and combining an element of community with increased privacy. As cooperative housekeeping also held the possibility that women might be relieved of their domestic duties, it was potentially highly appealing to both women and men. This book traces the history of cooperative housekeeping in England and considers its theoretical origins, its architecture and its effect on women's lives.

2 Associated Homes and Cooperative Housekeeping

Household work in the mid-nineteenth century was sheer drudgery. There was a great contrast between the highly mechanised, large-scale factory system of production and working methods of the home. Working-class women did all or most of the work themselves, as well as bringing up children and possibly doing paid work. Middle-class women certainly did some work in the home, the amount varying with the number of servants employed. Servants had to be supervised and children looked after, and although the availability of servants reduced the number of tasks to be performed by wives, there was a consequent decrease in family privacy. There were constant complaints about the quality of servants. The various utopian or religious schemes for changing home life provided partial answers to the household drudgery problem, but only for those people willing to change their lifestyles and convert to new doctrines. Conventional households looked for answers to current trends in society as they knew it.

The increasing concern with the quality of home life was reflected by the number of books published on household management and domestic economy. W. B. Adams reviewed a selection of these for the *Monthly Repository* in August 1834.[1] Adams, a prolific inventor, touched on several points which were to come up again and again in discussions of cooperation in housekeeping: the poor quality of servants, privacy, the education of children, industrialisation and planning. He felt the only remedy for the ills of domestic life was the introduction of, as he called it, 'social living'. This article is a very early adaptation of the alternative utopian/religious lifestyles to suit the conventional middle classes, and is notable for the introduction of most of the arguments which were to be deployed in favour of some form of cooperative housekeeping over the rest of the nineteenth century and on into the twentieth.

Adams's basic argument was as follows:

The simple proposition as to social living is, to perform all the household services, and prepare the necessary food of five hundred or fewer families, out of a joint-stock fund of labour and material, upon the same principles of economy and arrangement as are found so advantageous in our large manufacturing establishments. (p. 494)

Social living was to be conducted in a number of private houses – he suggested just 60 to begin with – arranged along a gallery from which access was obtained to two buildings housing the central facilities of the establishment. There was a central kitchen with all its equipment powered by a steam engine, including machines for doing laundry, shoe-cleaning, kneading bread and chopping meat. Hot water and gas lighting were to be supplied. There was a large dining hall, baths, a reading room and library. Food might be transferred from kitchen to dining hall on a pulley system. Each house was to have up to eight rooms and a garden; central heating was included. The rent of £80–£100 per year included domestic service, lodging for a family of five, heat, light and laundry. Adams calculated that this would be half the cost for the same arrangements made individually, working from a cost price of £300 per dwelling. He suggested the buildings could be built on a subscription plan or for profit.

According to this view of cooperative living, privacy was gained rather than lost. Servants lived in their own accommodation, not in the employer's house, and the buildings could be arranged so that gardens were not overlooked by other houses. Servants would be better trained and administered, and economies of scale would be possible in food production. Machinery would be used in the kitchen, which would itself be better planned. Wives would do no domestic work, leaving them free to deal with the children. The system as described was clearly meant for the middle classes, those who could afford the £80–£100 per year rent plus another £100 for food. For the middle-class man it had the merits of providing him with improvements in service and privacy for less cost, and ensuring that his wife never did 'aught to soil the purity of her hands' (p. 578).

The increasing confinement of women, particularly middle-class women, to the home has already been well documented.[2] Even working-class women were beginning to be included in the idealised view of home life, which emphasised the dependence of the housewife and the home as her sphere of influence.[3] Household work became a series of tasks to be supervised rather than undertaken herself. Communal life as seen by Adams incorporated mechanical efficiency, financial economy and higher standards of cleanliness and service, while improving the wife's position in relation to household work. The price to be paid for these advantages lay in the extent to which social living interfered with family life. Servants, of course, were also dramatically affected by these proposed changes. Instead of living in individual households and being on call, often for a wide range of duties, for a very long day, they would be working set hours for a centrally administered body. Whether these points improved the quality of the servants' lives depended upon their treatment by particular households. A system with reasonable hours of shiftwork would leave them free and relatively unsupervised, but central organisation of work might remove some of their little independence. The standard of servants' accommodation would depend entirely upon the generosity of provision made in the arrangements for setting up the social living system. Clearly if economies were needed, the element of rent paid for central services would be closely scrutinised.

Also in 1834, James Morrison put the working-class case for cooperation between households in his newspaper *The Pioneer*.[4] *The Pioneer* was an Owenite trade unionist paper, begun and edited by Morrison. Frances Morrison, the wife of James, was an Owenite and feminist, contributing to *The Pioneer* as 'A Bondswoman'.[5] The 'Page for the Ladies' began in March 1834,[6] the article on domestic cooperation being an early example, before the name was changed to 'Women'. In the article James (and/or Frances) Morrison suggested that working-class women could get together to form childminding associations, with each woman taking her turn at looking after the children. Nursery or play schools and communal laundries were also mentioned. The emphasis in the article was on cooperation between households, not the employment of servants or any form of communal living itself. The sheer amount of women's labour was to be decreased by association, which was seen simply as 'the method of procuring additional comforts to the poor man, by the union of women' (p. 263). This is an interesting, although possibly inadvertent, use of words. The main contrast between the articles of Adams and Morrison lies in the absence of any working-class suggestion for communal living. All other financial differences in provision of buildings and servants are easily explained by reference to the relative resources of the two groups, but particularly in an Owenite paper this absence is surprising. The eventual collapse of the Owenite community at Orbiston in 1827 may have discouraged further thoughts of communal life.

These two 1834 articles were followed around the half-century mark by a small burst of publications on cooperation in housekeeping. W. B. Adams again, writing on 'Human Progress' for the *Westminster Review* in 1849,[7] saw a future of rebellious servants or increased use of 'mechanical appliances and labour-saving processes' (p. 21). Adams felt that housing was 'lamentably deficient' in comparison with factory building, suggesting a large block containing flats, central kitchen, dining hall, baths, washhouses, library and schoolroom. Power was from a steam engine, and there was also to be a small gas works, providing waste heat for the central heating system. Single people and families could live in the block, eating in the communal dining room if they wished. Adams emphasised the technical advantages of the system, with its instant hot and cold water, quick access to food and simple furniture. 'There could be no dirt, with hard slate surfaces for floor and walls' (p. 19). The steam engine powered a variety of grinding, chopping, cleaning and pumping machines in the kitchen. Adams, taking a long view of human progress, envisaged improved housing conditions for all classes and the independence of domestic servants. Adams's system of communal living had as its purpose the cutting of household costs and the provision of good lodgings and allied facilities.

Mary Gillies had tried to preempt criticism of the idea of communal living in her 1847 article in *Howitt's Journal*.[8] Her description of a communal plan was drawn from the Adams article of 1834, but she concentrated her defence on the matter of privacy. Having mentioned the cares of middle-class women and the narrowing effect of domestic drudgery, she went on:

When anything resembling Associated Homes is mentioned, the idea of living in public is apt to occur; but this is quite erroneous. Were it otherwise, it would be fatal to attempt to introduce them, for English habits are formed on the very contrary basis. The English enjoy the family circle, the power of privacy, quiet, and seclusion; and any scheme of living that failed in securing these would at once fall to the ground . . . Every man's house might be as exclusively his own, as completely 'his castle', though under the same roof with fifty others, as if it stood on one side of a street, in a row with fifty others. (p. 271)

She goes on to criticise thin party walls, bad drainage, draughts, insulation and individual cooking arrangements. In a second article[9] two months later, Gillies gave a detailed description of a family club, with individual apartments, housekeeper, servants and schoolteacher. The club or associated home was intended for middle-class families, and was an apparently logical solution to the housekeeping problems of the time. The combination of cheaper housekeeping with better service and increased privacy should have been an instant success.

To judge by her lengthy description of the relative privacy of associated homes, Gillies had realised the inherent unacceptability of her argument to many of the English middle classes. During the late 1840s the first tenement blocks for working-class families were being erected in London.[10] These blocks were built by organisations such as the Metropolitan Association for Improving the Dwellings of the Industrious Classes, formed with the intention of improving housing conditions while still making a small (4 or 5 per cent) profit on investments. The housing was fairly successful, but the various organisations found it increasingly difficult to build to a high standard in the city centres, because of the high cost of land. As later blocks were built with fewer facilities, families who could afford it moved to suburban villas, the workers using the new train services to reach the city centres. Thus tenement blocks, initially associated with charity, later acquired a poor reputation for housing standards. They also failed to dispel the impression of overcrowding which had come to be associated with poor housing conditions as a result of government reports such as the 1842 *Inquiry into the Sanitary Condition of the Labouring Population of Great Britain*.[11]

In addition to this impression of forced communality and charity associated with living in apartment blocks, there were also the utopian overtones of communal living. The ideas of Fourier for communal living in a large block, with consequent changes in family life, had filtered over from France to Britain. By the mid nineteenth century, most of Europe, except Britain, was involved in revolutionary changes. In Britain the only revolution was industrial, but numerous small experimental communities were set up, often in the English countryside, and these were reported in the national press.[12] This atmosphere of imminent change must have appeared threatening to those of the middle classes who were beginning to accumulate wealth. Any small changes in family lifestyle which could have paved the way for revolutionry changes were likely to be rejected. Even the luxury flats, first seen in London in 1853,[13] were not a great success. Over 20 years after their introduction critics still felt these 'horizontal dwellings' would mean the total absence of home life, would be troubled by noise from above and contaminated by cooking smells.[14] There was also the problem of lift access to higher floors 'which, although delighted in by our American friends, yet not one person in twelve over here cares about much'[15] and of servants congregating unsupervised on the back stairs.

Altogether, associated homes, particularly in the form of apartment blocks, seemed almost designed to conjure up a range of unpleasant feelings for the villa or town-house dwelling middle classes. It would take a very strong economic argument to move them from their relatively inefficient but comfortable privacy. For those poorer members of the middle class such as the 'destitute gentlewoman', some form of associated home might be the only alternative to cheap and unsatisfactory lodgings. Harriet Martineau, the political writer, described the life of a woman living alone in London on £50–£60 per year:[16]

> Her health is almost certain to fail. She cannot afford to eat meat more than three times a week; . . . She is obliged to stint herself in fuel. She lets the fire go out on any pretence . . . She takes less and less exercise.

Martineau's solution was the associated home, where around 20 ladies would club together to provide each with a room in a large household, and a shared sitting room and library, with communal meals. Her main point was the benefit to be gained from the company of others. Martineau may have been prompted to write this article by a pamphlet sent to her from London in March 1850.[17] The object of the pamphlet was to raise support for a 'club mansion' for ladies over the age of 30, the daughters or widows of gentlemen, with small incomes. The mansion was to be a large house with a garden; each lady would have her own room, but meals were to be taken communally. The idea had come to the author after seeing a model lodgings house for the poor. Again, there is the unfortunate connection in the public mind between associated housing and charity or the poor.

It is interesting to note that Martineau lived in a detached house in the Lake District, which she had designed herself. She chose the site in 1845, and

> Then came the amusement of planning my house, which I did all myself. [She pondered:] . . . how to plan the bedrooms so that the beds should not be in a draught, nor face the window nor the fireplace, etc. . . . The whole scheme was fortunate and charming. There is not a single blunder or nuisance in my pretty house: . . . [18]

It was very unusual for a woman to be involved with designing a house at that time. During the mid-nineteenth century it was felt that only certain areas of architecture were suitable for women, particularly interior design and decoration.[19] Even by the early twentieth century, architecture was considered to be an all-male profession; only 12 women architects were listed in the 1891 census of London. Martineau moved to Ambleside in order to work in peace and quiet, but she was at the same time interested in improving the conditions of the local people. She gave lectures to the mechanics of Ambleside and began a building society which eventually erected 15 cottages.[20] She clearly had no personal inclinations towards communal living – her house had three bedrooms, a kitchen, sitting room and study, just enough space for Martineau and her maids[21] – but her ideal of domestic life did include young servants she could train and improve.[22] Her article on associated homes carried the same message of improvement, giving weight to the view that communal living was something to be recommended to and undertaken by others.

The working classes were the subject of another article by Mary Gillies in March 1847.[23] She outlined the workings of a rather idyllic associated home for the working classes as seen through the eyes of its inhabitants, ten years hence. There were 100 homes in the block, with one to five rooms in each. Hot and cold water was piped to every floor, while meals could be eaten in the dining hall or in individual rooms. Cooking and washing were performed centrally. The labour for these tasks consisted mainly of the 12 to 16 year-old girls of the home:

> . . . they were employed in every kind of service within the household, and were thus trained for their duties as wives and mothers, as well as to the work of domestic servants, needle-women, nurses, teachers, assistants in shops, or whatever occupation they might choose. (p. 172)

Both boys and girls did service work until the age of 12, when the boys were apprenticed out to various trades. No married women with children went out to work, but they could work within the associated home on tasks 'compatible with their duties as wives and mothers' (p. 172). Men did no household tasks, but had time for classes after work. Gillies emphasised the economic advantages of the system, which she saw as being a paying proposition for both speculator and tenants alike. But her final point was

> the great improvement that Associated Homes make in the condition of women. Women are raised by them, from anxious toil-worn drudges, to their true place in the world . . . Now . . . our children know what it is to have mothers. (p.174)

Under this system, mothers were still completely responsible for the care of their children (when not at school), house-cleaning and clothes-mending; they were relieved only of the cooking and laundry. This would certainly have been a considerable improvement in their working conditions, particularly when combined with better housing, but the system did not lead to equality of opportunity for men and women in paid work.

Isaac Doxsey's 1868 article in *The Co-Operator* [24] also stressed the twin aims of economic housekeeping and improved services. He envisaged ten or twelve working-class families combining to share a large building with homes for each family and a shared dining hall and washhouse. Every wife would take turns at cooking for the entire establishment, leaving the other wives free to tend their children. He felt they would improve each others' cooking skills, have more time to devote to cleaning the house and, as an extra benefit, would be able to make the common hall so attractive to the husbands that they would not want to go to the pub. Nowhere is there any mention of men undertaking any domestic or childcare duties. An earlier contributor to *The Co-Operator*[25] suggested cooperative living for young single working men, as wives would always want to be mistresses in their own homes, thus ruling out any thoughts of domestic cooperation. *The Co-Operator*[26] and *Co-operative News*,[27] both organs of the British cooperative movement, were frequent sources of articles on domestic cooperation in the 1860s and 1870s. Edward Vansittart Neale, a leading figure in the cooperative movement and particularly the Christian Socialist movement, began to advocate associated homes in 1860,[28] although it was 1872 before his plans were widely publicised. *The Co-Operator* published several articles on an American initiative in domestic cooperation, the Cambridge Cooperative Housekeeping Society, in 1869;[29] English advocates of domestic cooperation were naturally interested in working experiments from other countries.

The Cambridge Cooperative Housekeeping Society had been started by Mrs Melusina Fay Peirce on 6 May 1869. Peirce had written a series of articles in the *Atlantic Monthly*[30] on the subject of cooperative housekeeping, and the Cambridge Society was her attempt to turn theory into practice. Peirce had been married six years when she began to write about middle-class women in American society, her husband, Charles, being a lecturer in the philosophy of science at Harvard.[31] Her argument in *Atlantic Monthly* began by pointing out that middle-class women no longer carried out the production of food or other goods used in the home. They had become unproductive consumers, not even paying by their labour for the necessities they consumed. This state of affairs was encouraged by their husbands and fathers, although women were being increasingly criticised by them for being vain and frivolous. Peirce felt that the time had come for educated women to search for work appropriate to their abilities, so that the relations between men and women could be made more equal.

Women in general had no capital to begin farming or manu-facturing ventures, which left the retail trade as the only avenue open to women. Capital would still be a problem as would lack of time and the general prejudice against women engaging in trade. Peirce proposed to overcome all these obstacles by means of cooperative housekeeping, an application of cooperation to the domestic economy. She suggested groups of 12 to 50 women getting together (with the permission of their husbands) in order to supply the whole group with food and other goods. Cooked food would be provided and services such as laundry and sewing would be carried out. Profits from the scheme would be returned to investors in proportion to their original investment and amount purchased. Members of the association would perform mainly supervisory functions for fixed salaries, and the work would be organised into three departments: kitchen, laundry and sewing. Peirce suggested a central cooperative laundry, organised in the same manner as the many existing commercial laundries. There was to be a central building specifically for sewing, complete with everything from workrooms and fitting rooms to dining room and gymnasium. The most important cooperative building, the kitchen, was to resemble commercial kitchens, while the meals were to be taken round to the associated houses by horse and cart.

The whole plan depended upon the approval of the husbands for its success, which implied, as Peirce said, that there was no room for error in its functioning. The number of servants per household would be reduced, as only the house-cleaning remained to be done. The servants were to be employed by the central organisation, thus the difficult mistress/servant relationship would be improved. Peirce saw housekeeping as providing a suitable career for single women, while giving those women not interested in housekeeping the opportunity to develop their talents in other fields such as art and medicine. Although she insisted that women must earn their own living and be organised among themselves, she was not in favour of universal suffrage. She put forward the idea of women-only meetings, culminating in a Feminine International Parliament. Her reason for taking this view was the limitation of male thinking:

> So far, therefore, from women's wishing for manhood suffrage as an enlargement from their present limitations, they ought rather to scorn it as something too narrow for their sympathies and aspirations, as, in fact, directly imprisoning them in all the prejudices, hates, mistakes, selfishness, greed, and lies of these grand but detestable masculine nationalities that have filled the world with woe and slaughter, ruin and barbarism, since the day that Cain first murdered his brother Abel . . . Nay,

rather let all women meet on common ground as *women* . . . (Feb 1869, p. 170)

Peirce felt that a few women within the existing male institutions would simply be overwhelmed. She saw cooperative housekeeping as a first step towards financial independence for educated women; servants were to have better pay and conditions. Unfortunately Peirce erected the entire complex plan upon a base of male approval. The proposed constitution of the cooperative housekeeping society stated that the highest authority of the society was to be the Council, made up of all the male heads of families involved. In the end, this was the undoing of the Cambridge Cooperative Housekeeping Society; in April 1871, after much male opposition to the whole idea, the Council of Gentlemen dissolved it unanimously.[32] Without a source of capital under their own control, it was highly unlikely that the scheme could succeed, as it involved changes in the men's lifestyle with the ultimate prospect of complete independence for their wives. No doubt the postulated female parliament would have been derided by the men of the time, but in an age without servants and when the image of home life has changed dramatically, it is the point which seems most relevant to current events.

In contrast to the English vision of apartment blocks for associated homes, Peirce envisaged an altogether more open plan. Instead of enclosing squares with houses, she sited the houses in squares with trees, grass and flowers all around; she aimed for a healthy and beautiful environment for both families and workers. The cooperative housekeeping centre, with its laundry, sewing room and kitchen, was to be situated centrally, within easy reach of all houses in the group. She suggested a large block with an internal grassy courtyard for these facilities. Of the earlier English plans for associated homes, only Morrison's system consisted of individual houses with a central facilities block, and this was probably because the plan was intended for working-class families who were able to cooperate but could not afford new buildings.

Although Peirce used the English cooperative movement as a model for her society, it was a middle-class rather than a working-class organisation. Most importantly, the instigator of the idea actually put it into practice; it was not a philanthropic gesture or a purely utopian idea, but a working proposition. Peirce was arguing for women's eventual financial independence, but her starting point was the more innocuous aim of improving household service and efficiency. Her book, consisting of her previous articles, was published in England in 1870[33] and was influential precisely because of its apparently non-revolutionary outlook. Reactions to the book will be considered in the next chapter. Peirce was far from being an extreme feminist; she was not in favour of universal suffrage, and wanted to involve men in the cooperative housekeeping organisation. Her faith in male judgement led her to allow them the power of veto in the new society; she assumed that they, too, would see the long-term benefits of women taking a wider interest in life outside their own homes. She was wrong in this vital respect, and thus the whole ultimately subversive plan collapsed. However, it proved to be a fruitful source of ideas in England.

3 Mrs E. M. King and the English Response

The final article of the *Atlantic Monthly*'s series on cooperative housekeeping appeared in March 1869. Although published in Boston, Massachusetts, the magazine was widely read in England, and must have found its way into many middle-class homes where wives and daughters were trying to cope with the impossible demands of housekeeping. Domestic manuals still emphasised the idyllic qualities of the English home, the 'world-received type of domestic bliss', while 'Health and happiness, joy and sorrow, are more or less dependent on the good or evil of [the wife's] presence.'[1]

Mrs Beeton's *Book of Household Management*, the ultimate handbook for the status-conscious housewife, was first published in 1861. Although it assumed every family could afford a small army of servants, the onus was still on the mistress of the house to set high standards for housework and behaviour; 'The happiness, comfort, and well-being of a family' depended on the mistress's knowledge of household duties.[2] In practice, home life for the middle-class wife was an endless round of hard and dirty tasks, performed with inefficient tools and probably with the help of an ill-trained, unenthusiastic maid. Rich families could employ many servants and realistically aspire to the Mrs Beeton standard, but middle-class families were caught between rising expectations and inadequate resources. The housewife was the subject of complaints from her husband, on the one hand, while being exhorted to aim for perfection on the other.

Branca[3] has shown that towards the end of the nineteenth century increasing numbers of middle-class families were facing financial problems. The average middle-class woman, assisted by only one maid, spent most of her time on household chores: 'All her days and many evenings were spent in scrubbing, dusting, tending to fires, for six to ten rooms in a three-to-four storey home, plus doing the cooking, shopping, washing, and sewing required for a family of five.'[4]

By the second half of the nineteenth century, the enormous

demand for servants was increasingly being met by the training of previously pauper or criminal girls in various philanthropic institutions. Middle- and upper-class women had always promoted domestic service as an escape from poverty, and eventually tens of thousands of these girls were going into service annually.[5] The girls were overworked, poorly paid and unused to the middle-class lifestyle;[6] although providing an extra pair of hands in the house, they did not solve the housework problem. Indeed, they probably added to it by introducing a difficult personal relationship between mistress and servant.

The industrialisation of household tasks had progressed slowly in comparison with manufacturing processes in general. Gas had been in common use in towns since the 1860s,[7] but its main domestic use was lighting; the open or closed coal range remained the predominant method of cooking throughout the nineteenth century.[8] Electricity did not arrive on the domestic scene until the 1880s.[9] This slow process of modernisation was not the result of lack of invention, as Ravetz has shown.[10] It was more the outcome of a change in attitude towards new technology, which had taken place after the Great Exhibition of 1851. During the first half of the century there was still an eagerness for material progress, but 'The thrust of new values borne along by the revolution in industry was contained in the later nineteenth century; the social and intellectual revolution, implicit in industrialism was muted, perhaps even aborted.'[11] This reaction against technological progress both impeded the introduction of new domestic appliances and emphasised the role of the wife as guardian of the purest values, those of the home. The unchanging home routine was part of the image of England, an old England, green and pleasant, comfortable and civilised.[12]

The middle-class woman was constantly attempting to reach imagined housekeeping standards of bygone days – 'the lost art of housekeeping'[13] – or ever higher levels of cleanliness. The domestic economy movement of the 1870s sprang from the widespread feeling that English standards of housewifery were declining.[14] Thus the time was ripe in 1869 for a new housekeeping initiative which managed to combine the ideals of housekeeping with greater efficiency, but in a manner which did not destroy the image of the middle-class woman around which the home was based. Later in the century there were to be a variety of movements which challenged to some degree the aspirations of

Victorian home-making.[15] In 1869, however, Mrs Peirce's idea of cooperative housekeeping offered some kind of hope to beleaguered housewives and their husbands. In spite of the basically subversive quality of her ideas, Peirce's suggestions were acceptable as they did not involve communal living and worked within the capitalist system. Her system was a sophisticated and much enlarged version of the many schemes for associated homes which had been almost completely ignored by the middle classes in the past. In the press reaction to the *Atlantic Monthly* articles there is a sense of relief at finding a possible escape from the housekeeping impasse. An apparently conservative idea was right for a time of consolidation; a small domestic change to mirror the great industrial revolution.

Even as the final article in the *Atlantic Monthly* series was published in March 1869, the first English reaction to it appeared in *Chamber's Journal*.[16] The tone of the article was one of muted approval, particularly of the 'sensible, womanly' spirit in which it was written, without any advocacy of 'Woman's Rights'. The article summarised Mrs Peirce's plan at length, noting that this was the first use of the term cooperative housekeeping. Not until 1868 had 'cooperation', with its working-class and industrial overtones, been connected with the domestic world. The purpose of the scheme was described as being to economise in housekeeping while giving women the opportunity for more active employment than at present. Families were not to live together and share their possessions. The article did not go so far as to suggest an actual experiment, but mildly approved of the idea. It did point out the possible difficulties of having a male council in overall charge of the housekeeping society, noting that the eventual form of any such society might depend upon women's access to their own capital. Indeed, only one year later the Married Women's Property Act was passed, and then expanded in 1882.[17] These Acts gave women the right to own property for their own use, and entitled them to all wages they earned. The coincidence of the passing of these Acts with the increased interest in changes in housekeeping may have encouraged wives to consider new schemes more seriously. Books such as Edward Bulwer Lytton's *The Coming Race* also added to the general awareness of new possibilities in domestic life. Lytton's futuristic novel described an underground world with a great city. Domestic buildings were large, arranged around three sides of a court, and there was no need for servants:

'Four automata (mechanical contrivances which, with these people, answer the ordinary purposes of domestic service) stood phantom-like at each angle in the wall.'[18] This arrangement would have ideally combined complete privacy with perfect domestic service.

The *Co-Operator* continued to report on the progress of Mrs Peirce's Cambridge Association, while advocating cooperation between English housewives.[19] The (male) writer of this article was most enthusiastic about the application of cooperation, and the organisation of (women's) labour to cooking and washing. He envisaged a central kichen and store room, but no centralised housing. One of the first women to comment on Mrs Peirce's plan was Mary Hume-Rothery of Manchester. She devoted most of her 1871 article in *The Co-Operator* to enlarging on Peirce's original suggestion for all-female parliaments.[20] She felt the House of Lords might usefully be replaced by a female house of representatives, the consent of both houses being required to pass new measures. Interestingly, she ascribed her own failure to take part in the women's suffrage movement to her dislike of contemporary male politics, 'that arena of miserable party struggles and unprincipled shuffling of the political cards for personal objects'. She had her doubts about the practicalities of cooperative housekeeping, particularly concerning the ability of the scheme to produce enough revenue to pay all the workers originally suggested. She thought food delivery would be the biggest problem, although she indulged in her own flight of fancy, suggesting 'little food-freighted balloons, captive to aerial wires, floating from house to house on receipt of some telegraphic signal'. Overall, she condemned the details of the scheme as having no practical value, but applauded the theory behind it. She saw the organisation and cooperation of women, and the possibility of their paid employment, as valuable ideas.

Hume-Rothery was commenting on cooperative housekeeping for the middle classes, but the following year, 1872, saw a number of articles aimed at the working classes in the pages of the *Co-operative News*. This new paper was intended to be the national paper for all cooperators, whether producers or consumers.[21] In January 1872 'E. W.' suggested cooperative homes as minimal housing solutions for the poor, a cause to be taken on by philanthropists.[22] 'E. W.' likened cooperative homes to model lodging houses, the only additional facilities being a variety of recreation rooms and a cooperative store. Capital necessary for building was to be raised by public subscription. E. W. conceded that not all working men would be keen to adopt this mode of life, but they at least were: *'somewhat* more free from the idiotic slavery to "gentility" which renders people of the middle and upper classes so reluctant to adopt any practice until it has become "fashionable"'.

The choice of the 'model lodging house' format for the proposed cooperative home was unfortunate, in that it identified the new type of home with an earlier variation which was already disliked. Although blocks of model dwellings had only been in existence for two decades, they had a poor reputation and were unpopular with the artisan classes. Bodies such as the Society for Improving the Condition of the Labouring Classes (SICLC) erected a series of exemplary model dwellings, later to be modified by other semi-philanthropic organisations.[23] This first SICLC block for male lodgers opened in 1846, followed by the Streatham Street, London, 'Model Houses for Families' in 1850 (see Plate 1).[24] These blocks, or 'barracks' as they came to be known, usually had some communal facilities, often baths or washhouses, and tenants had to abide by a lengthy series of rules. The problem of providing dwellings for the poor in towns was discussed at the RIBA in December 1866;[25] several speakers expressed what they felt to be the feelings of prospective tenants of large blocks of flats:

> They had a decided objection to those large and formally conducted establishments where, as they considered, they were constantly under a supervision which was irksome to them.

> There was a certain amount of prejudice against these immense blocks of buildings; a great one on the part of respectable parents against promiscuous mixing together of large numbers of children during their play hours, by which they sometimes became contaminated, being beyond the parental influence and control.

> ... the poor ... were, as a rule, averse to living in those immense modern or model edifices. They wanted something approaching to a house of their own.

Earlier in the same year *Building News* criticised the building of model lodging houses as a solution to the problem of providing housing for the working classes.[26] The paper disliked the 'barrack-like form' of the dwellings made necessary by shortage of space and land values, but its main objection to flats was their bad influence on family life: 'The love and pride of home is associated with a desire of proper seclusion, and of possessing every convenience within its own limits' (p. 2).

Thus E. W.'s advocacy of the block form for cooperative housekeeping was not likely to find much favour with the working classes with their prior experience of model dwellings. However, it may have been calculated to attract the philanthropists, without whose money it would have been difficult to begin building. Even in 1872, philanthropic provision was seen as the only answer to the problem of housing the poor. Although the Torrens Act had been passed in 1868, allowing authorities to demolish insanitary houses, state housing was still several decades away. There was a feeling that the recipients of philanthropy sometimes chose to abuse their new amenities.[27] The attractions of cooperative housekeeping to a possible benefactor were the reforming aspects of the institution, the higher housekeeping standards, temperance and general high-mindedness of the social life. As the cooperative movement was particularly strong in the north of England, E. W.'s article would have been more likely to attract artisan support if it had suggested houses rather than flats. As Gaskell[28] has shown, there is a long history of dislike and distrust of tenement blocks in the north.

The possibility of rejection did not stop E. V. Neale from returning to the pages of *Co-operative News* in support of one of his favourite ideas.[29] His plan for an associated home involved a five-storey rectangular block of flats, part of the space in the centre of the rectangle being occupied by a building containing the communal facilities (see Figure 1). He emphasised the privacy of the flats, and included a central kitchen, laundry, bathrooms, dining room, library, smoking and billiard rooms and a nursery. There was also the possibility of adding schoolrooms or gardens. He intended the central passages of the blocks of flats to be lit from above, although this would have been so gloomy that gas lighting might well have been added. Privacy would depend on sound insulation between flats and the number of staircases included in the final building; more staircases would have increased the cost. Facilities in the central block would cause some problems because of the stairs. Not only would the kitchen and dining room have been on different floors, but women taking their washing to the laundry would also have to climb stairs unless they happened to live on the same floor. Children's play would presumably be supervised in the day nursery. The communal facilities were recreational (for men) and work orientated (for women); Neale was only a hesitant supporter of women's emancipation, preferring them to keep to the domestic sphere but unable to deny that they were entitled to vote.[30]

In his article, Neale did not give many details of life in the associated home, but went quickly on to discuss financial matters. He accepted that the initial expenditure was going to cause great difficulty, and suggested that associated dwellers should put their own money towards the building, and that the cooperative stores should back them up by investing their capital in the project. W. Morrison, a director of the Improved Industrial Dwellings Company, supported the idea of investment in housing for cooperators.[31] There was, however, little support within the cooperative movement for Neale's ideas. Although he produced a pamphlet in 1880 describing the French cooperative colony at Guise,[32] 'opinion within the English movement was taking the opposite path. Cooperators were interested in building, but building individual dwellings with no communal facilities; they saw the prospect of communal living as both impossible and unpleasant.[33] Neale's arguments for better facilities and increased privacy had been defeated, partly by financial problems and partly by adherence to the ideal of home as being distinctly different from the outside world. The model dwelling was a middle-class model, imposed upon the artisans. Cooperators had the same aim as the middle classes, a home of their own; with no middle-class associated home in existence, Neale's idea, although true to the original aims of the movement,[34] would by 1880 have seemed like a step backwards to cooperators seeking improvement in their lifestyles.

Mrs Peirce's original plan was, of course, directed at the middle classes, and one of cooperative housekeeping's strongest advocates in England was Mrs E. M. King. One of her earliest papers, on international disarmament, was given to the National Association for the Promotion of Social Science in 1872.[35] Mrs King was born in Meath, just north of Dublin, in 1801 and came to London in 1866 after raising a large family in Dorset. Her husband was

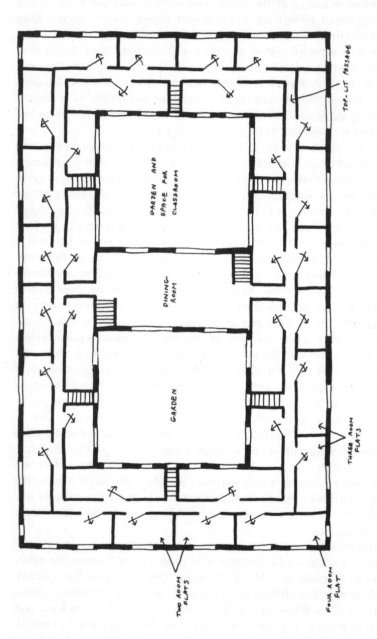

FIGURE 1 *Plan of the first floor of an associated home described by E. V. Neale (from E. V. Neale, 'Associated Homes',* Co-operative News, *27 Jan 1872, vol. 2, no. 4, p. 37)*

the vicar of Long Crichel, near Wimborne, which gave the family an income in 1860 of £400 per annum plus a house.[36] This would have put the family into the upper middle classes. Elizabeth Moss King was a prolific speaker and writer, a member of the British Association for the Advancement of Science and founding secretary of the Rational Dress Society. Her first public pronouncement on cooperative housekeeping was made at the annual meeting of the British Association in September 1873. She gave a paper to the 'Economics and Statistics' section entitled 'Confederated Homes and Cooperative Housekeeping'.[37] The paper caused quite a stir, being reported in *The Times* as the chief attraction of the day's proceedings.[38] The complete paper was published in the December 1873 edition of the *Contemporary Review*.[39]

Mrs King's first point was that home life was either imperfect (for the middle classes) or non-existent (for the poor). The main cause of this state of affairs was the lack of good servants, but this was simply a result of their bad working conditions and the need for them to live in the homes of their employers. She suggested that domestic work should be organised, giving scope to those women who excelled at housekeeping to superintend domestic staff for a number of homes. Servants would live in their own homes and work a shift system. Mrs King felt that this system would reduce the cost of employing servants while enhancing the status of domestic work. Associated or confederated homes were needed so that domestic service could be performed in shifts, but there would be other benefits to members. Domestic skills could be properly taught instead of mistress and maid being in relative ignorance, and mechanical aids could be used to the full. She suggested central heating, lighting, water and waste disposal services, all of which would be too expensive for individual homes. There was another factor holding back the introduction of labour-saving devices, however:

In carrying water to sleeping or dressing rooms – . . . very little economy of labour is thought of, because it is only women's labour that is expended, and economy of labour means only economy of money, not economy of muscle, health, or strength . . . But when housekeeping becomes, by co-operation and division of labour, an organized trade or profession, women's labour will then be thought worth economising.[40]

Confederated homes would also be more economical to run, through cutting out food wastage and bulk buying. Her final point in their favour was that they would take up less building land, leaving space for parks or gardens.

Mrs King gave no detailed plans for confederated homes, but concentrated instead on their long-term effects on society. She had read the work of Mrs Peirce, and although agreeing with her method of domestic reorganisation and the need for some form of associated home, did not appear to support Peirce's suggestion that wives should work in supervisory positions. King barely mentions supervision except to say that it would constitute a profession, while 'guardians of the children' are to be 'ladies in the best sense of the term', not to be considered as servants, 'but more as the companions and guides of mothers'.[41] This is far from an enthusiastic endorsement of domestic service as a profession fit for the middle-class wife. Cooperation or confederation was a means to improved home life, and also an improvement in the world situation. She disagreed completely with Peirce's idea of a separate political structure for women. She saw the associated home as being a halfway house between the privacy of home life and the political world, and felt that joint male and female management of associated homes would be a step towards bringing together the interests of the sexes. She did fear that men would simply take over completely in domestic life, if given the chance. Her only suggested safeguards against this possibility were that women were accepted as better domestic servants than men, and that men would soon come to realise that power over women in the domestic sphere was degrading.

Peirce had emphasised the employment prospects arising within and from the cooperative housekeeping system, but King made no mention of these for women confederated home-dwellers. She emphasised the unfairness of the individual home system to servants, but did not see middle-class wives as undertaking domestic work. This difference in approach between the American and English plans may have arisen as a result of the relative lack of servants in America at that time. The 1870 US census listed one domestic servant for every 8.4 families,[42] while even at the end of the nineteenth century servants were employed by about 20 per cent of British households.[43] In 1871, more than one in ten of all women in England and Wales were resident domestic servants.[44] American writers of the mid-nineteenth century had also stressed the inequalities in the mistress–servant relationship, arguing that women ought to stay at home and do their own housework.[45] This suggestion had hardly surfaced in England, where the combination of idealised home life and a strong ethos of service[46] ensured that the continued existence of servants in the middle-class home was taken for granted until well into the twentieth century.

A wide variety of papers, from the *Englishwoman's Review* to *The Queen*,[47] reported Mrs King's lecture at the British Association meeting. *The Times* went into some detail, commenting on the crowded room and the number of ladies present. The president of the meeting suggested that the time had come for an experiment in cooperative housekeeping, which he was sure would be very useful, although he declined to join it on the grounds of his conservatism. One of the speakers in the discussion was Lydia Becker, secretary of the Manchester National Society for Women's Suffrage. She was in agreement with the paper, adding that 'By means of proper combination a great deal of domestic drudgery might be spared, and the principle of the division of labour was not sufficiently applied in domestic work.'

Becker, the eldest of 15 children, had personal grounds for her enthusiasm. In 1855 her mother had died, leaving the family with the problem of running the household. Her father suggested she should become a governess, as she was too weak for household tasks. As she wrote to her aunt, 'All household work is absolute toil to me. I am not equal to it.'[48] In later years the Becker household had servant problems of its own; the family diary records the comings and goings of five female servants in just over a month, shortly after Lydia returned from her trip to Bradford for the British Association meeting.[49] Mrs King's view of women's responsibility for domestic work would have appealed to Becker, who had written, only six years earlier: 'It is true that the peculiar duty of woman is to mind the house, and attend to the comfort of the inmates; . . . '[50] This is consistent with her opinion that only single women should be entitled to vote, as they were able to be responsible for property.[51] Becker's advocacy of cooperative housekeeping was not reflected in the women's suffrage movement of the 1870s, perhaps because most of those involved were middle class and had not shared Becker's experience of domestic hardship.

In her response to Mrs King's lecture, Becker had appealed to men with experience of organising labour in industry to advise women on the division of labour in the home. This point in particular was attacked by *The Queen*[47] in a scathing reply to the whole idea of cooperative housekeeping. *The Queen*'s columnist extended Becker's argument to its logical conclusion, that women's sphere of influence, the home, could be better run by men; by 'common consent' this was clearly not the case. *The Queen*'s criticism rested on the expense of the scheme. If profitable, profits would go to a landlord or hotel-keeper, and if unprofitable, life would be uncomfortable: 'We may say of Mrs King's scheme that it would be as dear as an hotel, and as miserable as a boarding house, instead of being, as she seems to imagine, as cheap as a boarding house, and as comfortable as an hotel.' Mrs King was accused of simply bringing up the old idea of hotel-living in a new guise, and indeed, as she had included so few of the cooperative elements that distinguished the Peirce plan, this was a reasonable point. *The Queen* saw only discomfort in communal living, dismissing its social benefits; having reduced the plan to a form of cheap hotel living, it finished with the ultimate in English criticism, that the plan involved a different way of life.

> it may be said that it is from first to last so utterly opposed to all our habits, customs, ways of thought, modes of life, and, if Mrs King pleases, prejudices, that there is no real fear of the experiment even being so much as tried, unless some more than usually zealous amateur of social science is willing to try it at his own expense.

The Queen had also criticised Mrs King's lecture for its lack of a detailed plan for her cooperative home. This omission was rectified early the following year when she published plans and a long article in *Building News*.[52] She had asked the architect Edward W. Godwin to draw up plans for the cooperative home, and he produced a design for a large, three-storey house containing 21 family flats (two to four bedrooms), a dining room, kitchen and children's amenities (Plate 2, Figure 2). Mrs King suggested an extra floor with single rooms for guests or poorer

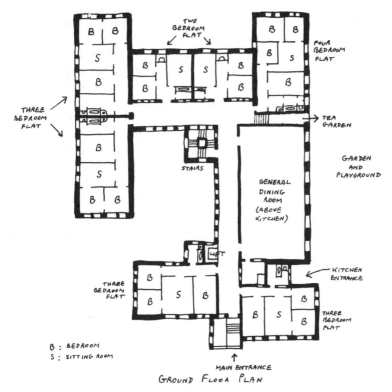

FIGURE 2 *Ground-floor plan of cooperative home designed by E. W. Godwin for Mrs E. M. King (from Building News, 24 April 1874, vol. 26, pp. 452–3)*

residents. The building was to be centrally heated from the kitchen range, well ventilated and provided with a lift. Each flat had its own bathroom and sitting room, the only communally used areas being the dining room and the room above it, presumably a library or common room. The entire building – 'neither a "huge barrack" nor a flaunting hotel' (p. 460) – would house over 100 adults and at least twice that number of children. Mrs King emphasised the privacy and isolation each family could expect, as a result of the high standard of construction of the building, and reminded readers of the advantages in terms of varied social life to be gained from living in close proximity to other families.

Godwin had apparently tried to design a building which looked as non-institutional as possible. The house was a rambling mass of gables, built of brick, with a tower and several groups of tall

chimneys. In shape it was almost quadrangular, the square possibly being broken to ensure maximum privacy for each front door.
The interior of the quadrangle would have been rather gloomy,
even more so with Mrs King's suggestion of an extra storey;
this, however, would only have affected light to corridors and
stairwells. To keep inter-flat noise to a minimum, Godwin
arranged the rooms to avoid sitting rooms and bedrooms in
separate flats sharing the same party wall; stairs and the lift
were on the inside of the main corridor. The performance of the
building would have depended not only upon the standard of its
construction, but also upon the arrangements for transferring food
from kitchen to dining room, which were not detailed. Apart
from the gloomy and probably useless central courtyard, all the
children's rooms and servants' areas were placed in the basement,
an odd decision given Mrs King's insistence on good provision
for children and the necessity for their inclusion in the cooperative
home. It did, however, accord with her desire that their accommodation should be 'planned in such a way that they may not
become a nuisance or an infliction to grown people' (p. 459).

At the time he received the commission from Mrs King, E. W.
Godwin's architectural practice was going through a quiet phase.[53]
Godwin was an unconventional man, the first architect of Bedford
Park and chief exponent of the aesthetic movement, holding that
the arts and everyday life were completely interrelated.[54] Apart
from his design for the cooperative home, there is no record of
any further involvement on his part in cooperative housekeeping,
but he was a supporter of the view that women should be allowed
to earn their own living. He went so far as to take a woman pupil
into his practice,and wrote a short piece in June 1874 for *Women
and Work* on the possibilities of the architectural profession for
women.[55] He saw no reason why women should not profitably
enter the profession, although 'An impulsive, gay, free-as-air,
lightsome sort of girl, is not the stuff for an architect. The right
sort being found, there is before her a wide field of usefulness.'
In this wide field he included the design of public buildings,
normally thought to be well outside the scope of aspiring female
architects. Godwin's aesthetic viewpoint led him to become
involved in the rational dress movement, giving a lecture 'Dress
and its Relation to Health and Climate' in 1884.[56]

The Rational Dress Society, with Mrs E. M. King as its secretary,
had been formed in 1881. The aim of the society was to encourage

the adoption of a style of dress based on comfort, health and beauty.[57] An exhibition of rational dress was organised in 1883, arranged and paid for entirely by Mrs King, who also designed a 'tricycle dress' with skirt and trousers.[58] Numerous figures from the artistic world became involved with the rational dress movement, including the artist and socialist Walter Crane, later an advocate of cooperative housekeeping. Lydia Becker wrote in 1888 in favour of keeping the corset,[59] an unexpected argument in view of her advocacy of the women's franchise. She maintained that the corset supported the heavy weight of outer clothing. The general climate of social experiment in middle-class artistic circles meant that proposals such as that of Mrs King for the cooperative home might at least be more seriously considered than earlier suggestions from more strictly political or religious sources. Both the aesthetic and rational dress movements emphasised health, comfort and beauty. Supporters of either might be expected to express interest in a proposal which offered improvements in those areas of home life, and had overtones of a better social life rather than pure, or puritanical, socialism.

There appeared to be no direct result from Mrs King's proposal and Godwin's plans, but these were the first architecturally correct plans for a cooperative home to be published in England. There was already a working group of cooperative houses in existence in London, at Stamford Hill. This group was mentioned by Mrs King in her 1874 paper to the Glasgow meeting of the National Association for the Promotion of Social Science.[60] They had apparently received 'favourable notice', but were not otherwise described; a pity, since this is the first known English example of a working cooperative home. Mrs King's paper had a more radical tone than her previous articles, suggesting that domestic economy opened up increasing possibilities for women's employment, something she had barely mentioned until this point. She foresaw the setting up of cooperative homes by men, with male needs in mind, and encouraged women to take part in the new developments before they could be completely excluded. As usual, she envisaged either cooperation between the sexes or male domination of the home, never a wholly female solution to the housing or servant problem. This 1874 paper was Mrs King's final venture in the field of cooperative housekeeping; after her involvement with the Rational Dress Society in the 1880s, she died in the later years of that decade.

The 1870s saw not only the first of many English articles on cooperative housekeeping, and one actual experiment, but also the visit of Melusina Fay Peirce to London in 1874–5. She visited a cooperative store and met Thomas Hughes and E. O. Greening, prime movers in the English cooperative movement.[61] There was, however, still no sign of her ideas being taken seriously by the cooperative movement in general. Similarly, no sponsor had come forward to erect a large cooperative home along the lines of Mrs King's plan; in spite of all the interest, the only experiment which had taken place was at Stamford Hill. The *Englishwoman's Review* had published a report of Mrs King's original Bradford paper, and continued to take an interest in the subject with its clear implications for women's domestic work. The emphasis in Elizabeth Ramsay's article in the *Review*[62] was on cooperative housekeeping as a solution to the servant problem. She could only see increasing difficulties in the employment of servants, noting that employment opportunities for women were growing.

The facts of the employment situation were complex. Women were increasingly finding clerical work,[63] but rather than an actual decline in the number of people available to perform domestic work, it appears that the work was being done outside the home instead of inside.[64] The location of employment changed, with more use being made of services such as laundries and restaurants. It is possible that the high point of domestic employment was reached in 1871,[65] well before the First World War, which is the date most often quoted.[66] There was also the problem of finding suitable servants; Prochaska has suggested a flood of cheap domestic labour split servant ranks into those who were expensive and experienced and those who were cheaper, less respectable and less acceptable to employers.[67] The overall employment pattern of domestic servants is by no means clear, with some middle-class families keeping no servants, while less wealthy families could afford cheap help.[68] Thus it seems that Elizabeth Ramsay was justified in her worries about changes in the nature of domestic service, if not for the simple reason she suggested, that of increasing opportunities for women in other fields.

Ramsay saw three solutions to the servant problem: families could pay servants more, put up with bad service or opt for cooperative housekeeping. Contrary to some previous advocates, she did not suggest cooperation as the solution for all families, saying it was best for the single or married couple without dependent children. She returned to the old theme of improvements in domestic machinery, first suggested in this connection by Adams[69] in 1834. She compared the substitution of servants by central heating, running water, washing and knife-cleaning machines to Edward Bulwer Lytton's domestic robots.[70] She felt that cooperative housekeeping establishments, like good clubs, would leave women free from trivial interruption. She suggested testing the arrangements on a small scale, with just two families cooperating, which would have been a more practical proposition than the large schemes.

The same year, 1875, saw another philanthropic middle-class suggestion that cooperation should be applied to the working-class housing problem. Dr Sigmund Englander, at the Brighton meeting of the National Association for the Promotion of Social Science, proposed that some type of work should be given to tenants of cooperative homes, so that they were able to pay their way and had an interest, housing, in common.[71] Cooperative housing was to reconcile privacy and individuality, as a means to human progress. At the following year's meeting, Miss Marie C. C. Morfit came up with a contrasting scheme for six solidly middle-class families.[72] Her slightly fantastic edifice (Figure 3) contained six six- to seven-person flats, all domestic offices, servants' living quarters, sick rooms and a games room. It had at least one glaring constructional defect, with its skating rink positioned in the attic. Disregarding the exact details of the building, it was an attempt to be more precise in listing the requirements for cooperative housing. She also costed the proposed experiment, allowing for nine domestic staff from manager to kitchenmaid, concluding that an annual payment from each family of just under £200 would cover all services and provide a 10 per cent return on investment for any landlord erecting such a building. The wages she proposed to pay the servants – £30 per annum for a cook, £15 for a housemaid – are comparable with wage rates quoted from other sources for the time.[73] Morfit's point was simply that with good planning and some slight cooperation, higher standards of domestic service might be achieved at a lower cost. There were no thoughts of improved social life, 'Nothing of the character of a hotel or club is contemplated' (p. 618), nor were changes proposed in the relationship of servant to employer.

Her building would have been unwieldly in operation,

40

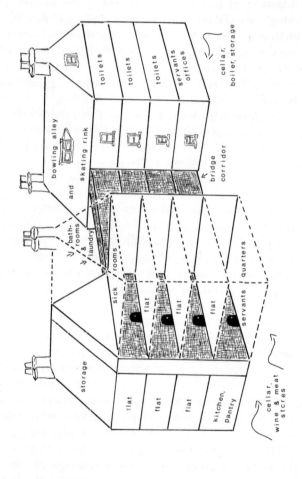

FIGURE 3 *Marie C. C. Moffit's cooperative house (from a description in Transactions of the National Association for the Promotion of Social Science, 1876, pp. 618–19; first shown in* Spare Rib, *Sept 1983, no. 134, p. 57)*

although enough facilities were included for six families. The flats themselves contained only a dining room, drawing room, library and three bedrooms, all bath and toilet facilities being in the rear annexe. The flats were therefore hardly self-contained, and it is hard to imagine members of the Victorian middle class being sociable in the central passage on their way to or from the bathrooms. Meals were to be hoisted from kitchen to dining rooms by lift, which opened on to an antechamber adjoining the dining room. With only three housemaids and one kitchenmaid, it is likely that staff would have found working conditions much the same as in an ordinary home. They would not have had to deal with coal fires, however, as all heating was provided from the central boiler.

Morfit was sure that for improvements in living standards and privacy by means of a minimal cooperation, 'Houses as at present constructed are unsuitable, and hence special buildings are requisite' (p. 618). Even as she gave her paper at the meeting of the National Association, a new type of flat was being erected in London: the catering flat. These flats had evolved from hotels; families could rent entire suites and be served meals in their rooms or eat in a dining hall. The object of the proprietors was to make a profit from servicing middle-class families who wanted their food prepared and their rooms cleaned without having to organise their own servants. The blocks of flats resembled hotels, and indeed the catering flat system was more like hotel life than cooperative housekeeping, as almost all the cooperative elements had been replaced; servants simply worked for the management rather than for individual families. At first the catering flats were popular, their cost being comparable to the cost of living in normal households, and the mistress of the house gained considerably:

> As she is thus relieved of all the anxiety of catering, and can be assured of always having the best of cooks, with experienced waiters or waitresses, it would seem that there is likely to be an increasing demand for this type of menage, which combines the privacy of the house with the advantage of experienced hotel management.[74]

Hall praised these flats in 1874, but at almost the same time their construction was being criticised. The largest block[75] was Queen Anne's Mansions, opposite St James's Park in south west London.

The ten-storey block, 'perhaps the most famous and horrifying of all nineteenth century apartment blocks',[76] was built in 1875. A further block, one storey higher, was added two years later in view of the great demand for the flats. Suites of two rooms upwards could be rented, the cost ranging from £60 per annum for two rooms to £300 per annum for six rooms. The journal *The Builder* was scathing about this 'huge tower', grumbling that 'The rent which these buildings command may perhaps be regarded as another inducement to continue Babel-like structures.'[77] Tenants, households in the upper-income range, had the use of a dining room and drawing room as well as their own set of rooms. The flats themselves were simply a series of rooms opening off a hall or short corridor. Other blocks of catering flats were built, and the Savoy Hotel began to let suites of rooms on a catering basis.[78] Although flat life in general enjoyed a short period of popularity in the 1880s, 'by the end of the century the Englishman was more firmly wedded than ever to the concept of his house with its patch of garden'.[79] As Tarn explains, interest in flats dropped swiftly after the turn of the century, and the vogue for catering flats also disappeared. It had little connection in principle with cooperative housekeeping, although superficially its practical development was similar.

While catering flats were fashionable, they were connected with cooperative housekeeping by articles such as Roswell Fisher's of 1877.[80] He stated the case for cooperative housekeeping as the application of economic principles to domestic life, rather than a social or socialist reform. Although he mentioned the success of catering flats, he felt that some form of cooperative management was necessary on grounds of quality and efficiency, as residents without their own kitchens could be exploited by a purely commercial firm. He saw the future of upper- and middle-class dwellings as being in cooperatively managed groups with ensured privacy, offering tenants freedom from domestic worries, economy and high standards of service. Fisher suggested that cooperative mansions would soon become one of the best property investments available, but there were still no investors prepared to mount a truly cooperative experiment. Augusta Webster remarked on the great interest in domestic cooperation, and the equally great lack of enthusiasm for practical measures: 'Our zeal has a vicarious vigour; it is to see co-operative housekeeping tried that we yearn, trying it ourselves is another matter.'[81] She criticised the obvious shortcomings of flat life, such as the lack of space and inadequacy of lifts:

It is not soothing, for instance, to the inhabitants of the remote and airy heights of a Westminster fourth or fifth floor flat, after having had to breakfast without milk, to learn, in answer to their resentful enquiries, that the milkman's conscience is clear, and the milk a quarter of a mile off in the fathomless deeps of an area of whose existence they are scarcely aware and whence it is about as likely to get to them as if it were in the opposite house's coal-cellar.[82]

Her greatest complaint was that cooperative cooking was not the norm, so that servants were still really in control of the establishment. She felt catering flats could therefore be a great success as long as the service was efficient, although she described Queen Anne's Mansions as an

appalling erection which, scowling over Westminster, grows and grows till it threatens to shut London out from the sun, with its tier upon tier of square flat windows, and its unpretending hideousness . . . perhaps it is a factory of domestic bliss.[83]

Her feelings about the mansions echoed the ambivalence of the entire article; it was clear that the time had come for a change in the nature of domestic life, but none of the alternatives were particularly palatable. J. J. Stevenson, a leading architect of the 'Queen Anne' movement,[84] summed up feelings about changes in domestic lifestyles in his two volumes on *House Architecture* of 1880. He felt that difficulties in obtaining servants 'may alter our system of living' but that 'it will be some time probably before . . . cooperative housekeeping become English institutions [sic]'.[85]

Over the entire decade of the 1870s there had indeed been little in the way of changes to domestic life, in spite of the publicity accorded to the idea of cooperative housekeeping. The rich had altered the basis of the original plan to produce catering flats, merely a slight change in hotel practice. Women were increasingly demanding housing suitable to their new status as workers, and it was in this area that the next developments were to take place. But for the vast majority of middle-class and working-class households, cooperative housekeeping was simply an idea in the pages of a magazine.

The main difficulty with Peirce's or King's original plans lay in the need for new buildings, either housing or central facilities. Most of the variations in the plans had also stipulated new build-ing, including those suggested by members of the cooperative movement. If an investor could obtain a good return from con-ventional housing, there was no reason for putting money into property which might prove unpopular. Likewise, the phil-anthropic investors would receive no greater return for the addition of communal facilities, which might be misused in any case. The most likely avenue for the further development of coop-erative housekeeping was the possibility of its being taken up as part of another movement, which would include a changing life-style as one of its aims. Members of the aesthetic movement were peripherally involved with cooperative housekeeping, as with Godwin's house design, but the movement itself found expression through art forms rather than lifestyles. Godwin did design houses for artists, but not to a cooperative plan.[86]

There was no clear source of funds for an experiment in coop-erative housekeeping; it was to be almost ten years before a company was formed to promote this type of housing for single women, and even longer until families were able to benefit. Mean-while the original problems of domestic life for women were as great as when the *Atlantic Monthly* articles had appeared and apparently offered a solution. The introduction of domestic appliances was slow and the servant problem was ever present; conflict between housekeeping practice and the idealised home worsened with the increased possibility of single middle-class women obtaining work outside the home. Their problem then was to combine paid work with the upkeep of high standards in the home. A combination of the mainly conservative English reaction to flat-living, or any change in home life, and the dif-ficulties of financing a building with overtones of socialism, toge-ther put paid to the idea of introducing cooperation into domestic life. It is a tribute to the strength of the idea and the problems of contemporary housekeeping that it did not simply fade into obscurity.

4 Homes for Working Women

The second half of the nineteenth century saw women begin to break free from the constraints of their domestic sphere of life. The range of activities it was acceptable for them to undertake gradually enlarged, and more women began to take paid jobs outside the home. Working-class women had, of course, always worked, whether inside or outside the home, and many middle-class women also had to do domestic work.[1] The upper and upper-middle classes had their charitable work, which could be fitted in around the household routine.[2] These domestic occupations were essentially for married women, although daughters were expected to do their share in the household before they left home on marriage. A society which perceived women only in so far as they were attached to men was therefore faced with a problem when the number of women exceeded men; in 1871, there were almost 600 000 more women than men aged 20 or older in England and Wales.[3] Fathers were responsible for their daughters until marriage, but if marriage was postponed indefinitely, this could result in a strain on family finances.

This situation provided women with the opportunity to attempt to earn their own living, but this was not to the taste of the professional organisations in particular. *The Lancet* in 1867 opined that women's place was in the home because they were less fit than men to encounter the obstacles of the world;[4] a *National Review* article of 1862 proposed that 'redundant' women should emigrate to the colonies in order to find husbands;[5] while it was 1898 before the RIBA elected its first woman member.[6] However, the number of women clerical workers increased dramatically towards the turn of the century. In 1901, 17 per cent of clerks in business and the civil service were women. The 1881 figure of 9205 had comprised only 4 per cent of the total, the rise in numerical terms being 60 891.[7] Advances were made in a wide variety of fields including higher education – Girton College, Cambridge, was founded in 1869[8] – and the long struggle for

women's suffrage reached Parliament in the 1860s. The organisational skills many women had learned in the course of their
philanthropic activities were useful in the suffrage movement.[9]

The world of work held many perils for women in the eyes of
conventional society. One of the most important of these was the
loss in status caused by a gentlewoman actually being paid for
working. Philanthropists evolved several schemes to circumvent
this objection, with women needleworkers, for example, either
working at home or only in workshops with their own class.[10]
The increase in women's employment brought with it the possibility that unmarried daughters of middle-class families might
meet and work with women whose moral standards differed. If
living at home, daughters could be supervised until marriage, but
the young single woman living alone was, in the eyes of her
family, in some moral danger. The early years of the nineteenth
century had seen the world of the mdidle-class woman shrink as
more and more restrictions were placed on her mobility, respectable women never walking but always riding in carriages; the
origin of this practice was concern about the sexual and social
purity of unmarried young women.[11] As more middle-class young
women took jobs in cities, finding suitable accommodation for
them became a problem. Lodgings had to satisfy high standards
of cleanliness and moral security before they could be acceptable
to parents, while some – the 'needy gentlewomen' – had to take
whatever accommodation was on offer. The first issue of *Women
and Work* in 1874 quoted from several letters received from poor
women desperate for work, and noted the difficulties of finding
somewhere to live: 'Sometimes the parents (not unnaturally)
object to a daughter leaving home – very often the applicants
themselves dread "lodgings" in a strange place.'[12] The journal
helped women find places in families, but failing that, a young
woman might easily find herself in the position desribed by H.
G. Wells in *Ann Veronica*, written after the turn of the century but
only too well reflecting the situation in the 1880s and 1890s:

Such apartments as she saw were either scandalously dirty or
unaccountably dear, or both. And some were adorned with
engravings that struck her as being more vulgar and unde-
sirable than anything she had ever seen in her life ... The
windows of these rooms were obscured with draperies, their

floors a carpet patchwork; the china ornaments on their mantels were of a class apart.[13]

One of the first attempts to provide accommodation for 'struggling or lonely ladies, whose life in lodgings is often a misery and not a home'[14] was made by Lady Mary Feilding in 1878. She adapted a six-storey block of artisans' rooms in Kensington for the needs of women with small fixed incomes, teachers and students.[15] There were about 50 rooms in all, let singly or in groups, furnished or unfurnished. These flats were intended to be for the poorer class of gentlewoman, the lowest rent for a single unfurnished room being 2s 6d per week. The service charge was 9d per room per week, which covered the work of a housemaid and of cooked dinners delivered to the tenant's room. There was no communal dining room or sitting room, as Feilding believed that ladies wished 'to choose their acquaintance, which becomes impossible when meals are taken in common. When all else that made home is gone, it is still something to have your own room for your castle free of intruders . . .'[16] A woman could rent one of the cheaper rooms for £9 15s per annum, inclusive of dinner; she would have to provide her own breakfast and tea, do the associated washing up, and dust the room.[17] Feilding went on to provide more rooms of the same type in Chelsea, as they had been successful and paid their way; the overall rent for the block was £350 per annum, paid to the National Dwellings Company.

In spite of the success of Feilding's experiment at the lower end of the ladies' housing market, it was ten years before a company was formed to meet the housing needs of wealthier single women. The level of service in Feilding's houses was basic, no facilities were offered apart from tenants' own rooms, and the gas was turned off and the house closed at 11 p.m. every night. Possibly speculators felt that building to a higher standard and, more importantly, providing an improved level of service, would result in reduced profit margins. Demand for housing of a more luxurius type had not yet been proven. Women's magazines had shown a consistent interest in housing problems of all kinds, including the provision of central kitchens, and associated homes,[18] and in August 1887 the subject of the monthly prize competition in *Work and Leisure* was the design of a block of associated dwellings for single women earning from 20s to 90s a week. The magazine was disappointed to receive only two poor responses, but decided to suggest its own design, in the hope that it would be taken up by an investment company.[19]

The 'Castle in the Air' was to have flats of varying sizes to suit all incomes, the only women excluded being those widows with young children. There was to be a restaurant, shared with local customers, and a ladies' waiting room, 'the need for which is so urgent in many parts of London', also open to all on payment of $\frac{1}{2}$d. There was a laundry, servants' rooms and a common room, and the entire building was to be managed by a lady superintendent. Labour-saving fittings were to be included. Although the plan was unexceptional, being only the latest in a long line of similar suggestions, it at last produced a reaction in the form of the registration of the Ladies' Dwellings Company Limited on 6 April 1888. Letters of support for the idea of a cooperative home had reached the editor of *Work and Leisure*, Louisa M. Hubbard, following the publication of the plan.[20] She and her associates then developed the idea and proposed in November 1887 that a Ladies' Associated Dwellings Company should be formed.[21] A circular to this effect was included in the December 1887 issue of *Work and Leisure*, and by April the company was registered under a slightly different name.[22] It was estimated that supporters of the project would need to raise the sum of £30 000 to buy a suitable site and erect a 200-room block.

The Ladies' Dwellings Company and another company, Ladies' Residential Chambers Ltd, which was registered in 1889, were able to obtain funds and successfully erect buildings. Harriet Martineau had suggested this type of building in 1850,[23] so what were the factors which made it possible only after a period of nearly 40 years? In those four decades, women's employment had increased steadily: thus, by 1887, there was an even clearer need for accommodation for single women with the power to earn their own living. The efforts of one strand of the Victorian women's movement had been successful in 1882, when the Married Women's Property Act, 1882, was passed. This act set out the rights and responsibilities of women with respect to their own separate property, but just as importantly, its passing changed women's attitudes and attitudes towards women. Emancipation had become a state of mind.[24] Women involved in the campaign to change the property laws soon began to fight for other feminist causes,[25] particularly as the suffrage campaign itself declined from

1884 until near the turn of the century.[26] Housing, as well as education and employment, began to be seen as a practical method of improving women's position. Single women in particular would doubly benefit, as the availability of accommodation would enable them to take up places on courses and work opportunities. Married women could see the provision of this type of accommodation as part of the women's movement in general, provision for their daughters, or as an insurance against widowhood for themselves. Although housing was not seen as one of the most important issues of the late nineteenth-century women's movement, it warranted constant reports in journals such as the *Englishwoman's Review* and *Work and Leisure*; even *The Queen* took a strong interest in the matter. Women directly involved in the campaign for women's suffrage did take an interest in housing, for example Lydia Becker, but the fields of education and employment received more publicity. Within the middle classes, housing need was great only for single women; many of the supporters of women's suffrage were more than adequately housed, so that the subject was not one of such immediate relevance.

The first block of women's flats to open was built in Chenies Street, Bloomsbury, by Ladies' Residential Chambers Ltd. The opening, on 20 May 1889, was attended by a number of well-known figures in the women's movement, including Lydia Becker, Clementina Black, Elizabeth Garrett Anderson, England's first woman doctor, and Lady Stanley of Alderley, promotor of women's educational advancement. Several titled ladies were present, including Viscountess Harberton, the founder, with Mrs E. M. King, of the Rational Dress Society in 1881.[27] The building itself (see Plate 3) was a six-storey-high block containing flats of two to four rooms, all self-contained. There was a common dining room and kitchen on the basement floor, and cooking was to be carried out on the cooperative housekeeping system.[28] Elizabeth Garrett Anderson hoped 'that the food would be of a much more appetising and attractive character than that to which ladies living alone were usually accustomed'.[29] Rents varied from 10s to 25s per week, depending on the number and position of rooms, and there was a monthly charge of 10s for use of the dining room. There was a small kitchen within each flat, but tenants could buy moderately priced meals from the cooperative kitchen. There had been some discussion by the directors of the company as to the scale of charges for rooms,[30] but although the rents were relatively high (Feilding's rooms had a maximum weekly rental of 4s), the directors' decision was vindicated by the number of applications for places. In 1890 the Chambers had 18 residents, in 1891 17, including one Margaret Sharpe, a doctor; they were continuously occupied until the Second World War.[31] The red-brick building was designed by J. M. Brydon, who went on to build the Hospital for Women, Euston Road, in 1894.

The design of the building was intended to provide the women with independent flats, reached by an impressive stone staircase, and the benefits of cooperation in the form of good, cheap meals in the cooperative dining room. There was a caretaker, but no mention was made of a lady manager or superintendent; the method of managing the building is unknown. The Chambers appeared to be successful, to judge by their continuous occupation, the only possible disadvantage in design being the position of the dining room in the basement. Although this made the serving of food far simpler than if the kitchen was situated below the dining room, this did mean that the room was rather gloomy. This may have discouraged women from using it, especially as they had some facilities for cooking in their own rooms. The large, solid, red-brick exterior of the flats was suf-ficiently impressive to assist in establishing the Chambers as a respectable place for young single women to live. No doubt the well-publicised visit of inspection by the string of titled guests on opening day also helped in this process.

In August 1889 the Ladies' Dwellings Company opened Sloane Gardens House in Sloane Gardens, just off Sloane Square[32].The six-storey building was on a grander scale than the Chenies Street Chambers, catering for 106 women and providing a public restaurant, reception room, music rooms and studios. There was a lift, thus rents for all floors were much the same, varying between 6s 6d and 8s 6d per week. This put Sloane Gardens into the medium-price range of women's accommodation. Rent included service, but meals had to be eaten in the restaurant, as servants were not expected to wait on tenants in their own rooms. With the exception of a laundry and any mention of labour-saving equipment, the plans of the building bore a strong resemblance to the ideas as originally set out in the 'Castle in the Air' article which effectively began the project.[33] As suggested, there were single cubicles for hire, as well as sets of rooms, a lady housekeeper was present, and the street front consisted of four shops.[34] After the house had been open three months, the only complaint was that charges were too high for the 'working gentlewoman'.[35] As the object of the company was to provide accommodation as a profitable and philanthropic investment, this was no surprise; Sloane Gardens was a fashionable area. Even as the flats were opened, the company was contemplating the erection of a second block, probably in a less expensive area.

Ladies' Residential Chambers soon followed up their initial success at Chenies Street with another block of flats at York Street, Marylebone (see Plate 4). It was opened in May 1892,[36] and soon a series of clubs and homes for women was opening in London. There was a residential club just off the High Street, Kensington, and two more in Earl's Court, all of which were opened by 1891.[37] Another opened in 1895 in Oakley Street, Chelsea, where the second of Feilding's homes was situated.[38] Often these clubs were no more than two houses with a dining room in common, where ladies could hire rooms or simply be casual members. Outside London, similar clubs and homes were being opened, for example in Sheffield in 1889 by Mrs Fenn.[39] Several of the smaller clubs were founded by women, possibly making use of their own property to obtain an income from the new market of single working women.

The tenants of the York Street Chambers (see Figure 4) were 'principally artists, authors, nurses and other workers'.[40] The six-storey red-brick U-shaped block contained flats and bed sitting rooms arranged around its outer edge, the inner edge being lined with corridors, stairs, spare rooms and bathrooms. The common dining room, as with the Chenies Street flats, is in the basement, its few windows being below street level and partly facing on to the gloomy inner court of the building. This dark, north-facing court would have had little use apart from providing the stairs with some natural light. The kitchen was also in the basement, only a few yards from the dining room. There were three ladies' flats in the basement, as well as the servants' rooms; these can hardly have been popular (unless very cheap) due to the proximity of both smells and servants. There was lift as well as stair access to the other five floors, each of which held 10 to 11 flats. Several pairs of flats shared a front door and pantry, but were otherwise self-contained. The toilet opened off the pantry, an unusual

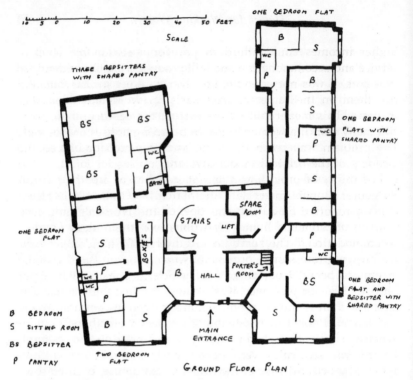

ONE BEDROOM FLAT

SCALE

THREE BEDSITTERS
WITH SHARED PANTRY

ONE BEDROOM
FLATS WITH
SHARED PANTRY

ONE BEDROOM
FLAT

ONE BEDROOM
FLAT AND
BEDSITTER WITH
SHARED PANTRY

B   BEDROOM
S   SITTING ROOM
BS   BEDSITTER
P   PANTRY

TWO BEDROOM
FLAT

GROUND FLOOR PLAN

FIGURE 4 *Ground-floor plan of ladies' residential chambers, York Street,
London (redrawn from Sydney Perks, Residential Flats of all Classes,
Batsford, London, 1905, fig. 156)*

arrangement, and there was only one bathroom for all 13 flats on
the ground and basement floors. The rooms were adequate in
size: a typical sitting room measured 12' × 15', and a bedroom
11' × 8'; all had fireplaces. The strongest point of the design was
the relative privacy of each flat, only one tenant on each floor
having to walk past another front door to reach her own. The bad
points were the lack of bathrooms and the siting of the basement
flats, for both tenants and servants. The flat opposite the dining
room, at the north end of a dark corridor and with its bedroom
window opening on to the courtyard, would not have been a very
pleasant proposition. Entrance to the flats was made relatively
secure by the siting of the porter's room next to the hall.

Flats such as the Residential Chambers and Sloane Gardens
House were a success for both professional women and the philanthropic companies which erected the buildings. Women on

higher incomes could afford to pay for a reasonable level of service and accommodation and still produce a small dividend for investors. It was not possible, however, to erect similar flats and run them on the same serviced basis for women with smaller incomes. This meant that by the turn of the century, there were still many working women living in boarding houses or lodgings. The problem was much the same as that which had faced the builders of the original model dwelling houses for families, the impossibility of providing a decent standard of accommodation for poorer people. An article in the March 1900 issue of *Nineteenth Century* reported on an investigation by the Women's Industrial Council of women's living conditions and their ideas of ideal accommodation.[41] The survey covered over 600 London women, mainly in professional occupations, and found their average income to be £129 per annum, of which they paid £28 (22 per cent) in rent, or just over 10 shillings per week. Over half the total lived in a single room, generally seen as uncomfortable and lonely. Rooms in residential chambers were thought to be expensive, as well as badly managed and providing poor food. Their oppressive rules were mentioned in several comments. In spite of this clear dislike of the available residential chambers, an overwhelming majority of women surveyed wanted to live in some form of 'combined dwelling'. They wanted no more strict rules and segregated communities ('pusseries'), and felt that management should be undertaken by committees of residents. The presence of men was seen as a method of upgrading standards of food and accommodation, a rather sad comment on the experience of a decade of housing intended to help advance women's opportunities.

The ideal accommodation for women, yet another 'castle in the air', was to be a large building situated in Bloomsbury, housing about 200 men and women. Tenants could rent one to four rooms, studios and music rooms would be available, and there would be a variety of common rooms and a dining hall. A servants' block would be attached to the main building, and a lady warden would run the establishment and be responsible to a committee of residents. The author felt such a building could be constructed for £30 000, and would be a profitable investment. As one woman worker put it: 'A wholesome existence with perfect freedom is all that is required' (p. 481).

The idea of a mixed and well serviced castle in the air probably foundered on grounds of cost. The women in the survey had, not unnaturally, wanted to pay slightly less for better accommodation than they already had. The most interesting part of the survey lies in its endorsement of the idea of combined dwellings. Cooperative life was

> in an early, even embryonic, stage of its history. The twentieth century will witness its development. For women at least all efforts in that direction have been more or less clumsy, certain ancient notions clogging the wheels of advance. When these are removed, co-operative life will develop easily . . . (p.479)

The first two decades of the twentieth century saw great advances for the idea of cooperative living, but none of these developments took place in central London. Several more blocks of women's rooms and flats were built, the idea of mixed accommodation being perhaps rather too progressive for the mainly small philanthropic companies which funded them. These blocks were intended to be substitute homes, where women could rent either flats or single rooms;[42] one of the later blocks was Nutford House, just north of Hyde Park, built in 1916 (see Plate 5).[43] It was (and still is) a six-storey building of unusual purple brick, its windows dressed with red brick. As originally planned, its dining room was in the basement, close to the kitchen, and directly under the entrance to the ground floor.The social room, library and lounge were on the ground floor, all the bedrooms being on the first floor and upwards. They were simply a series of single rooms, ranged along a corridor which ran the entire length of the L-shaped building.

Nutford House was described as a residential club, and its system of single rooms and communal dining hall did not really keep to the spirit of the original idea of cooperative housekeeping, which demanded that households should cooperate in order to economise and save time. The air of impermanence surrounding life in single rooms might have been dispelled in those buildings such as the Residential Chambers where entire sets of rooms could be rented, and certainly Chenies Street and York Street do come closer to the ideal of a cooperative flat. Sloane Gardens House also had a mixture of single rooms, cubicles and flats, but the majority of the accommodation was single room. The residential chambers were not able to provide meals in tenants' rooms, management was not under the control of tenants, and they existed in order to make a profit for their shareholders, although investors may often have felt their motives to be philanthropic as the dividend was not large. True cooperative living implied a home plus communal elements; self-management, non-profit-making (any profit was to be ploughed back), and no enforced communality. The turnover at Chenies Street, where over half the residents left after the first year, may have reflected dissatisfaction with the level of cooperation. However, the chambers were an example of cooperation at the minimal level in domestic life; unlike the case of catering flats, at least the tenants ate together and motives were social as well as economic.

There was clearly still an accommodation problem for women workers, particularly the lower paid, well into the twentieth century. Although various grades of rooms, flats and clubs existed for better paid workers, the National Association for Women's Lodging Homes felt there was insufficient accommodation at all levels. The Association saw cooperative living as a safer form of housing for women, but noted the usual drawback, lack of capital to begin with, even on the part of those women who might be able to afford higher rents.[44] Companies were still being formed specifically to house women, such as Lady Workers' Homes Limited (registered July 1914), but the trend of women's housing was away from communal living in the residential chambers manner. The newer blocks often contained only single rooms and a canteen, with other facilities like laundries and common rooms, and were more hostels than collections of homes. The main thrust of cooperative housekeeping had moved on by the turn of the century, and was concerned with changes in family lifestyle. Although housing specifically for women was to be an important part of the cooperative housekeeping movement, it did not lead the way towards changes in house design. The break away from traditional housing was led by people wealthy enough to be able to experiment with lifestyles. Most working women had no capital and little choice of housing. The form of cooperative living offered by the residential chambers was socially acceptable and fairly economical; it broke no housing barriers, but it did give a secure home to women working for emancipation in many areas of their lives.

5 Socialised Domestic Work and the Garden City

In the 15 years following Mrs E. M. King's proposal for a cooperative home in 1874, much was written about housekeeping methods but few practical improvements were introduced. Middle-class wives were still dealing with the problems of coal ranges, gas lighting and difficult or unobtainable servants well into the 1890s. Although some parts of Kensington were supplied with electricity for lighting in 1887, it was after 1900 before this became the norm, with the consequent reduction in dirt and cleaning.[1] Suburban living had become more widely available from 1880 onwards,[2] and wives with new houses and housekeeping problems provided a growing market for the plethora of women's magazines concerned with upkeep of the home. The *Housewife* began publishing in 1886, *The Mother's Companion* in 1887 and *The Ladies' Home Journal* in 1890, and these were followed by many more,[3] with articles frequently concerned with home management and the servant problem. The teaching of domestic subjects was becoming more common, their importance in the school curriculum increasing in the 1880s and 1890s,[4] while the theory and practice of domestic economy was taught widely in evening classes by the late 1890s.[5]

This increased concern with housekeeping problems reflected their intransigent nature. The experiments of catering flats and residential chambers had been found to function well for specific groups of people who did not wish, or were not able, to live in individual houses. Households wishing to retain complete independence had been offered no clear, practical solution to their problems which involved only a minimum of changes to their lifestyle. There was as yet no constituency for communal living in any form, and no means of raising capital for cooperative buildings of this type. As the nineteenth century neared its end, the development of cooperative housekeeping became more conceivable as a result of the growth of social and political movements which advocated changes in lifestyle. In 1889, however, the only opportunity for change in household organisation for the middle classes was that provided by various food delivery services, some cooperatively managed. This form of cooperative housekeeping again kept to the minimum the elements of communal social life and mutual cooperation, but did ensure that the idea of domestic cooperation was not forgotten.

One suggestion for 'cooking by co-operation' was made by Mrs H. T. Johnson in the pages of the *Englishwoman's Review* in 1889. Her first article[6] proposed that 100 families should combine to rent a central kitchen, where dinners would be prepared and sent out in felt-covered heat-retaining tin boxes. Wives would order and pay for dinners on the previous day. Households would therefore economise by not employing a full-time cook, burning less coal and buying food at wholesale prices. For wives in particular, Johnson saw advantages in this scheme:

> The mistress of the household would save time in shopping as well as in the disagreeable duty of supervising an inexperienced cook. Such time she could more valuably employ for the good of her family.

Her article caused such interest that 'several friends' requested her to go into more details of the costing of the scheme. This she did,[7] showing that the capital costs of setting up the central kitchen could be covered by the purchase of a £10 share by each of the 100 families involved. Meals could then be prepared and delivered for less than one penny per dinner plus the cost (at wholesale prices) of the food, assuming households to consist of five members, each consuming two cooked meals a day. This calculation included a 5 per cent return on investment for shareholders; clearly meals at this price would be cheaper than home-cooked meals after fuel and the service costs were taken into account. Mrs Johnson suggested that the scheme would be most successful in areas such as West Kensington, where the streets were lined with houses costing from £80 to £100 per year to rent. The scheme was intended to apply to members of the middle classes, freeing wives from domestic duties but not helping them to find paid work outside the home, rather increasing the time they could devote to their families.

Mrs Johnson (of Liverpool) invited interested parties to write to her, but apparently nothing came of this idea. Ten years later, however, *The Queen* reported that a Women's League had been set up in a London suburb, with the object of starting a public kitchen where a few good cooks would be employed to cook dinners for all households involved.[8] *The Queen* felt that the scheme would not save enough money to be a practical prop-osition, as breakfast and tea still had to be prepared at home, and suggested there was a greater need for shops where the occasional cooked meal could be bought. In fact, there was a real demand for food delivery schemes, as had been shown only a few weeks earlier with the announcement of the opening of the Queen's Club Gardens distributive kitchen.[9] Queen's Club Gardens is a large West Kensington square, completely surrounded by five-storey blocks of red-brick flats. Tennis courts and lawns fill the centre of the square, giving it an open and spacious feeling in spite of the almost continuous wall of tall buildings encircling it. The distributive kitchen was run by Miss Watson and Miss Daunt from Victoria Mansions, on the east side of the Gardens (see Plate 6), where their Victoria School of Cookery was situated. They used earthenware containers to keep the food hot during delivery. As the square is not more than 200 yards long, it would have provided an ideal setting for a distributive kitchen, the only problem with delivery being the height of the flats. Even *The Queen* felt this system was an improvement on trying to cook in small flat kitchens.

By 1902 another cooked food service was in business, the Lon-don Distributing Kitchens Ltd, working from Westminster Palace Gardens. The company's kitchens were described in a well-illus-trated and highly enthusiastic article in *The Lady's Realm*.[10] The company, not a cooperative venture although described as offer-ing a new form of cooperative housekeeping, would provide breakfast, lunch, afternoon tea and dinner for one person from 3 shillings per day. There was also a bargain offer of meals for three adults for a week for only one guinea. According to one contemporary household management text, a household of three could eat more than comfortably on £2 per week, so that even taking into account the cheapness of food around the turn of the century, the one guinea offer probably represented good value.[11] The Distributing Kitchen was originated by John Ablett, who had seen a similar arrangement at work in Boston, USA, and was managed by Mrs Daubeny 'whose heart and soul are in the work' (see Plate 7). Customers could choose from more than 60 soups, 250 vegetable dishes, 100 ways of cooking eggs, 98 salads and an equally vast range of main dishes; Indian cooking was a speciality. Cooking was by gas, and according to the article, in February 1902 there were several hundred customers. Meals were delivered by electric car, its interior warmed by smouldering charcoal. Separate dishes were packed into divided trays, which were then placed on top of a hot water tin in food-carrying boxes lined with green baize. Demand for the service was so great that further branches were to be set up all over London, and it was also possible to hire a butler and parlourmaid. The emphasis in the article was on escaping from the disadvantages of incompetent and expensive domestic servants, so as to create more time for personal enjoyment, rather than to care for the family (and certainly not in order to be able to work outside the home). The young wife was seen as having many interests other than her home:

> She likes a home of her own, the freedom and luxury thereof; but she regards her storeroom as a nuisance and her domestic duties as a bore. She joins her rifle-club, goes in for golf and hockey championships, and deplores the decay of domesticity – in her servants! (p. 514)

She had not been trained to cook, and would not want to cook for her new husband even if she had been trained; she had no 'housewifely soul':

> British women may have other and super-excellent virtues, but they never have been, and never will be, good cooks and housekeepers, with hearts centred in gridiron, store-room, and pantry. Their housewifery is done as a matter of stern duty. It is rarely a labour of love, as it is with their Continental sisters. The distributing kitchen system had to come; it is a necessity of the times, and it is a logical idea. (p. 520)

The working-class alternative to the cooked food delivery service was the cooked food shop. There were many varieties of these shops, each catering for a particular group, from the cooperative stores for the richer artisans to soup kitchens for the very poor. Some shops were run for profit, others were cooperative concerns or philanthropic efforts to provide the poor with nutritious food. Feeding the poor was seen as a suitable object of philanthropy in the late nineteenth century, particularly as it could be combined with inducements to lead a more respectable and sober life. Captain Wolff published his plan for feeding families in 1884,[12] suggesting that the health of the working population could be improved by a system of philanthropic restaurants. They would also encourage temperate habits, and the influence of the middle-class ladies serving food would lift the 'lower classes' 'from the suffocating atmosphere of vice and reprobation to a well-regulated, sober life – to thrift and happiness' (p. 61). Meals could either be eaten on the premises or taken home, and tickets for a week's supply of meals could be bought on a Saturday, immediately after wages were paid. A version of this system, providing take-away meals only, was put into practice in Worcester in 1886.[13] It proved popular and self-supporting, dinners consisting mainly of pea soup or Irish stew and suet pudding.

A report was published in 1894[14] of the success of restaurants for the working class in Vienna, which served over 20 000 people every day and which were run by philanthropic companies. The author of the article, Edith Sellers, suggested that £500 spent on starting a 'people's kitchen' was a wise investment, as 'The underfed, it is well to remember, are a dangerous element in any community' (p. 753). She proposed a people's kitchen in London,[15] but found nobody willing to come forward with the initial capital for such a large-scale venture.[16] English initiatives were more concerned with preventing intemperance than improving nutrition. The People's Refreshment-House Association was founded in 1896, with the object of decreasing the normal family expenditure of 6 shillings per week on alcohol.[17] Managers in their public houses were on a fixed wage, but were allowed all profits from any food they sold.[18]

Cooperators had continued to suggest schemes for improving the domestic situation of the poor, particularly since the founding of the Women's Cooperative Guild in 1883, when the emphasis changed from large-scale cooperative homes to shops, restaurants and laundries. The cooperative women's movement was at first called the Women's League for the Spread of Cooperation, and was initially 'regarded with some suspicion and even antagonism by male cooperators'.[19] The founder, Alice Acland, felt she had to be cautious in the early days of the Guild:

The women who were fighting for the rights of women (in 1883) were sometimes strange in their personal appearance. Cooperative menfolks were fearful that I intended to lead their wives and daughters to adopt similar styles of dress and speech.[20]

At first there was a great deal of tacit opposition from male cooperators, who felt women might begin to interfere with matters which they had previously managed alone; E. V. Neale did, however, support the Guild.[21] Margaret Llewelyn Davies, general secretary of the Guild from 1889 until 1921, found initial opposition to women's participation greatest in the north of England:

> In the South, the women were more easily and quickly accepted as fellow workers, and such an expression as 'Let my wife stay at home and wash my moleskin trousers' would not have been heard at a Southern Conference.[22]

The Guild was first concerned with specifically domestic subjects, and only towards the end of the century did cooperation on a more political level become important. In 1893 Catherine Webb, founding secretary of the Battersea branch of the Guild, gave a paper to the Guild's annual congress conference showing how cooperation could be applied to domestic life.[23] She suggested cooperative laundries, washhouses, bakeries and restaurants, and quoted working foreign examples. She felt cooperative kitchens would be successful if staffed by good housekeepers. The Guild produced a 'popular paper' on cooperative housekeeping, which gave as its object the promotion of cooperative washhouses, bakeries, kitchens and gardens, and speakers were available in 1894 and 1895 to lecture on the subject to local meetings.[24]

Margaret Llewelyn Davies heself suggested cooperative coffee and cooked meat shops in poor neighbourhoods, where good dinners would be available for 3d to 5d, and cooperative restaurants for wealthier areas.[25] In reply to this, Mrs Knight of the Guild pointed out that cooperative cooking was always popular in theory, but in practice nobody wanted to make the experiment at their own branch.[26] The reasons given were that the men worked close enough to home to return there for meals, that the neighbourhood was not really poor, or that the women were too busy cooking their families' meals to work in a cooperative kitchen. Several factors worked against the acceptance of coop erative kitchens; previous experience of the poor quality of coffee shop food did not encourage further experiment, and communal eating still held associations with slum dwelling. Before the turn of the century, male cooperators had a fairly inflexible view of the role of their wives, which probably did not include their involvement in cooking for other men. Finally, it is possible that women were not attracted to the idea, seeing the Guild as offering them the chance of participation in the wider political world, rather than an extension of their domestic responsibilities. As the influence of Margaret Llewelyn Davies increased within the Guild, concern with domestic matters decreased and was replaced by interest in broader social reforms.[27]

The Guild publicised the experience of its own members, for example in relation to the provision of maternity and child welfare services, in order to speed reforms. Cooperators were not drawn from the poorest section of the population, and towards the end of the century many bodies concerned with social reforms came into existence. Housing societies such as the Peabody Trust, founded 1862, and others which had been in operation since the 1850s and 1860s, had not made great inroads into the problem of providing better housing, and thus generally improved living conditions, for the poor. There was a renewal of interest in the problem in 1875, after the passing of the Cross Act which allowed authorities to buy and clear areas of slum dwellings. Philanthropic private enterprise continued to be the main source of housing for the poor until 1890,[28] while societies such as the Commons Preservation Society (founded 1865) and the Metropolitan Public Gardens Association (1883) dealt with the provision of open space. The overall moral, physical and spiritual welfare of the poor was seen as a problem to be defeated by sending the better educated into poor areas to teach, learn and inculcate standards by their exemplary behaviour. The first university settlement, Toynbee Hall in Whitechapel, was founded in 1884 and soon led to the establishment of many others.[29] Canon Barnett and Dame Henrietta Barnett brought Oxford and Cambridge graduates to the Whitechapel settlement to investigate the living conditions of the poor, and to provide education and recreation for them. There was an element of communal living at the Hall, in that all meals were taken together, but the atmosphere was more of an Oxbridge college than a cooperative home. The staff were maids rather than menservants, and residents had to be 'warned that offers to carry the heavy trays or fetch the coals were liable to generate mistaken notions'.[30]

Canon Barnett felt that charity breakfasts, soup kitchens and night shelters were mere 'sops' to the suffering poor, the solution to family impoverishment lying in self-help.[31] He did, however, invite six destitute children to eat daily at Toynbee Hall, more as a reminder to the residents than a response to general need. When, during the winter of 1885–6, a general relief fund was started at the Hall, 'The result was disastrous. Ne'er-do-wells from all parts of the country flocked into London; the idle left their work to obtain "something for nothing" . . . ' [32] The Hall acted as an inspiration for the founding of other settlements, including Hull House in Chicago, initiated by Jane Addams in 1889. She had visited Toynbee Hall in 1888,[33] and with two associates set up Hull House to provide a base for workers in the immigrant community of Chicago. She later helped to start the Jane Club, a residential cooperative housekeeping club for women factory workers.[34] The Barnetts visited Hull House in 1891, both Hull House and Toynbee Hall acting as centres for the exchange of ideas on social reform.

Octavia Hill and William Morris were both dinner guests of the Barnetts,[35] Dame Henrietta Barnett having worked with Octavia Hill from 1869 in the Charity Organisation Society,[36] formed to coordinate charitable relief work. Hill began her career in housing management with the financial assistance of John Ruskin, who had attempted to create a feudal community with the farming ventures of the Guild of St George in the 1870s.[37] Hill believed that tenants and housing standards should be improved simultaneously,[38] and suggested that for the 'more ignorant and destructive class of people, unaccustomed to the use of even simple appliances', one-room flats were adequate, as two- or three-room flats were too dear for most families. In reply to this, William Morris accused Hill and other philanthropists of seeing working-class aspirations as revolutionary.[39] He saw the reason for poor housing as, simply, poverty. Morris, the power behind the founding of the Society for the Protection of Ancient Buildings in 1877, had clear ideas on the future shape of working-class housing. If great cities had to exist, then the poor should not be forced to live in 'bare, sunless and grim bastilles' but in tall blocks of flats with 'vertical streets', leaving sufficient space for beautiful gardens between blocks.[40] There would be cloisters, covered play areas and ornaments, while

> Inside the houses, besides such obvious conveniences as common laundries and kitchens, a very little arrangement would give the dwellers in them ample and airy public rooms in addition to their private ones; the top storey of each block might well be utilised for such purposes, the great hall for dining in, and for social gathering, being the chief feature of it.[41]

He saw 'no insuperable difficulty' in providing lodgings for the poor with good public cooking and washing rooms, and beautiful halls 'as in the Colleges of Oxford and Cambridge, which it would be pleasure merely to sit in'.[42]

Morris was at his most politically active in the 1880s, lecturing for the Socialist League all over the country, writing for its paper and taking part in demonstrations.[43] His 1888 essay, 'How We Live and How We Might Live', contrasted present and future homes; he saw contemporary life as mean, shabby and dirty: 'It is profit ... which condemns all but the rich to live in houses idiotically cramped and confined at best, and at the worst in houses for whose wretchedness there is no name.'[44] Future socialist life might be lived on a communal basis, if individuals wished to club together. The communal hall of the future would be

> alive with the noblest thoughts of our times, and the past, embodied in the best art which a free and manly people could produce; such an abode of man as no private enterprise could come anywhere near for beauty and fitness, because only collective thought and collective life could cherish the aspirations which would give birth to its beauty, or have the skill and leisure to carry them out.[45]

Morris himself was in favour of communal living, seeing no advantage in home ownership for its own sake, although he was aware that his view was not universally endorsed:

Whether a working-class man would think his family possession of his wretched little room better than his share of the palace of which I have spoken, I must leave to his opinion, and to the imaginations of the middle class, who perhaps may sometimes conceive the fact that the said worker is cramped for space and comfort – say on washing-day.[46]

Morris did not go so far as to include communal housing in his utopian dream *News from Nowhere*, written in 1890. The redbrick and tile-roof terrace housing had a communal garden, while larger, detached houses were set in private gardens. There were communal halls where meals were served, and where women waited on the men; Morris justified this arrangement by elevating the occupation of housekeeping to a position of respect. Women did what they could do best: 'don't you know that it is a great pleasure to a clever woman to manage a house skilfully, and to do it so that all her house-mates about her look pleased, and are grateful to her?'[47]

Without the constraints of the large and ugly city, in *News from Nowhere* Morris portrayed his ideal housing as small, detached and surrounded by garden, although with a beautiful communal hall close at hand. He had perhaps become disillusioned about the probable success of communal living in any more complex form after the disintegration of the Socialist League in 1889, following internal arguments.[48] Morris was aware of the existence of the women's movement, but his own family circle kept to a traditional division of labour. In the evenings Morris himself would engage in political discussion with friends from the Socialist League, while his wife and daughters worked at embroidery or served tea. May Morris, the younger daughter, was also active in the Socialist League but rarely gave her own opinions at meetings.[49]

Morris wrote *News from Nowhere* in reply to another utopian novel, Edward Bellamy's *Looking Backward*. Bellamy's vision of a state socialist future, published in England in 1889, was a great success.[50] It inspired the Nationalist movement in America, its object being to remove class conflict and political argument by extending the collective socialist state to include all areas of life. *Looking Backward* envisaged Boston in the year 2000 as a city in a socialist state which owned all property, individuals being

rewarded equally whatever their job.[51] Families still lived in separate houses, although large houses might be shared by several
households; rents varied 'according to size, elegance,and location,
so that everybody can find something to suit'.[52] Meals were taken
in large communal halls, but home life was kept simple: 'To save
ourselves useless burdens, we have as little gear about us at home
as is consistent with comfort, but the social side of our life
is ornate and luxurious beyond anything the world ever knew
before.'[53]

Bellamy had written on the reform of domestic work,[54] and gave
rather grudging support in *Looking Backward* to the idea of women
doing paid work outside the home. Women were spared domestic
drudgery by the cooperative housekeeping system and were
allowed to work in jobs specially adapted for their needs. Women
in the future Boston had been given 'a world of their own, with
its emulations, ambitions, and careers',[55] but were only permitted
to work as it improved their overall health.

Nationalist clubs were formed in England immediately after the
publication of *Looking Backward*, and the Nationalisation of Labour Society was founded in London on 3 July 1890. By October
of the same year a monthly magazine, *Nationalization News*, had
commenced publishing.[56] Morris detested Bellamy's centralised
utopia, seeing in it the prospect of any easy life in return for a
reduction in individuality.[57] *News from Nowhere* was serialised in
The Commonweal, the paper of the Socialist League, from January
to October 1890, and Bellamy's incorporation of communal living
into his utopia clearly affected Morris's views on the matter. He
had earlier been enthusiastic about the possibilities of communal
living for those unfortunate enough to live in towns, but in *News
from Nowhere* implied that it was 'nothing but a refuge from mere
destitution'.[58]

Nationalization News gave prominence to articles concerned with
the practicalities of setting up experimental utopian colonies. By
April 1893, a site for a cooperative colony had been selected, at
Hockley, just north of Southend.[59] The scheme never came to
fruition, but several other progressive colonies were established,
mainly in the countryside in the 1880s and early 1890s as a return
to the 'simple life' became the vogue.[60] The country cottage cult
was particularly strong amongst intellectual women in the 1890s,[61]
when the farm colony movement was beginning, with the object
of putting unemployed city-dwellers to work in the country.[62]

Small groups of cottage farmers settled into their rural dream homes, while larger groups formed agrarian communes. The theoretical background to this upsurge of rural communality was provided by the writings of Morris, John Ruskin, Edward Carpenter and Kropotkin. Kropotkin first published his suggestions for socially organised production in 1888.[63] He argued for small-scale self-sufficiency, decentralisation and workers taking part in both agriculture and industrial production. *News from Nowhere* had portrayed a future where work was fulfilling and pleasurable, while Ruskin's Guild of St George had been created to begin the return to an economy based on crafts and agriculture.[64] Carpenter lived out his own version of the simple life in his cottage in the hills south of Sheffield, his books suggesting practical alternatives to city life.[65]

Carpenter found life on his smallholding hard work, as did many of the migrants to the countryside who had arrived with the idea of setting up an egalitarian community.[66] Most of the schemes and organisations involved in the 'back to the land' movement in the last quarter of the nineteenth century stopped short of altering the nature of the sexual division of labour. Carpenter, however, was one of the few men who advocated changes in the way domestic work was performed, feeling that great social changes were necessary for women's complete emancipation to become a reality. In 1896, he saw signs that public institutions were beginning to take more responsibility for education and childrearing,

> . . . and even here and there we may discern a drift towards the amalgamation of households, which by introducing a common life and division of labor [sic] among the women-folk will probably do much to cheer and lighten their lot.[67]

Public bakeries and laundries would decrease drudgery, and, additionally, 'We see no reason indeed why [the man] should not assist in some part of the domestic work, and thus contribute his share of labour and intelligence to the conduct of the house . . .'[68] Although socialism involved the creation of new forms of relationships between the sexes, many of Carpenter's friends disliked the idea of men doing 'women's work', and found it very disturbing to see Carpenter's homosexual partner, George Merrill, taking great pride in the housekeeping at their Sheffield home.[69]

Carpenter found it easier to take part in domestic work when shared with Merrill, rather than under the control of the women who had previously looked after the cottage.

Another and more popular socialist advocate of communal living in the 1890s was Robert Blatchford, whose *Merrie England* sold nearly one million copies after its initial serialisation in the *Clarion*, the socialist weekly in 1892–3.[70] Blatchford realised that domestic work was hard and tiring for working-class women: 'Poor Mrs John Smith, her life is one long slavery. Cooking, cleaning, managing, mending, washing clothes, waiting on husband and children, her work is never done';[71] but he did not recommend that men undertook any of the work. His own marriage was extremely conventional,[72] and he saw 'more comfortable homes' as being achieved through some degree of communal living. He suggested a street of 100 working-class families should replace their individual kitchens with communal facilities:

> We set up one laundry, with all the best machinery; we set up one big drying field; we set up one great kitchen, one general dining hall, and one pleasant tea garden. Then we buy all the provisions and other things in large quantities, and we appoint certain wives as cooks and laundresses, or . . . we let the wives take the duties in turn.[73]

There is no hint here of any change whatsoever in the sexual division of domestic labour, and it is quite possible that the prospect of an improved, although still conventional, lifestyle was one of the points which encouraged male readers to buy the book. Carpenter's vision of a socialist society certainly implied that men should do more domestic work.

Edward Carpenter was a member of the Fellowship of the New Life, founded by Thomas Davidson in 1883 to practise a 'new life' based on love, wisdom and unselfishness. Their early meetings centred round the setting up of some form of Owenite community, to be situated in Bloomsbury (or possibly Peru), but after a few months a split occurred, the members more interested in immediate social reforms leaving to form the Fabian Society in early 1884.[74] The Fabians were an elite group of the expanding salaried middle classes, believing that social reform could be achieved by an efficient socialist bureaucracy, in which they would play an important part. Over a quarter of their membership in 1890 consisted of women, and there were also a number of artists and writers.[75] The Fabians, particularly Beatrice and Sidney Webb, were anti-utopian, preferring gradual reform to utopian revolution,[76] but in spite of the Fabians' generally philistine reputation, they had a continuing programme of discussion on the arts. They concentrated on literature, to the exclusion of more utilitarian arts and crafts, and had occasional lectures on architecture and town planning.[77]

One of the Fabian Society's guest speakers in 1896 was the American writer and lecturer, Mrs C.P. Stetson, better known (after her second marriage) as Charlotte Perkins Gilman. Gilman was a regular speaker on the American Nationalist circuit, also lecturing to women's clubs and suffrage groups.[78] The purpose of her first visit to England in the summer of 1896 was to attend the International Socialist and Labour Congress, where she met several members of the Fabian Society. She liked the Fabians, 'that group of intelligent, scientific, practical and efficient English Socialists' wearing their 'knee breeches, soft shirts, woollen hose and sandals'.[79] This description bears more relation to Edward Carpenter than Sidney Webb, and indeed Carpenter met Gilman at the congress, presenting her with a pair of leather sandals he had made himself.[80] Carpenter, although never a Fabian, was always ready to speak at their meetings.[81] Gilman also met William Morris at the congress, later becoming a good friend of May Morris.[82] She was invited by the Webbs to their house in Suffolk, and in September 1896 Beatrice Webb proposed her for membership of the Fabian Society.[83] The Fabians found Gilman's ideas stimulating, and encouraged her to write a book.[84] She returned to America in November 1896, and began work on the book, concerning the economic relations of the sexes, on 31 August of the following year. By 8 October, she had finished the first draft, the publishers calling it *Women and Economics*.[85]

Women and Economics was published in England in 1898,[86] and was the *Fabian News* choice for 'Book of the Month' in January 1899. The argument of the book rested upon Gilman's basic contention that women were economically dependent on men, and that because of the restrictions of the domestic role, women had been denied the opportunity to specialise and organise their work.[87] She felt the path of human progress lay through greater organisation, and that individual freedom was a necessary step towards cooperation. 'The priestess of the temple of consumption',[88] the female consumer, had a reactionary economic influence, encouraging useless production and perverting world economic development. The new American woman was ill suited to the generalised nature of domestic work, and women's potential would be wasted until home industries were organised like any other industry.

Gilman realised that 'Economic independence for women necessarily involves a change in the home and family relation.'[89] She argued that changes would improve the quality of home life, by allowing the partners in a marriage economic independence and thus social equality. Home industries would be carried on by professionals:

> This division of the labor of housekeeping would require the service of fewer women for fewer hours a day. Where now twenty women in twenty homes work all the time, and insufficiently accomplish their varied duties, the same work in the hands of specialists could be done in less time by fewer people; and the others would be left free to do other work for which they were better fitted ... [90]

Unlike Melusina Fay Peirce, Gilman saw one of the benefits of organising domestic work as freeing women for paid work of all kinds. Gilman was not in favour of cooperation between families, seeing domestic tasks as being related to individuals; cooking for families had grown up simply as a matter of convenience, and was not integral to family life. Women could be expected to choose professions which might be combined with motherhood,[91] and babies would spend several hours a day in kindergartens. Women city-dwellers and their families could be accommodated in apartment houses, the flats being kitchenless with meals being served in a common dining room or individual flats.[92] Cleaning would be performed by workers hired by the management, and nurses and teachers would take care of the children. The whole establishment would run on a profit-making basis, fulfilling a growing social need. In the suburbs, kitchenless houses could be grouped together and connected by a covered way to the central hall. This type of arrangement would provide family privacy combined with collective advantage. Kitchenless homes would require less cleaning than ordinary homes, so that an 'invasion of professional cleaners' would be a great improvement on the permanent presence of family servants. The new home would retain the 'sweetness and happiness' of home life while removing the domestic industry.

Gilman saw social contact as being provided by the many necessary adjuncts to kitchenless houses, the common library, baths, gymnasia, workrooms and play rooms. There would be free association between people along lines of common interest, producing a social life far more natural than contemporary 'society'.[93] Her feelings about truly communal life had been influenced by a two-year period from 1874–6 when, as a child, she had lived in a three-family cooperative community. She concluded that 'Cooperative houskeeping is inherently doomed to failure. From early experience and later knowledge I thoroughly learned this fact, and have always proclaimed it.'[94] Gilman had spent much of the summer during which she wrote *Women and Economics* on a farm in New Hampshire, as the guest of Miss Prestonia Mann, a Fabian socialist. Miss Mann invited a group of friends to the farm each summer, and although two maids did most of the cooking and some cleaning, the guests did the other domestic tasks. Gilman eventually concluded that the cooperative approach to domestic work left women with too great a responsibility for the home,[95] and the efforts of male guests to perform their domestic tasks no doubt hastened this view:

> It was immensely amusing, the cheerful good-will and colossal ignorance of these co-labourers. Even the laundry work we did, putting the clothes to soak over night, and attacking them with washing-machine and wringers next day. Good Mrs McDaniels and I were the only ones present who knew how to wash, and we exchanged sad glances to see gallant college professors and high-minded poets toiling at the wringers while buttons flew away and spots remained.[96]

Cooperative housekeeping had been advocated by several American women since Mrs Peirce's first experiment in Cambridge. In 1870, Victoria Woodhull wrote that housewifery was becoming a branch of industry, as women became more independent, and predicted that future homes would be in vast hotels catering for 1000 people. She saw this as a more economical mode of living and a sign of progress.[97] Mary Coleman Stuckert gave a paper to the Women's Congress of the 1893 Chicago World Fair on cooperative houskeeping.[98] She had been attempting to arouse support for a cooperative house in Denver over the previous 15 years, and showed a model of the proposed building in the Woman's Building at the Fair. It was to house 44 families, with a communal kitchen, laundry and kindergarten, and servants were to be hired for the entire community. Gilman's suggestion of apartment houses for families had earlier been made by an American Nationalist architect, J. P. Putnam.[99] He envisaged a variety of suites of rooms, with and without kitchens, or with direct connection by dumb-waiter to the central kitchen. He felt there would be great cost savings, freedom from management of servants, complete privacy and the advantage of increased social intercourse in the public rooms.

The reaction of English reviewers to the new lifestyle proposed by Gilman was mixed. *Fabian News* thought the book was a passionately sincere work of propaganda, without 'one practical proposal in the volume from cover to cover'.[100] The *Englishwoman's Review* also thought the book would stimulate discussion, but criticised the 'occasional rather colloquial style' and hesitated over Gilman's contention that an independent woman would make a better mother.[101] *The Humanitarian* said these were not new ideas, and doubted their practicality: 'It would be cruel to cast a doubt on this Utopian picture, but we fear that a course of "co-operative cooking" . . . would destroy the "sweetness and happiness" of these Stetsonian homes.'[102] Gilman, however, felt that the book had been warmly received when she revisited England in the summer of 1899. She carried out many speaking engagements, becoming 'quite a lion' as she put it, and kept in contact with the Fabian Society.[103] Members of the Society differed widely in their attitudes to communal living, reflecting the Society's origins in breaking away from a movement dedicated to evolving a new lifestyle. Beatrice Webb herself felt she was, 'of course, disqualified for the ordinary communal life by my need for privacy as an intellectual worker. For me a private sitting-room is not a luxury, but a necessity . . .'[104] Clearly the advocates of communal living, with their promises of increased privacy, had had no influence on her.

Other Fabians were more enthusiastic. An advertisement appeared in the May 1899 edition of *Fabian News* offering places in a cooperative home in Canning Town,[105] while Daniel McEwen, a London member of the Society, produced a memorandum setting out the plans of the Associated Dwellings Company.[106] The object of the company was to 'combine the comforts, privacy and economy of home with the advantages of a good hotel' by building blocks of flats with shared facilities. Flats were to be of varying sizes, to suit families or single people, and were to be completely self-contained. They were intended for the middle-class market, being cheaper than the West End mansions but more comfortable than artisans' blocks; that is, they were 'specially designed to provide for comfort and pleasant appearances at low rates'. The company intended to pay a 5 per cent dividend, any further profit accruing to the tenants.

It seems that the scheme came to nothing, but by the turn of the century even Hermann Muthesius, in his survey of English domestic architecture, considered flats with communal dining rooms interesting enough to remark: 'Many regard these flats as the homes of the future.'[107] He felt that cooperative housekeeping flats for women, in particular, 'have proved their worth and have met a universal need'.[108] He saw the increasing popularity of flats as resulting from the influence of foreign and especially American ideas, the faster pace of life and, possibly, the servant problem. He concluded that flat-building was still in an experimental phase, the requirements of the public being uncertain, with some households unlikely ever to contemplate flat-dwelling: 'There is a firm belief all round that it is out of the question for a family with children to live in a flat. A flat always puts an Englishman in mind of an hotel.'[109]

Arguments about the future of society increased around the end of the nineteenth century, with Gilman's *Women and Economics* being widely read and discussed.[110] The German feminist Hedwig Dohm had written in 1873 on communal kitchens, laundries and kindergartens, and her work was translated into English in 1896.[111] She felt that communal kitchens would provide opportunities for those people who enjoyed cooking to cook for all, this view perhaps having been inspired by her experience of the boredom of middle-class domestic life. Not all writers were in favour of the communistic approach to social life. Eugene Richter's *Pictures of the Socialist Future* was a satire by the leader of the German Liberal Party, translated into English in 1893. In Richter's socialist state, houses were allocated by the 'universal dwelling house lottery', and meals were eaten at state cookshops. All cook-shops served exactly the same fare, all portions were identical, tables were cramped and time allowed for eating was severely limited.[112]

In England, several small-scale 'utopias' were built towards the end of the nineteenth century, as wealthy industrialists put their ideas about improved living and working environments into prac-tice. The early industrial villages were built specifically to house factory workers, but Port Sunlight (1888) and Bournville (1895) marked the change in emphasis to improved housing conditions for the population in general.[113] Port Sunlight, near Birkenhead, was founded by William Lever to provide cheap housing for employees at his nearby factory. It suffered from its founder's excessive paternalism; in one instance the front gardens of the houses were taken over by the central management, because Lever did not like to see them used as chicken runs, or with 'the family washing . . . unblushingly exposed on the railings'.[114] George Cadbury moved his chocolate factory to Bournville in 1879, and began building the village in 1895. He intended the low-density housing with gardens to be suitable for all workers, not just those he employed. Bournville's architect, W. Alexander Harvey, saw the gardens as being an antidote to the evils of drink, where 'the tenant himself may add to the beauty of his home, and at the same time enjoy fresh air and recreation'.[115] Both the housing and gardens were popular, with only two tenants in the first ten years being given their notice because of lack of cultivation of their gardens.[116]

The emphasis on bringing 'men into touch with the soil', as George Cadbury put it,[117] as well as the low housing density of the new industrial villages, were reflections of the 'back to the land' movement in conventional industrial and suburban housing. This movement, the industrial villages, the temperance movement and various utopian writers were all influences on the developing ideas of Ebenezer Howard, founder of the garden city movement. Howard was born in London in 1850. The son of a shopkeeper, he took several jobs as a clerk before he and two friends left for America in 1871. They spent some time farming in Nebraska, but after this venture failed, Howard moved to Chicago where he worked as a court reporter.[118] He returned to England in 1876, working as a shorthand writer and improving his experimental shorthand typewriter. He inhabited the world of middle-class London radicals, taking particular interest in the questions of poverty and land reform. Two of his friends began the Brotherhood Trust in 1894, with the intention of bringing cooperative stores and workshops to the East End of London.[119]

In 1888, Howard was lent a copy of Bellamy's *Looking Backward* by an American friend. He read it in one sitting and was highly impressed by the vision of a state founded on cooperation rather than self-interest.[120] He had a hand in persuading an English publishing firm to bring out the book, and became a founding member of the Nationalisation of Labour Society in 1890. *Looking Backward* stimulated Howard into producing proposals for a new community, in order to test out Bellamy's theories.[121] Howard 'had already taken part in two very small social experiments unsuccessfully'[122] as he put it, before 1888; these experiments may have been the Nebraska farming venture and the Brotherhood Trust. This previous experience of failure did not deter Howard from sending an outline of his plans for a 'Home Colony' to *Nationalization News* in early 1893.[123] The proposal was for a planned town on a 1000-acre site, set in agricultural land and encircled by a railway. There was to be a combination of centralised planning and individual initiative (a deviation from Bellamy's total state control), and provision of sites for libraries, schools, creches, swimming baths and a concert hall. The colony was never more than a proposal as the necessary capital was not forthcoming, but Howard continued to refine his plans for the ideal community.

His work was eventually published in 1898 under the title *Tomorrow: a Peaceful Path to Real Reform*, and reissued in 1902 with some revisions as *Garden Cities of To-morrow*.[124] Howard's garden city combined the best of country and city, as he saw it, bringing homes and work into the countryside so that the social life of the city would be possible in the healthy environment of the country. Good housing within walking distance of work would be available for even the poorest family, in contrast to the situation in the centres of English cities where poor families lived in small tenement flats.[125] In his book, Howard concentrated on the basic principles of the garden city, rather than giving specific details of the type of housing he envisaged, but he did refer to 'The very varied architecture and design which the houses and groups of houses display – some having common gardens and co-operative kitchens . . .'[126] The first draft of his manuscript, written about

1892, contained further description of the central kitchens.[127] The houses were to be built facing outwards around squares, with gardens in the centres. Some of these squares were to have dining halls in their centres, with kitchens overhead. Tenants of three or four blocks of houses might all share the same dining hall, while others would prefer to do their cooking at home using labour-saving appliances. Indeed, Howard saw the garden city itself as a labour-saving invention in that it combined the advantages of town and country life.[128]

Reviewers were not enthusiastic about *Tomorrow*, the *Fabian News* being particularly scathing on the subject of 'utopian' schemes.[129] In spite of this, with the help of the Land Nationalisation Society, Howard founded the Garden City Association on 10 June 1899, and began a programme of lectures on the garden city to groups throughout the country.[130] He spoke to the Fabian Society in August 1901, saying he had long been a socialist and felt that all land should be held by the community. He explained how *Looking Backward* had given him the necessary impetus to write *Tomorrow*.[131] Gradually Howard accumulated support for his scheme, eventually meeting George Cadbury and William Lever who were won over to his ideas, as it appeared their own plans would be furthered by the success of the garden city. The first conference of the Garden City Association was held at Bournville in September 1901,[132] and a paper was given on 'The Advantages of Co-operative Dwellings' by Harold Clapham Lander.[133]

Lander was an architect who was on the first executive committee of the Garden City Association (GCA), and was a member of its Council in 1901.[134] He was the son of the architect of the Jubilee Market in Covent Garden, and was initially articled to his father's firm of Lander and Bedells before going into practice on his own in 1895 at the age of 26. He lived in Tunbridge Wells, although his practice was in London, and was secretary of the Tunbridge Wells Fabian Society in 1896.[135] He lectured widely on the garden city after joining the GCA, and spoke to the Fabian Society on the problems involved in building houses for poorer families. He was an advocate of municipal housing, recommending a wide range of dwelling sizes to suit all types of family. He disliked tenements, but saw few acceptable alternatives to them for single people: 'Accommodation for single men and women can be provided more cheaply in the lodging-house, but the comforts of the home are wanting.'[136]

Lander ran his architectural practice along socialist lines, and although he at one time taught wood-carving to boys at an East London settlement, he was described by an ex-employee as 'the most aristocratic socialist I have ever known'. He never gave tips, not being a believer in casual charity, but although some considered him mean, the reverse was often the case:

> To a cottage for two old ladies who could only afford 'a square box with a lid upon it' a bay-window addition was put on before completion at the Architect's own expense and costing beyond any remuneration fee he had for the job, but added as necessary to the view and artistic effect.[137]

Lander had his clothes made by cooperative labour to ensure the workers were paid fairly. He was a friend of many leading Fabian Society members, including the Webbs, and was a close friend of Ebenezer Howard well before *Tomorrow* was published.

Lander's paper to the Garden City Association conference put the case for cooperative dwellings as an extension to the home of the benefits brought by cooperation to public life, particularly by municipal socialism. He considered the effects of cooperation on domestic economy and social life: 'There is little to be urged in favour of the present domestic system upon the score of economy.'[138] The system of individual houses led to wastage of fuel and labour, and increased construction costs. Flats, less wasteful of space than private houses, posed health problems as a result of overcrowding. Even in well-planned houses, untrained cooks were inefficient and wasteful in their food preparation,

> with the result that too often the husbands and sons as they grow up, instead of spending their time at home, adjourn to the public-house, driven there by the want of proper food and comforts which are not to be obtained under their own roofs.[139]

Lander saw human progress as leading towards greater fraternity, thus the need for new homes 'designed upon more generous lines to allow scope for the growth of a broader spirit of brotherhood'. He outlined a plan for a cooperative home, the public rooms to include a dining room, kitchen, laundry, bathrooms, recreation and reading rooms. Private apartments (sitting and bedrooms) would be grouped around the public rooms, perhaps in the form of a quadrangle. Catering and all services would be a matter for the management, and family privacy would increase with the disappearance of the residential servant. In working-class cooperative homes, a creche might be included, Lander assuming that working-class wives were likely to be working outside the home. He made no mention of specific benefits to women from the cooperative system, concentrating on improvements in social life and higher standards of cooking from professional cooks.

Lander referred to a number of experimental cooperative homes which were already functioning successfully, including a block of flats in north east London erected around 1870. These flats, with common billiard and recreation rooms and garden, were currently in great demand after an initial period of slow letting. It is possible that these flats constituted the experimental group of cooperative homes referred to by Mrs E. M. King in 1874, as they were situated at Stamford Hill, north London.[140] Lander also mentioned a contemporary plan for a cooperative home in west London, the building to be rectangular with a square garden in the centre. There was to be lavish provision of public rooms, including gymnasium, concert room, billiards, smoking and reading rooms, and swimming baths. Private accommodation would be in kitchenless suites of varying sizes, complete with small gas stove, and at the time of the conference it seemed that 'The scheme has the support of many well-known names including several artists.' This scheme may be identical with the plan put forward by the Associated Dwelling Company (see above), since this was instigated by a member of the Fabian Society and it is therefore likely that Lander, as a Fabian, would be aware of its existence. The scheme, or schemes, apparently came to nothing.

Lander concluded his paper by relating his theories on cooperative dwellings to the opportunity provided by the garden city project for encouraging 'the free development of the highest ideals of home and social life'. Lander had deliberately omitted to go into any detail on the precise plan of a cooperative home, feeling that several experimental designs should be tested, but another conference speaker did suggest that quiet quadrangles of houses, often with central buildings, offered the best possibilities for good urban architecture. This speaker was the architect and planner Raymond Unwin, who was to be, with his partner Barry Parker, the planner of the first garden city. In his paper to the GCA conference, Unwin argued that the design of houses in the new garden city should be determined by 'the chief requirements of health in the house, namely, light, air and cheerful outlook'.[141] He saw the large quadrangle of houses as fulfilling these requirements rather better than 'the dismal monotony of a narrow street', but in addition expressing the nature of the life within the housing:

> In the squares and quadrangles of our Garden City dwellings the spirit of co-operation will find a congenial ground from which to spring, for there association in the enjoyment of open spaces or large gardens will replace the exclusiveness of the individual possession of backyards or petty garden-plots, and will no doubt soon be followed by further association, to which the arrangement so admirably lends itself.[142]

Unwin suggested that Oxford or Cambridge colleges were fine examples of the architectural charm of quadrangles. He had spent much of his childhood in Oxford, but after considering becoming involved in settlement work in London, moved north to Chesterfield where he was apprenticed to an engineer.[143] He moved to Manchester in 1885, becoming secretary of the local branch of the Socialist League, contributing regularly to *Commonweal* and lecturing to socialist meetings. He spoke on the planning of new communities, influenced by personal contact with John Ruskin and William Morris, and knowledge of the farming experiments of the Guild of St George. He became a close friend of Edward Carpenter, often visiting Carpenter's smallholding.[144] Unwin returned to Derbyshire in 1887, working as an engineer for the Staveley Coal and Iron Company, which involved him in laying out small housing estates. In one of his *Commonweal* articles of the time, he expressed his feelings on seeing the Derbyshire estate of Sutton Hall, the Hall itself lying empty, surrounded by beautiful parkland. In the future, perhaps it would be

> . . . the centre of a happy communal life. Plenty of room in that large house for quite a small colony to live, each one having his own den upstairs where he could go to write, or sulk, or spend a quiet evening with his lady-love or his boon companion; and downstairs would be large common dining-halls, dancing-halls, smoking rooms – . . . [145]

Unwin discussed going into architectural partnership with his cousin Barry Parker in 1891, by which time Unwin appears to have become disillusioned with the possibilities of putting Morris's theories into practice through lecturing and planning working-class housing for the Staveley Company. One of Unwin's Sheffield lectures in spring 1888 was advertised by 1000 handbills, but hardly anyone came to the meeting.[146] In a letter to Parker's older sister Ethel in 1891, Unwin wrote:

> At one time I was sort of given up to socialism, it was my religion and I feel the loss of it as such. But I think it quite possible for some other side of the work besides agitation to take some place . . . [147]

He began to give priority to practical improvements to the environment above socialist theorising, and after marriage to Ethel Parker in 1893, the brothers-in-law went into practice together in 1896 in Buxton, Parker's home. Parker, four years younger than Unwin, was born in Chesterfield but trained at a London art school before being articled to a Manchester architect until 1893. He was in practice alone until joined by Unwin, their early work consisting of commissions for middle-class houses. They also designed interior fittings and furniture, working in the style of the arts and crafts movement. This movement was based upon the ideas and practice of Ruskin and Morris, Morris's own firm leading the way with high-quality design and reform of industrial practice. The distinction between designer and worker was removed, and emphasis placed on the fitness for purpose of products.[148] The Northern Art-Workers' Guild was formed in Manchester in 1896, so that Parker and Unwin were able to work in an atmosphere supportive of both their ideals and their practice. A wide range of craftwork was readily available to them.[149]

In the mid-1890s, Parker and Unwin took the first step towards putting into practice their theories on cooperation and housing with the production of designs for a cooperative dwelling at Bradford. These plans were reproduced, along with others for cooperative housing on a rural site, in their book, *The Art of Building a Home*, published shortly after the GCA conference in 1901.[150] Unwin was particularly concerned with the disappearance of unity and harmony from contemporary building, and saw

'artificial picturesqueness' as an individual response to uninter-
esting modern housing: 'In short, around all our towns are spread
patches of villadom of the beauty of which no one can cherish
any memories, but the ugliness of which causes them to be
regarded by many with a cordial hatred . . . '[151] For those who
were able and willing to move out of the towns, Unwin suggested
that the creation of country villages would fulfil their social and
physical needs within a pleasant environment. A site could be
purchased and developed along cooperative lines, and as the
settlement grew, various communal ventures would probably be
initiated. Unwin mentioned a laundry, transport and a school.[152]
The same plan would be feasible in the suburbs with a reduction
in the size of the gardens to allow for the higher price of land.

Unwin also attempted to apply the cooperative principle to
cottage housing in cities, but omitted any mention of how the
plans might be funded. He suggested the quadrangle as the ideal
format, giving character and dignity to city architecture. Each
quadrangle would be provided with a common room, 'in which
a fire might always be burning in an evening, where comfort for
social intercourse, for reading, or writing, could always be found'.
He envisaged the possible addition of a laundry and drying room,
bathrooms for the smallest cottages, and eventually a common
bakehouse and kitchen: 'From this to the preparation of meals
and the serving of them in the Common Room would be only a
matter of time; for the advantage of it is obvious.'[153] The advantages, economy of materials and effort, would also be available to
wealthier people seeking to escape from the cares of servant
management. Groups of houses could be built with access to a
central service building, meals served at home or in the dining
hall, and service provided. In short, cooperation would improve
the architectural environment of town or countryside.

The plans for the Bradford cooperative dwellings (see Figure 5)
show a rectangular arrangement of three-storey terrace houses
connected by a covered way to a common room. The houses vary
in size, having from three to five bedrooms, but all have baths
and sculleries. In all the cottages, the stairs opened directly off
the living room, which was designed to provide a large open
space in which small areas were enclosed for fireside seats and
desks. Front, and sometimes back, doors open directly into the
living room, giving a draughty, corridor-like feeling to the rear

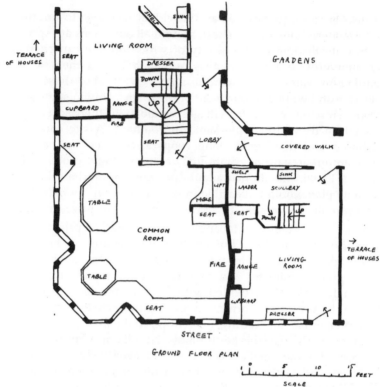

FIGURE 5 *Design by Barry Parker and Raymond Unwin for the common room of a quadrangle of cooperative dwellings in Bradford (redrawn from Barry Parker and Raymond Unwin, The Art of Building a Home, Longmans, Green, London, 1901, plate 7)*

of the room. Unwin felt that the 'useless front parlour' was a waste of space, but this view was not shared by working-class tenants, as he was to find in later years during the building of the first garden city.[154] Except in the case of the largest house, the scullery is squeezed into a small space on the inward-facing side of the house.

The common room took up two storeys of the common building, a gallery at first-floor height overlooking seating arranged along the walls. The kitchen was situated on the second floor and connected to the common room by a lift. Parker and Unwin also placed the laundry on the top floor, involving all users in a climb of two flights of stairs while carrying heavy washing. The floor area of the common room was a little over 400 sq ft, but this included space taken up by tables, seating and inglenook fire-places. If meals were eventually to be served to all tenants, prob-ably numbering around 150, they would not all be able to eat together due to lack of space; the central part of the common room is little larger than the living room of one of the terrace houses. Meals could, of course, be cooked in the kitchen and collected for eating at home, but if this system were to operate, it would be more efficient to locate the kitchen on the ground floor. The quadrangle of larger houses also shown in *The Art of Building a Home* had its common room, kitchen and laundry all located on the ground floor, with only a library, balcony and caretaker's flat on the first floor.

The Bradford cottages appeared in a more economic form in Raymond Unwin's Fabian tract of 1902, *Cottage Plans and Common Sense*.[155] Both Parker and Unwin were Fabians, and Unwin used the tract to advocate the communal use of space previously taken up with tiny backyards and narrow back streets. He suggested grouping cottages together round open spaces, thus affording each house a pleasant outlook and sunny aspect for its main rooms. Quadrangles could be laid out with central gardens, play-grounds or bowling greens to give variety. The housing (see Plate 8) shown in the tract was a two-storey terrace, the attic floor having small windows. Some houses had baths, those without used the shared bathrooms, and all used the communal wash-house and playroom. Unwin emphasised these simpler coop-erative provisions, but still thought that 'the bakehouse, and even the common kitchen would be matters only of time and the growth of self-restraint, and the co-operative spirit'.[156] One par-ticularly useful communal provision is the playroom attached to the washhouse, and divided from it only by a glazed screen. In this 1902 plan, the washhouse was situated on the ground floor of the quadrangle. By this time, Unwin was clearly coming to the conclusion that full cooperative housekeeping was not feasible. He explained his plans for quadrangles of working-class housing at a meeting of the Workmen's National Housing Council in November 1901:

He urged the benefit of common rooms and common laundries at each of the four angles of the square as a satisfactory solution of modified cooperative living, which can only be successful by judicious limitation . . . [157]

Unwin's early writing had emphasised socialism as an end in itself, with communal life being made possible through the construction of cooperative housing. By the time of the GCA conference in September 1901 Unwin had ceased to see cooperative housing as a means of spreading socialism, and increasingly saw it as an end in itself, an improved environment for the working class with the prospect of good views, sunny aspects and gardens. He still believed that 'architecture always reveals the life it clothes and reflects its ideals',[158] but because of his urge to produce real changes in the living conditions of the working class, he began to give priority to the form of housing over the lifestyle reflected in it, seeking immediate improvement rather than being satisfied with promises of a better future.

The GCA conference gave the idea of a garden city more respectability, and its realisation was brought closer with the formation of the Garden City Pioneer Company in 1902 to raise funds and acquire a site. In 1903 a site at Letchworth was bought and First Garden City Ltd was formed to organise its development.[159] A competition was held to find a suitable plan, and in February 1904 the Parker and Unwin entry was accepted as the company's plan. The building of Letchworth Garden City brought to fruition a quarter century of intense theoretical consideration and practical experimentation concerned with improving both living conditions and human relations. A number of industrial villages had been built, leading to improvements in housing standards and estate planning. Bedford Park, a middle-class London suburban development founded in 1876, had shown that good planning and a sense of community were appreciated by wealthier house owners. Its tile-hung, red-brick villas in large gardens were inhabited by an artistic elite, who nevertheless provided a living example of successful community planning.[160] The long working-class tradition of attempts to form communities was continued with the foundation in 1888 of Tenant Cooperators Ltd by Edward Vansittart Neale, a consistent advocate of cooperative housekeeping.[161] Neale had long felt that the surplus capital of cooperative societies should be used to build associated homes, and the co-partnership housing movement, as it became known, had its first success in 1901 with the erection of Brentham garden village in Ealing. The village was cooperative only in that the tenants were their own landlords, part of the building capital being provided by them. The growth of co-partnership housing ensured that more working-class tenants had control over the design and management of their housing. The average working-class lifestyle was still very different from that advocated by the 'back to the land' movements, but concern with land ownership was one factor which prompted Ebenezer Howard to suggest the garden city.

The opportunity to build new housing and new types of housing at Letchworth was ideal for the cooperative housekeeping movement, recently invigorated by the writings of Charlotte Perkins Gilman. Previous experiments had mainly concerned single women or had lacked funds for building. The GCA conference, and in particular Lander's paper, showed that there was now a real possibility of further experiments in cooperative housekeeping. After 25 years of debate, centred on the women's movement, the socialists and the Fabians, and elements of the 'back to the land' and arts and crafts movements, a constituency of mainly middle-class people existed who were ready and able to change their lifestyles. In earlier years, minimal forms of cooperation had been used simply to ameliorate the servant problem, as in the case of cooked food delivery services. The coming of the garden city was the catalyst which ensured that cooperative housekeeping could be seen as an end in itself. It remained to be seen whether cooperative housekeeping could fulfil the promises made in its name, especially those concerning women's freedom from the cares of domestic work and thus their opportunities to work outside the home. Many previous experimental communities had promised much, but had left the sexual division of labour unchanged; the advocates of cooperative housekeeping had been presented with the opportunity of the garden city to show that their experiment was a practical proposition which could change the lives of its participants.

6 The Cooperative Housekeeping Boom

The First Garden City of Letchworth might have seemed the ideal site for the introduction of housing with communal facilities, but the Barry Parker and Raymond Unwin plan for its development contained only traditional housing, albeit often situated in three-sided squares or quadrangles.[1] The houses were grouped for good architectural effect, as Unwin had suggested in his paper to the 1901 GCA conference, and arranged round large areas of open space. Any lingering wish Parker and Unwin may have had to encourage communal developments with new housing probably vanished when First Garden City Limited failed to attract sufficient funds to finance model housing schemes.[2] The Cheap Cottages Exhibition of 1905 provided increased publicity for the city, 60 000 people visiting the exhibition which aimed to show that good cottages could be built cheaply. A total of 119 dwellings were entered in the various competitions, the main prize being offered for a £150 cottage for an agricultural worker.[3] Parker and Unwin felt that building cheap cottages of a low standard would not solve the housing problem, insisting that 'no cottage that is not a good cottage shall be built at all'.[4] Their article on cheap cottages made no mention of communal facilities whatsoever, suggesting only that groups of cottages were economic to build.

The Cheap Cottages Exhibition provided the architect M. H. Baillie Scott with the opportunity to build an experimental pair of cottages which could be used for cooperative housekeeping. Scott designed mainly middle-class houses, concentrating on providing truly open spaces using built-in furniture and integrating utilities into the fabric of the house as a whole.[5] Scott's 'ideal suburban house', as described in *The Studio* in the mid-1890s, used folding screens to divide up the hall, dining room and drawing room areas, and placed a single set of stairs in a neutral zone of the house so that both family and servants were able to use them.[6] He saw simplicity, homely comfort and economy as important. Scott's open-plan living rooms were influential in the work of Parker and Unwin.[7] The pair of cottages entered by Scott in the Letchworth competition were far from cheap, costing £210 each to build (see Plate 9). 'Elmwood Cottages' as he called them still stand in Norton Way North, Letchworth, although flat-roofed extensions now replace the typical Scott roofs sweeping down low over the sculleries. He felt that the accommodation provided – three bedrooms, large kitchen, parlour and scullery (see Figure 6) – 'should not be too much for the average cottager to expect', and went on to say that

> They were designed as a protest against the merely utilitarian ideals of modern building generally, and the cottage exhibition in particular, and attempted to show how the beauty of the old cottage is not incompatible with modern requirements.[8]

His design was not taken seriously as a realistic model for an agricultural worker's cottage, however, being too expensive; it was more suitable for 'persons who have been caught with the "week-end" fever, and while seeking for a cheap cottage, are prepared to spend a good deal more on it than £150'.[9]

The internal plan of the cottages was unusual in that a connecting door was provided, enabling the two cottages to be used as one house, or for some form of cooperative living to take place.[10] The door was probably situated to the rear of the house in the party wall between the two parlours, although it is not shown on any of the available plans. Scott intended the parlour to be a relief from the everyday associations of the living room, and yet not entirely isolated or poorly ventilated. The wide doorway to the living room achieved this aim, and the window seats and dresser provided an uninterrupted space before the open fire. The living room floor was brick, the kitchen table scrubbed deal, the front door an elm slab, and old tiles were included to give more artistic character.[11] The cottages were more likely to please the 'week-ender' than an agricultural worker who might prefer a labour-saving closed range to an open fire, and a more self-contained parlour. The cottages were very soon occupied by a Dr H. D. Ledward, who used them as a single house.[12] The complete duplication of facilities would have made the cottages less than efficient when used as a single home, but the inclusion of the connecting door showed that Scott realised the possibilities of some form of sharing, cooperation or amalgamation while retaining a mainly conventional house plan.

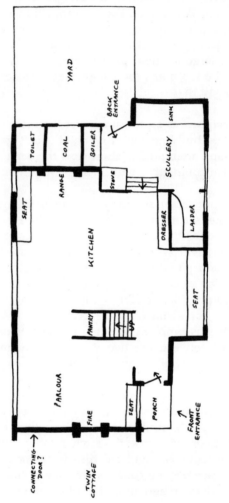

FIGURE 6 *Ground-floor plan of one of the pair of Elmwood Cottages, Letchworth Garden City, designed by M. H. Baillie Scott (redrawn from M. H. Baillie Scott, Houses and Gardens, Newnes, London, 1906, facing p. 103)*

Elmwood Cottages were not the first example of cooperative homes to be erected in Letchworth. Even before July 1905, the month in which the Cheap Cottages Exhibition opened, the occupiers of an adjoining house and cottage were undertaking an experiment in cooperative kitchen arrangements. This was described by Ebenezer Howard in a contemporary lecture as different from anything he had heard of before.[13] The large house was occupied by an industrious farm labourer and his 'equally industrious' wife, who intended to let out some of their five bedrooms to lodgers. The nursery of the adjoining cottage had been enlarged to form a small dining room, which was connected to the kitchen of the house, where all the cooking was done. The occupants of the cottage were a family consisting of a father, three daughters and a son, the father often being away from home. Some of the daughters slept in the spare bedrooms of the house, all these arrangements being made in order to solve the servant problem. Howard reported that the experiment had achieved both privacy and economy, the economy more through cooperation than in the cost of labour and materials saved during building of the shared facilities. In his view, it was obvious that the 'success of such ventures depends more upon the people who seek to cooperate than upon the inherent advantages of the schemes themselves'. Success in this case stemmed from the adaptable nature of the adjoining properties, which enabled the two households to live as an extended family while still maintaining their privacy.

By mid-1905, almost two years after the Garden City Estate had been officially opened, there was some disquiet within the garden city movement regarding the lack of plans for any form of cooperative housing at Letchworth, in contrast to the ideas put forward by Unwin and more particularly Lander at the 1901 GCA conference. In *The Garden City*, one commentator complained that the low housing density specified on the Parker and Unwin plan seemed to exclude a cooperative community.[14] He suggested that ten families would be enough to form an association, each family having an individual home but sharing a kitchen, dining room, nursery and laundry. The advantages would be a decrease in work, higher standards and a certain amount of choice for the wives: they could take turns with domestic tasks or stick to those they preferred. He added that the male cooperators would similarly divide up the rough work.

Earlier in 1905, the kitchenless home had gathered more publicity when H. G. Wells included it in his description of *A Modern Utopia*, serialised in *The Fortnightly Review*. The quadrangle was the most prevalent form of building in Wells' utopian town, all homes were equipped with labour-saving devices and the world was completely servantless. Hotels, clubs and various cooperative arrangements had decreased the popularity of the individual home. Flats and suites perhaps had small cooking corners 'but the ordinary Utopian would no more think of a special private kitchen for his dinners than he would think of a private flour mill or dairy farm.'[15] Wells, a Fabian, continued his speculations on the nature of utopia in his occasional columns in the *Daily Mail* during 1905. He rejected the idea of a cottage in a garden city as an ideal home because of Howard's intention that homes and industry should be provided together. Wells thought the coming of trams and cars would allow them to be 20 to 30 miles apart.[16] Wells was a garden city shareholder, but he went on to criticise the prevalence of detached cottages in Letchworth, seeing them as resulting from a distorted view of country life. He felt that the servantless cottage was 'impossible as a home for civilised working people' because of the sheer amount of hard work involved.[17]

The alternative to the 'cheap and nasty cottage', according to Wells, was the associated home, a traditional English form of living whose return would herald new social developments. He suggested that club membership would be the most practical method for experimenting with associated living, members paying a subscription and receiving the benefits of centralised facilities. These would include all manner of recreational, educational and medical services, and the usual central kitchen and dining room. Wells did not envisage his associated home as being suitable for everyone:

> I doubt if one could get average working men's wives or clerk's wives into such a place; they would be suspicious of each other, they would quarrel and refuse to speak, and do all sorts of nervous, silly, underbred things.[18]

He thought, however, that enough 'unpretending sociable people' would be prepared to try associated living and make a club financially viable. He suggested the 'Garden City people' at Letchworth should start the club, although it is not clear whether he was referring to the development company or the residents. In the final article of his series, Wells was more specific about the details of the residential club.[19] Architecturally it resembled an Oxford college, being in the form of a quadrangle. The walls were white pebbledash, the roofs red tiles. Individual living rooms were large, heated by radiators and provided with architect-designed furniture; various sizes of house were available within the overall terrace structure. Although Wells was 'absolutely indifferent' to questions of women's rights, he was keen on decreasing the workload of mothers, even suggesting that women relieved of many of their domestic responsibilities might be able to take up paid work (but only in the club kitchen or creche).

In terms of the continuing debate on associated living, there was little new in Wells' articles, but their publication in the *Daily Mail*, following the serialisation of *A Modern Utopia* and its eventual publication, gave the ideas increased publicity. This coincided with Charlotte Perkins Gilman's third lecture tour of England, during which her views on women and the home were widely reported. Her book *The Home, its Work and Influence* had been published in England in 1903,[20] extending the arguments of *Women and Economics* concerning the place of industry in the home. Gilman gave a course of six lectures in London during February and March 1905.[21] The first, 'The End of the Servant Question' caused a particular stir as Gilman repeated her proposals for the professionalisation of domestic work. The *Daily News* reported that 'She is saying, and saying boldly, what tired and distracted housewives are beginning to think, or at any rate to feel. And for that reason she is being amazingly run after by her sex.' The paper conducted a rather breathless interview with Gilman, describing her as

clever, practical, managing, not a sleepy peson who groans under the difficulties of domestic life, but a vigorous and capable housewife who has wrestled with its problems, and sees new and better solutions than have yet been realised.[22]

The *Morning Leader* mentioned the 'interested and fashionable crowd of femininity' who heard the lecture, while the *Daily Mirror* compared the proposals of Gilman and Wells, concluding that Gilman's aim of a servantless house had been detailed in Wells' *A Modern Utopia*, and that its realisation lay in the hands of builders and architects. The *Daily Mirror* was enthusiastic about the introduction of labour-saving devices into the home, whether servantless or not, but some reports were more sceptical. The *Daily News* referred to the earlier failure of the Distributing Kitchen in London, while *Society Pictorial* called her a crank. The *Sunday School Chronicle* correspondent, 'Marguerite', welcomed any plan which decreased household drudgery, but asserted that 'women are slaves at heart, and only truly happy in their slavery, if slavery be the word to apply to the service of love – the sacrifice of self in which they find their true element.'[23]

Gilman's hectic lecture tour and the publication of *A Modern Utopia* ensured that the middle class was aware of the possibilities of a changed lifestyle during 1905.[24] The Cheap Cottage Exhibition at Letchworth contained many experimental entries, and Wells' suggestion that a cooperative community should be initiated there doubtless helped to form public opinion of the garden city as a haven for strange ideas and stranger people.[25] Speakers at the first GCA conference in 1901 had, however, stressed the cooperative nature of the proposed housing schemes, ranging from grouped houses to fully associated homes, and in July 1905 an article appeared in *The Garden City* urging that steps should be taken to begin an experiment.[26] The author was Walter Crane, first president of the Arts and Crafts Exhibition Society, Fabian and participant at the initial GCA conference. Crane had met Edward Bellamy in the early 1890s, finding his views rather less extreme than those in *Looking Backward*, and had lectured for the Fabian Society.[27] He felt that collective homes could be designed to a beautiful plan, and later in 1905 published a plan for a quadrangle of collective dwellings designed by his son, architect Lionel Crane.[28]

The plan (see Figure 7) was for a simple square of 16 three-bedroom cottages, with access via a covered arcade to the dining hall and reading room. A washhouse and baths were provided, each cottage having its own toilet (although some of these were external, making inelegant and inconvenient additions to the basic plan). The ground floor of each cottage was taken up by a living room, from which the stairs opened; all cottages had an individual garden. Lionel Crane's plan included the essentials for

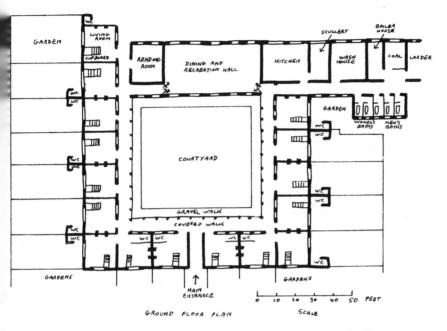

FIGURE 7 *Ground-floor plan of the quadrangle of cooperative dwellings designed by Lionel Crane for Walter Crane (redrawn from Walter Crane,* Ideals in Art, *George Bell, London, 1905, facing p. 116, by kind permission of Bell and Hyman)*

a communal dwelling, without any of the wide range of recreational or educational facilities specified in more ambitious schemes. The basic provisions may have been underestimated, with only two baths between the women of 16 households, and the serving of food made difficult by the omission of any direct contact between kitchen and dining hall. The exterior of the cottages was apparently undecorated, the plain design not reflecting any influence from Sir Ernest George, an early practitioner of the 'Queen Anne' style, in whose office Crane worked during 1895. Crane's work was mainly domestic; he had travelled widely in Europe before beginning practice in 1900, designed houses at Welwyn and Letchworth, and was made a Fellow of the RIBA in 1921.[29]

Walter Crane regarded the plan as a simple example of what could be done in designing a collective dwelling, the artistic treatment a contrast to the identical rows of 'small brick boxes with slate lids' being erected in towns. He felt that the best of contemporary flat design showed a trend towards the collective dwelling, which was becoming more acceptable as traditional ideas of home changed with the increasing complexity of cities. Collective dwellings would not only allow domestic work to be performed by professionals, but would give artists the opportunity to decorate large public rooms. Crane referred to an earlier proposal for a similar quadrangle of collective homes in a London suburb, which may well be the scheme described by Lander at the 1901 GCA conference (although this included a vast range of recreation facilities). As a Fabian, Crane would probably have been aware of the scheme put forward by the Associated Dwelling Company, and it seems likely that the idea of a community in west London resurfaced in a number of different forms in the early 1900s.[30]

The first real step towards the construction of a cooperative home in Letchworth was taken in 1904, when a leaflet, published anonymously from Hampstead, called for support in an experiment attempting to solve the servant problem. The proposal was aimed at raising interest in a cooperative kitchen, as opposed to a commercial distributive kitchen, and suggested that 25 to 30 houses should be erected around a central building; meals could be eaten at home or in the central dining hall. The houses would be supplied with centrally heated hot water, and all manner of labour-saving machines would be used.[31] Domestic economy and better food were the attractions of this scheme, aimed clearly at the middle classes who wished to move to Letchworth. In the early years of garden city development, First Garden City Ltd was in some financial difficulty, much of the house-building being undertaken by co-partnership societies. It was therefore unlikely that the company would be willing to invest in experimental communal housing schemes, leaving private funding as the only alternative. In *Tomorrow* Howard had mentioned cooperative kitchens, but had never shown as much enthusiasm for the idea as Lander, or indeed Unwin in his earlier writing. The publicity given to cooperative housekeeping in 1905 by Gilman's lectures and Wells, Crane and other members of the garden city movement increased the possibility of a viable experiment in communal living taking place.

On 18 August 1906 an illustrated article appeared in the *Daily Mail* in which Ebenezer Howard described the cooperative housekeeping scheme he had drawn up with Lander and others unidentified.[32] He envisaged a leafy, tree-strewn quadrangle of 24 houses with from one to three bedrooms. Each house contained a sitting room, hall, scullery with gas stove, and a bathroom as well as the bedroom or rooms, rents ranging from £30 to £40 per annum. One side of the quadrangle included the common kitchen, dining room and administration. Howard suggested that residents would save on servants' wages, food, labour and water heating, while sharing in the profits from the centralised cooking and enjoying increased privacy in their homes. The servants themselves would benefit from greater freedom, not being bound to a single home. The object of the scheme was

> to provide a home of comparative comfort and beauty for those numerous folk of the middle-class who have a hard struggle for existence on a meagre income – for those who require domestic help, but who can very ill afford it.

Lander, Howard's friend and designer of the scheme, had supported the idea strongly in 1901, but the need for public investment made it important that Howard should endorse the venture, giving it credibility. Wells, Crane and in particular Lander had advocated a communal housing scheme, and Howard knew of Gilman's ideas on the wastefulness of individual homes, so would have been receptive to their proposals.[33]

By late 1907 the project had reached a more definite stage, with the formation of a company, Letchworth Co-operative Houses, in the offing. Lander had changed the internal arrangements, and the scheme now gave potential investors the choice of four types of house, a bedsitter having been added to the range available.[34] Tenants were offered private gardens, the use of tennis courts, croquet lawns and a bowling green, and could eat vegetarian meals if they wished. Tenants could buy shares in the company, the cooperative nature of the project being revealed most clearly in its management structure. Domestic work continued to be performed by servants, but Howard hoped that under cooperative management it would 'assume a new interest and dignity'. By October 1907 the site, in Letchworth, had been selected and in 1908 the company was set up with a capital of £10 000 and Howard as one of four directors. Although First Garden City Ltd allowed the company to rent the site for a nominal amount, they were anxious not to be associated with the scheme in any publicity material.[35]

Lander's design was for a cooperative home for 32 households, and by 20 November 1910 the first eight houses were in use, to be followed by another eight before April 1912.[36] Howard's speech on the opening day stressed the advantages of the scheme for servants, with the benefits of division of labour, labour-saving appliances, improved working and living conditions and association with those of their own age. Miss M. B. Brown was appointed as manageress, her previous experience being gained as a housekeeper in a residential hostel in Stockwell, south London.[37] The building, designed in the form of an open quadrangle, was called Homesgarth (see Figure 8). On the opening day, Howard pointed out that the administrative area of the building was suitable for the complete community, and that although local people intended to eat in the dining hall, it would initially be difficult for the company financially. Some of the houses were already occupied as Howard spoke, and the tenants were apparently delighted with the scheme. Howard had accepted the criticisms that Homesgarth excluded children, saying it was merely a tentative experiment and that the lack of children 'condemns the whole thing'.[38] In the opening speech, he acknowledged that the scheme was not designed for those of 'very small means', but said that the real objective was to prove the idea successful and go on to provide similar accommodation for the working-class woman and her family.

The half quadrangle of Homesgarth still stands in Letchworth (see Plate 10), the covered way running round the inside of the houses. Lander's original design placed the dining room centrally, with flats and houses along the sides of the quadrangle (no bedsitters were built due to lack of demand). Lander had difficulty reconciling the demands of 'all the "cranks"' who were to live there, and who wanted particular types of windows and walls.[39] The interiors of the houses and flats were not unusual, each having a porch, sitting room, bedroom or rooms, bathroom and pantry, while the administration area contained the central kitchen (on the first floor to minimise cooking smells), dining room seating 50 to 60 people, reading and smoking rooms and staff accommodation. For an extra charge, meals could be taken at home rather than in the dining room.

Reaction to the opening of Homesgarth was enthusiastic if

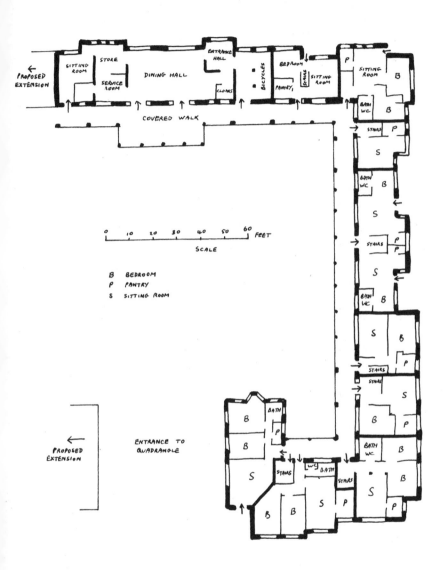

FIGURE 8 *Ground-floor plan of Homesgarth, Letchworth Garden City, designed by H. Clapham Lander (redrawn from C. B. Purdom, The Garden City, Dent, London, 1913, p. 101)*

slightly sceptical, with over 60 papers reporting the event. The *Westminster Gazette* had a typically ambiguous response, praising Homesgarth's solution of the servant problem as 'the beginning of a cooperative movement which may prove more revolutionary in its development than even the garden city ideal itself', while waiting to see 'whether the seclusive or the gregarious instinct triumphs'.[40] Lander himself described the scheme as suitable for single people or small families wishing for a wider social life than they could obtain in a hotel, combined with the privacy of home life.[41] Just over two years after its opening, Howard was able to write that 'all the dwellings are let and the tenants like the place immensely', but this success was not reflected financially as no profit was made.[42] Howard set about publicising the need for funds to expand Homesgarth from 16 to 32 houses, in the process combating press reports suggesting that cooperative house-keeping entailed loss of privacy. He had a personal interest in the matter, having moved into Homesgarth in 1911, and felt the scheme could be made to pay if the central facilities were to be used by 32 households as originally intended.[43] His *Daily Mail* article of 1913 produced a supporting article detailing the financial saving a Homesgarth resident could make (£24 per annum, i.e. slightly less than half the rent of the largest house), and stressing that the existence of the communal areas resulted in real privacy in the home. The dining hall was described as being very pleasant,

> with no suggestion whatever of the deadly constraint or the forced sociability of the ordinary communal meals of a board-ing-house or small hotel. Every Englishman's house is his castle, and if he is to live co-operatively he will do it on a tacit understanding that he carries his privacy into the common dining-room.[44]

The attractions of Homesgarth were seen as domestic economy, efficient service and increased privacy; to some prospective tenants, a cooperative home was simply an improved castle. Lucy Carr Shaw wrote enthusiastically to Howard after reading his *Daily Mail* article, saying she was

> nearly worried to death by the cares of housekeeping and the intolerable incompetency of servants ... One of your £64 houses presents itself to me as a paradise after the turmoil of private housekeeping.[45]

In spite of Howard's efforts, Homesgarth was never extended, and the working-class cooperative home which he had always envisaged as the next step in communal living was not built either. Howard had begun to publicise the need for a working-class scheme soon after the opening of Homesgarth, when he could point to the practical (although not financial) success of cooperative housekeeping. He suggested a development of 48 cottages, each with its own garden, with a central building comprising kitchen, laundry, creche and workshop. Instead of every housewife spending two to three hours a day preparing dinner, Howard felt that only 8 to 16 of them could manage the cooking for all the families, leaving the other women free to look after the children, or work in the laundry where 'labour saving machines would make the work a pleasure'. He estimated that the capital cost of the scheme would be £15 000. Apart from financial backing, Howard felt that committed tenants would be needed:

I shall have to get round me a group of strong-minded women who are anxious to experiment with the definite purpose of making it a success; who feel that under existing conditions of drudgery housework affords little or no chance of recreation or expressing their artistic or aesthetic tastes.[46]

In a later paper on the same subject, Howard's emphasis had changed from giving women free time to enabling them to take up paid work, although he added: 'they will at the same time be able to do far more for the comfort and happiness of their husbands and children than they can possibly do when all the drudgery of the cottages is borne by them.'[47] By 1913, when the article appeared in the *Daily Mail* and other papers, Howard's plan stipulated that the cottages should be grouped around three sides of a square, and that all domestic work should be performed by paid workers. This change from cooperative housekeeping in the original sense, with householders doing the work themselves, to a system of professionalised domestic work may have been prompted by Howard's experience of living at Homesgarth. Howard's increased concentration on women's domestic work in his post-1909 writing may have been influenced by his second wife Edith, whom he married in 1907.

Howard chose an opportune moment to raise the question of working-class cooperative homes, as in 1913 Charlotte Perkins

Gilman paid another visit to England, lecturing and resting at the home of May Morris.[48] Her lecture to the Fabian Society on 'The Economic Independence of Women' produced their largest meeting for some time; she spoke for the professionalisation of domestic work, and against 'the cooperative housekeeping delusion'.[49] Her work was very influential in the women's movement of the 1900s; Ada Nield Chew, socialist, suffragist and prolific writer, 'thought a great deal of her ideas'.[50] Chew's articles on the daily life of working women were amongst an increasing number appearing in *The Englishwoman* from 1910 onwards concerning housing and domestic problems.[51] In the years leading up to the First World War, a 'war with housework' was seen to be approaching, and cooperative housekeeping appealed to some women as a means of staving off daily drudgery.[52] Opinion on the servantless, kitchenless house ranged from the ovewhelmingly enthusiastic:

> The feminist flat is revolutionary, strikes at the root of the economic system, may involve vast readjustments of land tenure, communal building and taxation. But we are not afraid of revolution, for we are the pioneers of a sex revolution.[53]

on the part of a male supporter of the women's movement, to the conventionally dubious: 'Many women feel that if they give up having the family meat cooked at home ... they will be failing in their duty to their husbands and children.'[54] Personal experience of domestic crisis could give rise to greater acceptance of cooperative housekeeping, as in Lewis Mumford's case when, after being forced to cook for his family, he wrote an article extolling community cooking.[55]

Clearly the success or failure of Homesgarth, as the first practical example of a cooperative home for families, was of some public interest. C. B. Purdom devoted an entire chapter to Homesgarth in his book *The Garden City*, published in 1913. He accepted the need for 'a new kind of domestic policy, to bring back comfort into the home', but although he felt that it was too soon to assess Homesgarth, he somewhat grudgingly added: 'So far, it will be admitted, it has overcome most of its peculiar difficulties and offers promise of interesting developments.'[56] The *Pall Mall Gazette* commented on the high cost of the central facilities, and having acknowledged the precedent set by the ladies' residential flats in communal living, went on: 'And a co-operative home of this kind shelters eligible males from the attacks of wily females who might seek to entrap and lasso them with the noose matrimonial.'[57]

An architectural journal felt that kitchenless houses would fail, as people were too conservative to change their way of life, citing in support of this view the fate of communal washhouses.[58] Their unpopularity was well known; 'women revolted at the idea of washing their dirty linen in common', as one writer put it, and it was often impossible to take children into the washhouses.[59] However, this type of forced sociability during domestic work was far from the communal life envisaged in cooperative homes such as Homesgarth. Howard enthused about life at Homesgarth in his *Daily Mail* article, written from his private study there: 'Each house has its own garden – I see my wife (saved from housekeeping worries) is at work in hers now . . .'[60] No other accounts of early life there are available, but one visitor was told tenants liked Homesgarth 'very much', while in 1944–5 a friendly atmosphere prevailed at communal meals.[61] Howard himself left Homesgarth in 1921, moving to the second garden city, Welwyn, where he lived close to another cooperative home.

The 16 houses and flats which together with the central facilities comprised Homesgarth are now known as Sollershott Hall, after the road in which they stand. Modern flats have been added to the original development and alterations made to the interior, the communal meals and other functions having been discontinued soon after the Second World War as running costs increased. The Hall is now a peaceful square of traditional accommodation with attached clubhouse. It had taken, as *The Queen* suggested in relation to Mrs E. M. King's scheme in 1873, an 'unusually zealous amateur of social science' willing to put his own money into cooperative housekeeping in order that an experiment could take place.[62] Howard had been able to show that families were ready to change their lifestyle, and that cooperative housekeeping could function in practice. However, the experiment was not a financial success, as Homesgarth was never expanded to its theoretical optimum size. The small scale of the development, lack of shared staircases and provision of individual gardens ensured privacy. The greatest distance between sitting room and central hall, via the cloistered walk, was only 75 yards, so that attending the hall for meals took little time or effort, and meals could be served to rooms while still hot. The design of Homesgarth neatly combined houses and flats and would have remained compact had it been expanded to full size, although this would have resulted in a severely diminished view for the houses in the gateway of the quadrangle.

Homesgarth did not herald the revolution in domestic life which many observers had predicted. The 16 households lived as individual households except for the central provision of servants and communal meals. This was not cooperative housekeeping but socialised domestic work. Homesgarth catered only for the relatively well off, and its success could not be used as evidence in favour of similar schemes for the working class, which would have limited servicing and fewer facilities. Homesgarth has survived until the present because its design succeeded in combining privacy with an element of community, because it provided a pleasant place to live with its homely but unusual housing and cloistered green quadrangle. The onset of the First World War decreased the relative importance of the middle-class domestic crisis, and after the initial publicity Homesgarth continued in quiet obscurity. The garden city movement itself was still thriving, giving rise to numerous garden suburbs and maintaining the ideal of cooperation in new surroundings. The housing problem for single women workers, those pioneers of cooperative house-keeping, remained unsolved, and in 1909 another well-publicised cooperative venture aimed to provide housing for women in a new garden suburb. It appeared that middle-class families, although dissatisfied with their home lives, were more willing to think and read about change than carry it out; single women, often without the security of their own homes, were happy to take the opportunity of trying out cooperative life.

The site for the women's cooperative home was Hampstead Garden Suburb, originated by Henrietta Barnett as part of a plan to ensure that land adjacent to Hampstead Heath remained an open space. Barnett, wife of Canon Barnett of Toynbee Hall, first made public her suggestion in a letter to Hampstead's local paper in 1903, and enlarged on the idea in the *Contemporary Review* in February 1905.[63] In her projected garden suburb, Barnett hoped that 'all classes would live together under right conditions of beauty and space', envisaging a planned estate including houses of all sizes, each with its own garden, as well as cooperative stores, bakehouses, baths, washhouses and refreshment rooms.[64]

She also mentioned quadrangles of cottages, associated residences for young men (with common gardens) and a working lads' hostel. The Hampstead Garden Suburb Trust Limited was set up to carry out the scheme, Raymond Unwin having been involved in producing preliminary plans from January 1905.[65] His first layout for the suburb was drawn up in February 1905, and included several quadrangles of housing for particular groups such as widows, single ladies and working lads, as specified in Barnett's original description.[66] Although some of the family housing was planned around greens, there were no cooperative homes for families. The building of the suburb began in early 1907, Parker and Unwin's own quadrangle of flats for the old being opened in October 1909.

This development, called The Orchard, consisted of 57 flats with shared baths, washhouses and baking ovens, and was built for Hampstead Tenants Ltd, a co-partnership society (see Plate 11). The flats were intended to house two people, probably either a couple or a widow and child, but had only a single living room with bed recess and a scullery.[67] Meals were not eaten together, so that although facilities were shared, the development could not be called a cooperative home. It did represent Parker and Unwin's best attempt at building their ideal quadrangle, and was indeed a beautiful building in spite of its low standard of accommodation.[68] During the building of The Orchard, Unwin may have regained some of his diminishing belief in the value of good housing as an aid to the spread of cooperation. His *Town Planning in Practice*, published in 1909, referred to the growth of the tenant co-partnership movement and the probable need for 'something in the way of common rooms, baths, washhouses, recreation-rooms, reading-rooms, and possibly eventually common kitchens and dining-halls'.[69] Unwin even included a drawing of a 'group of cottages with a cooperative centre'[70] (see Plate 12), which bears a strong resemblance to The Orchard with tiled roofs, tall chimneys and large gables. He was convinced of the advantages of the central laundry, but felt that the question of the common kitchen and dining-hall was more difficult, while accepting that individual cooking was clearly uneconomic. He concluded:

We should need a volume in order adequately to discuss the advantages and the difficulties of co-operative living. Along certain directions it is clearly possible, even with the present prejudices, to secure by co-operation very great advantages to the individual; but such a form of life can only be developed tentatively . . . [71]

Several sites for cooperative dwellings had been marked on Unwin's original plan for Hampstead Garden Suburb. Henrietta Barnett selected one of these to be the associated homes for working ladies, marking the plan 'Here will lie a quadrangle of villas round a green'.[72] Her idea for a cooperative women's home stemmed from her knowledge of the housing conditions of women working with the poor in the East End of London. They were often uncomfortable, 'in drear neighbourhoods lodged in rooms overfilled with furniture and attended pehaps by disagreeable landladies'.[73]

Having decided on the site, she consulted Unwin, 'who sketched out an ideal quadrangle', which she then took to the Improved Industrial Dwellings Company (IIDC).[74] The IIDC had been founded by Sydney Waterlow in 1863, with the aim of showing that the building of working-class housing could be a profitable proposition. It concentrated on building tenements with communal sculleries and lavatories for the artisan class in its early years, later changing to self-contained flats, and by 1894 Waterlow felt able to tell the annual meeting that the IIDC had achieved its aims.[75] Barnett persuaded the IIDC to adopt her idea, finding that they agreed with her proposals for a common room, restaurant meals, tennis courts and a shared staff of servants. She also ensured that they included other features she regarded as essential: a separate bath for each flat, separate sitting and bedrooms, and individual gardens.[76]

M. H. Baillie Scott designed the women's home for the IIDC, and Waterlow Court, as the quadrangle was called after the founder of the company, was officially opened on 1 July 1909. Henrietta Barnett described the building as 'quaint and interesting', thus damning a superb building with extremely faint praise.[77] Scott's first design for a quadrangle of houses was published in 1906, the year after the erection of his Elmwood Cottages at Letchworth. This scheme, which he later said constituted an early version of Waterlow Court, comprised 12 houses arranged in the form of an open quadrangle. All cooking, service and heating functions were centralised, with a covered way leading from the houses to the central hall. It was a cooperative home for the middle class; each house had an average of two sitting rooms and four bedrooms, and a bus was included in the scheme to enable it to be built in the country where land prices were relatively low. Scott saw the problem of designing a cooperative home as one of obtaining the benefits of cooperation while maintaining the advantages of privacy. To this end, he included fires in the sitting rooms for those who wished to cook at home, and recesses in the dining hall for families wishing to eat away from the central table.[78] The two sitting rooms were connected by a wide doorway making the ground floor almost open plan, in a similar manner to the parlour and living room of Elmwood Cottages. The larger, through sitting room had windows facing on to both the interior of the quadrangle and the garden, while the bathroom was placed on the first floor, opening off a dressing room attached to one of the bedrooms.

The central building contained the two-storey wood-panelled dining hall, with kitchen below and servants' accommodation above. There appeared to be no provision made for a lift service from kitchen to dining hall, and food would have to have been carried up a flight of stairs, into the serving room and then under the covered way into the dining hall, a time-consuming process. Externally, the upper stories of the cooperative home were half timbered, the overall E-shape making it reminiscent of an Elizabethan country house. The houses would no doubt have proved pleasant and spacious to live in, and the entire scheme workable if enough money had ever been available to staff the house, garden, stables and bus. Any savings made from cooperation in cooking and heating would probably have been taken up by the high level of servicing required by the design and situation of house and garden.

Although Scott did not deny the importance of comfort and convenience in the home, he criticised the plethora of labour-saving devices advocated by H. G. Wells, saying they 'all seemed inspired by that inhuman calculating demon which lurks in all mechanical devices'.[79] He preferred 'good, simple, honest things, well and strongly made' to what he saw as the pretentious vulgarity of much contemporary villa-building.[80] His design for Waterlow Court reflected these attitudes, and his liking for the plan of house and central court which he traced back to the days of fortified dwellings [81] (see Plates 1, 3 and 14, Figure 9). The Court was, and still is, a beautiful, cloistered quadrangle of flats set around a peaceful grass square. The inside of the square is white plaster, the outside brick and half timbering with a tiled roof. It contained 50 flats for professional working women, each with living room, bedroom or recess, bathroom and scullery with cooker. Some larger flats had two bedrooms. There was a central dining hall, common room and kitchen, a servants' hall and other accommodation for the housekeeper and servants. A single-storey servants' annexe was built at the southern corner. Scott took great pains with the details of the internal decoration, including wooden latches for doors and the use of a heart-shaped motif on metalwork and staircases. The living rooms appeared spacious, dominated by open fires (see Plate 15).

Residents paid from £1 14s 0d to £3 5s 0d per month rent, depending on size of room, and an additional 3 shillings per week was payable for service. The central kitchen, sited above the dining hall to which it was connected by a lift, provided breakfast, lunch, dinner and supper. Vegetarian dishes were available at lunchtime, costing 3d or 4d, and were very popular. Meals could be taken in rooms for an extra charge of 1d or 2d, or residents could cook their own food.[82] Both rent and meals were inexpensive, causing one ex-resident to comment 'They were thoroughly spoilt for almost nothing.' The provision of meals was a necessity in some cases, as residents were unused to cooking their own food. One wealthy voluntary worker moved to the Court in 1919, when 'She couldn't cook very much. She could boil an egg – if pressed, and she could make a cup of tea.'[83]

The dining hall (see Plate 16) was oblong, with french windows opening on to the garden, oak panelling and an open fire. A long table stood in the centre of the room, with smaller tables around the walls, almost as Scott had described for his 1906 design. In the period after the Second World War, residents who had come to the Court in its early years tended to sit at the centre table, with later arrivals using the side tables, although nobody had a particular seat. At that time, the atmosphere had changed from the communal spirit of the early days, when the women got together to produce plays in the grounds of the Court, to one which was not especially friendly. Women at the Court could lead completely independent lives; they were rsponsible for ordering their own food if they cooked in their flats, payment of servants,

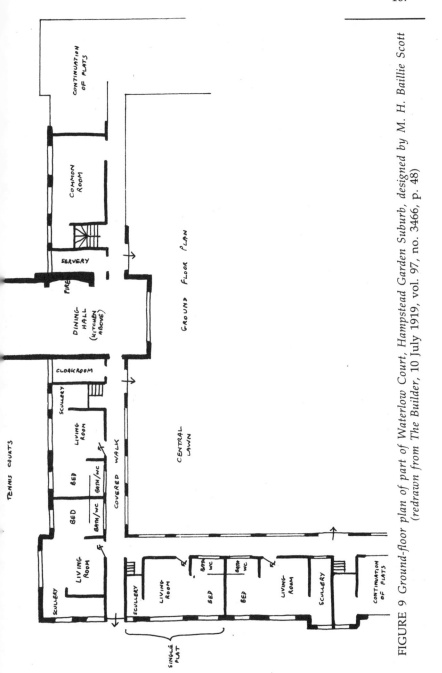

FIGURE 9 Ground-floor plan of part of Waterlow Court, Hampstead Garden Suburb, designed by M. H. Baillie Scott (redrawn from The Builder, 10 July 1919, vol. 97, no. 3466, p. 48)

and arranging for laundry to be cleaned, as no communal laundry was provided. Women had to leave if they married, and men were not allowed to stay at the Court overnight; the brother of one resident, who spent his army leave at the Court, had to jump from the window of his ground-floor room every morning to avoid discovery. At the time when sleeping out of doors was the fashion, the management committee allowed residents to do this providing they were up before the milkman came. The standard of service at the Court was such that women merely had to shout down to the maids' cottage, or wave a handkerchief from their window, for breakfast to be brought up to their rooms.

Waterlow Court continued to be used as flats for women until 1954, when the IIDC sold them to a commercial company. Communal meals were stopped in the early 1960s, and the flats are now in owner occupation. Many alterations have been made, and there are drawbacks to its use as modern homes, such as the poor sound insulation, lack of central heating and the small kitchens, especially in corner flats. In spite of these defects, the flats are very popular, Scott's design standing the test of time, changing expectations and physical alteration. The Court lies at the end of a secluded close, surrounded by its own gardens and lawns. Scott's design ensured that residents of all flats could reach the common rooms under cover, and his inclusion of ten separate staircases ensured that the minimum of noise would be generated on each one. No staircase serves more than six flats. The living rooms of ground-floor flats had no porch or lobby, opening directly on to the covered walk, and had residents been noisy this arrangement would have caused ground-floor dwellers some inconvenience. The inclusion of a large bath in every flat was unusual for 1909 (this was one of the points Henrietta Barnett had insisted upon), but the flats could be cold, as open fires were the only form of heating provided. Although Raymond Unwin's sketch of an 'ideal quadrangle' of associated dwellings has disappeared, the building produced to Scott's plan seems almost ideal for its original purpose. It certainly proved very popular, turnover of residents being low, and the current demand for the flats bears out Scott's view that the survival value of buildings is greatest where the architect's imagination is controlled by tradition.[84]

The initial announcement of the building of Waterlow Court was met with widespread approval in the press. One female columnist declared that 'The way ladies live after working hours is of more importance than the question of how or where or when they work.' She added that women could become careless under poor living conditions, being reduced to cooking sausages before the bedroom fire. Young women might be able to cope with this kind of home life, but older women could not. 'She falls, in fact, below her natural birthright of a lady; and her companions know it.'[85] Another paper felt the Court would provide an 'ideal residence for women of small means, compelled to live in or near London'.[86] The official opening day brought further praise, but also some criticisms from the socialist *Clarion*. Its columnist Julia Dawson called the Court an 'Adamless Eden', attacked its policies of temperance and excluding children, and concluded that both the Court and Homesgarth were intended solely for wealthier women.[87] This, of course, was true. Henrietta Barnett's attempt to start a cooperative home for working-class families met with the same fate as Howard's. The many files relating to her proposed 'group of small houses for families to be served by a Communal Kitchen' have long since been destroyed.[88]

Many of the residents of Waterlow Court in its early years were feminists or suffragists, and communal living, particularly the communal kitchen, was a subject of debate in the women's movement before the First World War. An early issue of the suffragist paper *Common Cause* suggested Institutes of Domestic Service should be established, to act as training centres for servants, cooperative kitchens and servants' clubs. The Institutes were thought to have 'the makings of a really large fortune' provided the necessary capital could be raised, but the plan still referred to servants as constituting one particular class of women. The plan might have raised the status of domestic service, but hardly to the level at which it became an acceptable profession.[89] *Common Cause* was also in favour of day nurseries for the children of women workers, with associated cheap restaurants. Yet another edition of Gilman's *Women and Economics* was published in 1909, the ensuing reviews taking communal living as their main point of contention. An anti-suffrage reviewer attacked Gilman's specious projects, glorified hotels and the system of socialised domestic work, while a more sober response in *The Englishwoman* put the position of the woman worker:

> The communistic kitchen is not always a success, as some of us know from bitter experience, but at any rate it provides a

meal which is infinitely preferable to the repast of tinned fish and tea which is often the only kind of meal that a fagged-out woman feels energetic enough to prepare.[90]

Gilman was not the only writer to attack women's position in the household. Cicely Hamilton's *Marriage as a Trade*, published in 1909, criticised the lack of alternatives to marriage for women: 'The housekeeping trade is the only one open to us – so we enter the housekeeping trade in order to live. This is not always quite the same as entering the housekeeping trade in order to love.'[91] Utopian fiction of the time also referred to domestic work; in Christopolis, a socialist utopia based on the garden city, domestic servants had been abolished. Husbands and fathers devoted 'some time and effort to the necessary labours of the household', but not so much that it interfered with their paid work. Wives and mothers still maintained ultimate responsibility for the home.[92] In *Nutopia or Nineteen-twenty-one* (published 1908), a Great Strike of British Women takes place in 1911, resulting in women's rule for Britain.[93]

Towards the end of the nineteenth century, women's magazines had carried reports on continental experiments involving communal kitchens and the provision of cheap food. Their interest was maintained into the 1900s, with articles on cooperative cooking in America and tenement homes in Paris, to name only two, appearing in *Englishwomen's Review* and *The Englishwoman*.[94] One such communal scheme in Austria or Germany, comprising housing and associated laundry, creche, dining room and library, was visited by two young Englishwomen around the turn of the century. They were so impressed with this idea that they initiated a cooperative home of their own after their return to England.[95] The women were Ruth I. Pym and Miss S. E. Dewe, who had met when schoolgirls at Cheltenham Ladies' College. Ruth Pym then studied history at Oxford, before she and her friend and constant companion Miss Dewe travelled abroad.[96] They moved to Letchworth in 1911, sharing a house on Norton Way South near the town centre, and Pym taught at the Letchworth Modern School for Girls. They were great friends of Ebenezer Howard, who was then living at Homesgarth. As well as being a board member of First Garden City Ltd, Howard was a director of the Howard Cottage Society, formed in August 1911 to promote working-class housing through co-partnership.[97] Both Pym and Dewe had private incomes, and were able to suggest to the Howard Cottage Society, possibly through Howard himself, that a cooperative housing scheme should be erected. The two women offered to provide the capital cost for the building of an initial seven cottages with common dining room and kitchen, an adaptation of the scheme they had seen on the continent.

On 31 July 1914 the board of the Howard Cottage Society approved the communal scheme, for which Pym and Dewe were to provide about £1600, guarantee the Society against loss if the houses proved hard to let, and pay for their conversion to conventional housing if the scheme was a failure. The Society undertook to build the houses to a design by Courtenay M. Crickmer, and to deal with their administration, although all lettings were to be nominees of Pym and Dewe.[98] The Society approached the Public Works Loan Board for a loan to assist with the scheme, which Pym and Dewe intended to house single business and professional women. The Board refused to sanction the loan, on the grounds that the proposed 13 shillings per week rent was too high for working-class housing, even including an allowance for dining room charges. The Society replied that they had found no difficulty in letting some houses in advance to a teacher, two typists and a laundry manageress; this doubtless merely confirmed the Board's view that the houses were not intended for the working classes, and the loan was refused.[99] Although the Society told First Garden City Ltd that 'the proposed experiment in co-operative housekeeping on a small scale will be another point of interest in the town',[100] they ensured that they minimised their own risks in undertaking the scheme. At First Garden City's instigation, they arranged that party walls should be constructed so as to allow connecting doors to be erected; thus, if the cooperative scheme failed, the houses could be enlarged and revert to use as traditional housing.[101] First Garden City compared this design to that used by Baillie Scott in Elmwood Cottages.

The first seven cottages of Meadow Way Green, with their common dining room and kitchen, were erected in 1914, to be followed by a further pair (also to Crickmer's design) in 1916. These cottages, together with a single house to the east of the original seven, formed the northern half of a quadrangle of cottages stretching across Meadow Way. The entire quadrangle was completed only after the First World War. On completion, Meadow Way Green North comprised nine cottages and one flat, each containing a living room, scullery, bathroom, WC and either two or four bedrooms. There was no central heating, all the cottages having individual hot water systems. To the rear of the quadrangle were private gardens, the area enclosed by the cottages being used as a communal garden. There was no covered way between cottages and dining room, which was situated in the centre of the block of seven dwellings (the single flat was placed above it), with the central kitchen at its rear (see Plate 17). The dining room itself was small, only about 14 ft square; furniture for the communal rooms was supplied by the Howard Cottage Society. The architect, Courtenay M. Crickmer, had moved from London to Letchworth in 1904. He had a mainly domestic practice, designing many cottages in Letchworth and Hampstead Garden Suburb. In 1912, he became a Fellow of the RIBA and won the *Daily Mail* Workmen's Cottage competition.[102]

Total rent for the cottages worked out at 13 shillings and 7 pence per week, including rates, 2 shillings and 6 pence service charge and 8 pence for garden work.[103] Only the midday meal was provided communally, a woman being employed to cook and wash up; another woman cleaned the cottages one day a week. Administration of communal activities was carried out by a tenants' committee, which met monthly. The system for provision of meals differed from those in use at other cooperative homes, in that it involved true cooperation on the part of the tenants. Each one was responsible for the catering for two weeks in turn. The hired cook did the cooking and washing up, but the tenant planned the menus, ordered the food, kept the accounts and paid the bills and the cook. During the Second World War, it also involved getting up very early in order to buy fish. A resident who arrived at Meadow Way Green North in 1940 said that the good, two-course midday meal then cost 1 shilling. The system worked efficiently; each cottage kept a small book in which was entered the number of meals taken, and these were handed to the tenant housekeeper every weekend. Money was collected in over Monday lunch, and the books returned. Provision of a cooperative meal was only ended in 1976, when the rise in catering wage rates and the availability of cheap convenience foods made the system uneconomic.

The system could also break down if tenants began to eat

elsewhere, but the pleasant atmosphere of the dining room, the cheap meals and the convenience of the arrangement ensured that it survived. Several of the tenants worked at the nearby Letchworth Grammar School and were able to return to the Green for lunch. In later years, when a greater proportion of the tenants were retired, although the provision of a meal was convenient, the administration became too much for some tenants to cope with. The vetting process for new tenants was aimed at ensuring that they would be compatible with existing tenants, and that they accepted the need for cooperation; if a tenant missed too many meals, the system became uneconomic. Ruth Pym and Miss Dewe interviewed all prospective tenants, asking about their background and current employment. Apart from the teachers, tenants included a librarian, a governess, a secretary and a missionary. Pym and Dewe rented 7 Meadow Way Green soon after it was built (it was an end cottage in the original seven) and retained it until after the Second World War. This long period of residence was not unusual, as several other tenants moved in when in their thirties and stayed until their eighties.

During the First World War, Ruth Pym was in France doing welfare work for the forces. On her return, she and Dewe started a British restaurant in Letchworth, the Crossways Cafe, which was a popular although not a financial success. In 1920, Pym suggested to the Howard Cottage Society that the southern half of the Meadow Way Green quadrangle should be completed, and this was eventually done in 1925, the same year that electricity replaced gas lighting on the north side (see Chapter 9). Ruth Pym became the warden of the Letchworth Settlement in 1931, Miss Dewe running the Settlement Library, having earlier been warden of the Letchworth Girls' Club.[104] As warden, Pym became well known for her organisation of a wide range of events, including plays, pageants and conferences. The constant round of activities at the Settlement became known as 'Pymming and Dewing'. Pym, a friend of Barry Parker, who was then president of the Settlement, resigned as warden in May 1938 at the age of 65. She and Dewe continued to deal with the Green lettings until 1944, when they were taken over by the new housing manager of Howard Cottage Society. Ruth Pym died in 1946, leaving behind her an efficiently-run cooperative home which was also a tremendously popular place to live, with a long waiting list. The Green is now open to male tenants as well as female, and the Howard Cottage Society intends to turn the disused kitchen and dining room on the north side into a bedsitter.

Soon after the Meadow Way Green quadrangle was completed, C. B. Purdom, author of *The Garden City*, wrote that 'There can be no hesitation in saying that it has been eminently successful . . .'[105] He later added that further similar schemes should be initiated, as they met an obvious need.[106] He attributed the Green's success to its small size, and this was certainly relevant to the ease with which the cooperative dining room functioned. However, there were other factors, not least the personalities and presence of Miss Pym and Miss Dewe. They were in a position to be able to select tenants specifically in order to keep the cooperative system working, and to be socially compatible. In the early years, prospective tenants had to be employed before they could be considered. All tenants were comparatively affluent, and thus able to participate in the cooperative meal. The design of the cottages themselves, and their position close to the centre of Letchworth, add to their current desirability. The cottages are peaceful, have their own gardens and are well designed internally with walk-in pantries and wood-panelled cupboards. The Green, because of its size, could and still does provide an attractive combination of community and privacy. Even after the cooperative meal had been discontinued, the quadrangular layout of the cottages ensured a certain amount of contact between residents.

Barry Parker attributed the basic plan of Meadow Way Green, with its common rooms and garden, to Ruth Pym and Miss Dewe.[107] Pym and Dewe's involvement with housing and changes in the organisation of domestic work mirrored the increasing interest taken in these matters by the women's movement in the 1910s. Although Charlotte Perkins Gilman disliked being described purely as a suffragist, she was renowned in suffrage circles and her views on socialised domestic work found many supporters in post-Victorian England.[108] Ada Nield Chew, writing in 1914, advocated organising domestic work without it becoming a profession solely for middle-class women. She wanted to discourage the idealisation of the home and was against the teaching of domestic subjects to schoolgirls. She saw

> the line of progress, as far as it is clear to the present writer, is for married women to insist on demanding the right to paid work, and to refuse to perform domestic jobs simply because

they are wives.[109]

Chew was a radical suffragist, but this group of the women's movement was not the only one to be interested in housing and domestic work.[110] *Votes for Women*, the paper of the Women's Social and Political Union, which was composed largely of middle-class suffragettes, published an article on 'The Burden of Housework' in 1911, inspired again by Gilman. It bemoaned the sacrifice of women's talents in housework, resulting in the exclusion of women from affairs outside the home; woman became the 'comfort-machine'.[111] In 1912 *Votes for Women* was replaced as the official paper of the WSPU by *Suffragette*, a weekly edited by Christabel Pankhurst.[112] In August 1913 *Suffragette* reprinted Ebenezer Howard's article on the possibility of starting a working-class cooperative home, first published in June 1913.[113]

Christabel Pankhurst followed this with two articles on cooperative housekeeping and working-class women. She argued that domestic work performed in separate little kitchens 'is enough in itself to provoke a women's revolution'. She saw women's ill-health as being caused by needless drudgery, and recommended cooperative kitchens where women would be able to work fewer hours and produce better and cheaper food. She referred to Howard and Homesgarth, saying its success was being hindered only by 'the unimaginative conservatism of those who could provide the necessary capital'.[114] Pankhurst went on to attack male attitudes to saving money through cooperative housekeeping: 'The apathy and even hostility of the enfranchised working men where cooperative housekeeping is concerned is a thing to marvel at . . . '[115] She saw the organisation of domestic work as a field ripe for profiteering, unless reformers stepped in first to encourage cooperation between consumers. It was not only on the domestic front that working-class men were against change; many of them felt that trade unions should act to exclude women workers rather than fight on their behalf.[116]

The only popular application of cooperation to working-class housing was the system of co-partnership, whereby tenants took shares in the society owning their houses, and were entitled to benefit from any rise in property values. They were also able to exert some control over the design of houses and the planning of estates. Members of co-partnership societies were not committed to any further form of cooperation, and the advantages of cooperative housekeeping described by its middle-class advocates may have appeared as disadvantages to working-class men. The cooperative home still had overtones of model dwellings, and the rise in status consequent on living in a large house and being able to afford a parlour could not be equalled by a move into a set of rooms within a larger group. Men who were against women doing paid work were unlikely to be in favour of their undertaking domestic duties for other families. The argument that cooperative housekeeping would allow women the opportunity to take paid work operated against its acceptance in some male circles. In fact, from a solely male point of view, the system of individual households worked perfectly well, thus the need for change was only apparent to those who felt that women should not bear the entire responsibility of children and home alone. Although the publicity for cooperative housekeeping always emphasised the opportunities it offered women, it was rare to find women being encouraged to take paid work.

In the period leading up to the First World War, the women's movement generally began to take a greater interest in domestic problems, and this was to be accentuated during the war. The movement was split along class lines; the radical suffragists of the north were socialist working-class women who found little in common with the mainly middle-class WSPU, and indeed Christabel Pankhurst felt that the support of the WSPU by working-class women would deny them the backing of non-socialist suffragists.[117] This division was reflected in their expectations of possible domestic reorganisation, the working-class women first wanting to ensure that decent housing and ample food was available, while being less concerned about communal social life and finding talk of standards of service totally irrelevant to their own homes. The promise of improved conditions of service for domestic workers had attracted no great support, and the reaction to the proposed professionalisation of domestic service was muted or suspicious. Professionalisation might imply a loss of working-class jobs to middle-class women. It was logically impossible for middle-class women to promote domestic service as a profession in itself with equal status to any other, and then refuse to take up paid jobs in service themselves. This, however, was the situation just before the First World War. The cooperative homes which existed were cooperative only in a financial sense, with the exception of Meadow Way Green; cooperators ate together but did not cook together. Even at Meadow Way Green, cooperators supervised while drudgery was left to the hired cook.

Middle-class objections to cooperative housekeeping were often hidden by enthusiasm for the principles involved; increased privacy, better service and domestic economy were universally acceptable as being improvements in home life. Behind its initial acceptability lay the communal basis of the idea, the socialist overtones leading on to the loss of the individual home, which seemed to be the root of the doubts about the idea. The entire edifice of Victorian ideals of home as castle, and woman as the angel within it, could be threatened if the individuality of the home were to be diminished. A cooperative home implied changes in lifestyle and self-image, and in spite of the many rational arguments in its favour, only a few middle-class households had both the money to make the experiment and the commitment to the cooperative principle. The position was very different for single working women, for whom the cooperative home provided an environment that was socially acceptable, affordable and comfortable.

The occupiers of pre-First World War cooperative homes were satisfied with their accommodation and the small element of communal living it involved. The architects of the various developments had successfully adapted old building forms, the collegiate quadrangle and monastery cloister, to meet the demands of contemporary communal living. The adaptation was flexible enough to allow further alteration as expectations changed, without losing the original spirit of the buildings, which combined community with privacy. Promoters and supporters of cooperative housekeeping experiments were less successful in their aims, as no large-scale reorganisation of domestic life took place. Early residents of both Waterlow Court and Meadow Way Green confirm that it was not the prospect of cooperative housekeeping which attracted them, but the convenient situation of the developments and the standard of accommodation. Communal meals were useful and sometimes enjoyable, but no more.

The case in favour of cooperative housekeeping was not proven by the pre-war experiments in Letchworth and Hampstead, although good housing had been produced almost incidentally. Garden suburb developments sprang up all over Britain before

1914, increasing the likelihood of further cooperative house-keeping experiments taking place.[118] Unwin's reputation as a planner grew, and new developments were often based on his layouts. The quadrangle or village green of Unwin's earlier years also became a common feature: the prospectus of Woldsea, a projected garden village on the Lincolnshire coast, read in 1909: 'Where it is found possible to build a picturesque quadrangle or a cloistered square, that will be done.'[119] It was not, however, necessary for cooperative housekeeping experiments to take place in garden suburbs. Suburban housing was equally suitable, if a cooperative centre could be included, and the success of this rather different style of cooperative housekeeping will be assessed in the following chapter. The coming of the war drew attention away from domestic concerns, but the need to ensure that supplies of food reached the population brought a resurgence of interest in communal feeding schemes. The garden city movement continued to grow in strength, and its advocates, and those of cooperative housekeeping, carried on their programme of publicising their ideas before and during the war.

7   Alice Melvin of Finchley

The first large-scale experiment in cooperative housekeeping in the London suburbs was initiated in 1909 by Mrs. Alice Melvin (see Plate 18). Melvin was an enthusiastic supporter of the garden city movement and had planned a number of working women's hostels.[1] She saw cooperative housekeeping as a means of decreasing the amount of domestic work performed by wives, solving the servant problem and ensuring that wives were able to take an interest in non-domestic matters. She lived in a large red-brick terraced house in Finchley, surrounded by other tightly-packed rows of houses.[2] In October 1909 she was asked to give a lecture on cooperative housekeeping, and it was this event which stimulated her to formulate a plan for putting her ideas into practice:

> For fifteen years the idea of co-operation in housekeeping has been simmering at the back of my head, but it did not take shape till last October. I was asked to explain my dream to the Finchley Women's Guild.[3]

The response to the lecture was so great that the Brent Garden Village (Finchley) Society was formed in 1910, with the object of buying the Brent Lodge estate in Finchley and building a cooperative village. At the centre of the estate was Brent Lodge itself, a large house where at one time Angela Burdett-Coutts, the philanthropist and builder of model dwellings, lived. The society intended to turn the Lodge into the central building for the village, and eventually managed to raise the purchase price of £10 000.

Several newspapers reported widespread interest in Melvin's scheme, and membership of the Society reached 140 in its first year of existence. Receipts, however, only totalled £3526, and the Society had to ask for extra time to raise funds to pay the first instalment on the estate.[4] Alice Melvin, secretary of the Society, wrote a pamphlet publicising the scheme in mid-1910, and support came from eminent people including local councillors and doctors.[5] The Society's intention was to build 114 houses of varying sizes and four quadrangles of flats for single people. Brent

Lodge was to be converted to house the cooperative kitchen, dining hall, nursery and laundry, and the servants' quarters.[6] The Lodge was to be connected to the houses and flats by a covered way. The demand for accommodation in the village was such that over 30 houses were reserved even before purchase of the site had been completed, and by January 1911 59 houses and 46 flats had been taken.[7] The houses were sited around an area designated as tennis courts, the covered way running at the rear of the houses which all had private gardens. This arrangement bore a close resemblance to Charlotte Perkins Gilman's ideas for a suburban group of kitchenless houses, detailed in her *Women and Economics*.[8] Melvin supervised the design of the houses herself, ensuring they had no long passages. Each house was to have a combined scullery and kitchen containing a gas stove, and individual water-heating systems were to be provided.

As the plan became reality, some features were altered or dropped. The covered way was never erected, and the houses with their workrooms, or combined scullery/kitchens, were replaced by houses built to conventional plans, although they were compact, as originally intended. The Society's architect was P. Woollatt Home of Finchley, and his unusual design for the first block of flats on the site was unfortunately never built. An application for planning consent for the block was made in February 1911, the plans showing flats with a sitting room, bedroom and a small room called the 'wash-up', containing cooker, sink and pantry. The block, to be known as Cedar Court (named after the fine cedar tree standing in the grounds), was joined by the covered way to the Lodge, and showed the influence of the arts and crafts movement in its external design. Both the houses of the village and Cedar Court combined brick, half-timbering and pebble dash and displayed tall chimney stacks. The flats had a balcony above the covered way. The internal layout of the flats was rather gloomy, the rooms leading off a dark central passage, but the 'wash-up' room showed the commitment of the architect to the idea of central services. There were to have been 17 flats as well as servants' accommodation in the original Cedar Court, but Woollatt Home's plan was replaced by a more conventional design in July 1912.

Several of Woollatt Home's houses were built, and still exist, recognisable by their chimneys and half-timbering (see Plate 19). The first house was occupied on 13 November 1911, the event being reported in *The Times*.[9] The house, one of those built without a kitchen, was taken by the secretary of the Society, now a Mr W. Leslie Booth. He appeared to be pleased with the dining arrangements, saying: 'For lunch today I had my soup, my pork chops, my potatoes, cabbage and bread, pudding, and cup of coffee – one and twopence! A four course dinner costs 1s 6d, with dessert from our own orchard.'[10] A tenant who chose to eat all meals in the central dining hall would pay between 7s 6d and 12s 6d a week, on top of the rent which varied from £32 to £63 per annum for houses, rather less for flats. The village was aimed at attracting tenants with incomes of £100 to £600 per year, and servants could be hired from the Lodge for 4½d per hour. The early days of the village attracted publicity, some reports doubtful about the loss of privacy and the need to dress for dinner, set against the economies and avoidance of cooking smells. The *Daily Telegraph*, although agreeing that the system was economically advantageous, was against any excess of good fellowship, seeing it as weakening individualism.[11] An article in *The Englishwoman* approved of Brent Garden Village because of its provision for children and single people.[12]

By 1914, there were 33 households living in the village and a block of flats had been built next to the Lodge.[13] The plans of the flats, by local architects Taylor and Huggins, had been approved in August 1912. Their design, unlike Woollatt Home's, was conventional with a full-size kitchen, and the two-storey L-shaped block of 12 flats was erected next to the Lodge, dispensing with the need for a covered way. It was known as Cedar Court and is still in use as flats today (see Plate 20). To the north-west of the Court stood the laundry, now demolished, while the stable block and kitchen garden remain. The Lodge has also disappeared, but the village housing still stands, the street plan approximating to Alice Melvin's original concept.[14] Although Melvin initiated and planned Brent Garden Village, she never lived there, and had ceased to be secretary of the Society by late 1911. Even as the first house in the village was occupied, she was busy setting up three further cooperative housekeeping schemes. The change in plan of Cedar Court, from almost kitchenless to conventional design, may reflect a change in the aims of the Society after Melvin left the secretaryship. The communal functions may have declined in importance, leaving the production of good suburban housing in a pleasant environment as the main object of the Society. Only one block of flats out of the original four was built, the remainder of the Society's land being taken up with terraced and semi-detached housing.

Although much of the publicity material for Brent Garden Village was written without specific mention of feminist ideals, the village did create some interest in the feminist press. The *Freewoman*, a weekly radical feminist review,[15] carried a series of letters in early 1912 on cooperative housekeeping, culminating in a plea for more support for the village written by A. Herbage Edwards.[16] Edwards had been involved with the village since its inception, seeing the organisation of domestic work as the basis of the feminist position. She reported that plenty of tenants could be found for the village, although there was still difficulty in raising capital. Men would not invest in the village, so Edwards appealed to wealthy women to use their money to free other women from drudgery. Edwards tried to publicise the 'struggling pioneer scheme' by speaking to the Fabian Women's Group in June 1913 on the 'Reorganisation of Domestic Work'. She mentioned the Brent experiment, and suggested that groups of people could easily begin other cooperative schemes by renting several houses for their own occupancy and one extra house to serve as the central kitchen and dining hall.[17] Servants could be managed centrally, and houses would be smaller and easier to clean without kitchens. Women freed from complete responsibility for domestic work in their own homes might become involved in the organisation of domestic work elsewhere, or take industrial or professional jobs. Edwards saw this type of scheme as the basis for many others of varying sizes which would cater for all incomes.

After setting up the Brent scheme, and ensuring that it was at least partially successful, Alice Melvin went on to found the Society for the Promotion of Co-operative Housekeeping and House-Service. This Society aimed to introduce cooperation into housekeeping and to turn domestic work into a profession suitable for educated working women. Its inaugural meeting was held in London on 15 November 1911, two days after the first tenant had moved into a cooperative house at Brent Garden Village.[18] Melvin, honorary secretary of the new Society, explained her views on housekeeping in the pages of the *Freewoman* in 1912, beginning her first article with a quotation from Charlotte Perkins Gilman.[19] Melvin felt there had been a qualitative change in housekeeping, resulting in the disappearance of all interesting domestic tasks and leaving the housewife with nothing but drudgery. Relations between mistress and maid were invariably poor, because 'in no case is she recognised as a member of a craft, having a definite status, definite rights, and a clear claim to an independent life of her own'.[20] Cooperative housekeeping would provide a remedy by giving staff training, allowing them to specialise, paying fair wages and giving time off. Eventually colleges of domestic science might be set up. Melvin also suggested that domestic workers should form a union.

Applying the principles of cooperation to housekeeping would remove the need for women to choose between marriage and career:

> There is no real reason why the marriage of two individuals should involve the confusion of the external machinery of their two lives. They should be able to have their cooking, sweeping, and cleaning done for them, and this, moreover, at a cost less than that of running a separate establishment.[21]

Melvin envisaged schemes similar to working women's flats for educated workers, and larger schemes in the manner of Brent Garden Village. Houses would be provided with labour-saving devices and would be constructed so as to be easy to clean. Melvin thought that the individual home had reached the limits of its development, but prejudice against change, arising from ignorance of the advantages, had prevented cooperative housekeeping from being more widely introduced. She had found builders unwilling to build cooperative houses in spite of the proven demand, and owners unwilling to let to cooperative housekeeping societies. The problem, as usual, was that of finding the necessary capital. Melvin's new Society had found some builders and landowners willing to cooperate if the Society could put up sufficient funds, and she mentioned two estates and a quadrangle of flats as being good prospects for development.

One of these estates was to be at Ruislip, and was described as a miniature town, a logical outcome of the garden city movement, in which all housekeeping would be done by a staff of servants. The town was to be known as Melvin Park, after its inventor and acting manager, and the estimated cost of the venture was £7000. Tenants would be required to buy shares and could live in houses, flats or a residential club. The architects of

Melvin Park were Gilbert H. Lovegrove and A. Wyatt Papworth, an east London practice specialising in educational buildings and flats. Both Lovegrove and Papworth were involved in another of Melvin's cooperative housekeeping ventures, and Lovegrove, a councillor then aged 33, addressed the inaugural meeting of the Society for the Promotion of Co-operative Housekeeping and House Service.[22] The report of the meeting mentioned the success of Homesgarth, as detailed by H. Clapham Lander, but it is not clear if Lander was actually present at the meeting.[23] By 1911, in addition to his previous involvement with the garden city movement, Lander had become honorary architect to the Co-operative Garden City Committee. The Committee had been formed in 1908 to encourage the introduction of garden city principles into housing schemes initiated by the cooperative movement.[24]

Melvin Park, Alice Melvin's most ambitious plan, was never built, and only existed as an ideal solution to the servant problem:

> The servant worry, the cooking trouble, the nursing difficulty – all are to be swept away as if by a magic wand. All that need be done is to become a tenant in the new Garden City at Melvin Park, Ruislip, which ere long will arise to earn the blessings of the tired wife.[25]

Although cooperative housekeeping was described by Alice Melvin and its other advocates as bringing an improvement in the working conditions of servants, little is known of the reactions of servants to this new form of service. Kathlyn Oliver, at one time the secretary of the Domestic Workers' Union of Great Britain, criticised cooperative housekeeping as it abolished drudgery only for the middle class, allowing households to share luxuries they could not afford individually. She agreed with Melvin in her wish to improve the status of domestic work, but was doubtful that cooperative housekeeping would result in reduced hours of work for servants. She felt more work might be crammed into the servant's day, and disliked the idea of working for several mistresses rather than a single one. Oliver conceded that the new system would give servants a wider outlook, but felt that 'a domestic would degenerate into a machine which would be sent here or there to do the dirty work for the "superior" people who were above such work'.[26] Although Melvin replied that cooperative housekeeping would definitely result in shorter hours of work and proper status for servants, clearly this could only occur if the economics of the schemes were such that enough servants could be employed without discouraging prospective tenants by high service charges.

The building of Melvin Park was to be preceded by a smaller scheme situated in Golders Green and consisting of serviced residential flats.[27] By November 1911, 16 tenants had already been found for this new venture, and on 10 August 1912 the Melvin Hall Co-operative Housekeeping and Service Society (Golders Green) Limited was registered as a friendly society. Alice Melvin was the secretary, and among the founding members were the architects of Melvin Park, Papworth and Lovegrove, two other married women, and Percy Hodges and Harry Bone, who were already sharing their Golders Green home with Harold and Alice Melvin. Melvin Hall itself was open by December 1912, and Alice Melvin became its manageress, Hodges briefly taking over as secretary to be followed by Bone in early 1913.[28]

The Hall was situated close to Hampstead Garden Suburb on the site of a sanatorium, which may well have formed the main building of the Hall, a 'Victorian warren of a place' with three floors and a basement.[29] The Hall contained just over 30 flats, the communal kitchen and dining room being in the basement. Staff and some residents lived in a pair of semi-detached houses close to the Hall, which had its own large garden. Melvin Hall continued to function as serviced flats with communal meals until 1964, when the Society was dissolved and the Hall demolished to make way for a new block of flats. At the time of its dissolution the Society was still profitable, employing eight foreign domestic staff who served the 'excellent' breakfast, dinner and weekend lunches and took care of other domestic work. Residents normally ate in the dining room, which was furnished with a number of small tables, as at Brent Lodge. All residents (who could be male or female) took shares in the Society, and were carefully vetted before acceptance. By 1964, residents were paying £6 to £7 per week for board and lodging.

Melvin Hall was certainly a successful example of cooperative housekeeping, although the cooperative element extended only to catering and central servicing. It was a popular place to live even in the 1950s and 1960s, being full until its dissolution. Alice Melvin lived at Melvin Hall in the early years, but was not content with two cooperative housekeeping experiments and embarked on a third in February 1912, well before the Melvin Hall Society was registered. This third scheme involved converting Frognal Priory, a 20–room mansion built for a millionaire in 1892, into a cooperative home. The Priory was situated close to an underground station in Hampstead, and Melvin envisaged rooms available for men and women, costing from 10s 6d per week.[30] Nothing came directly of this idea, as the price of the freehold of the Priory was probably too high for any prospective cooperative society to raise. Two years later, however, a society was set up with its offices in Priory Road, south Hampstead. This was the Second Melvin Hall Cooperative Housekeeping Society (Golders Green), which, after a change of name, became the Melvin Cooperative Residential Society (Hampstead) Ltd and was registered as a friendly society in March 1914.[31] All but one of the eight founder members lived at Melvin Hall, and four were women. Melvin was a founder member, but Harry Bone was the Society's secretary.

Members took £5 or £50 shares in the Society, which took over five houses in Priory Road, two at the Hampstead end and three adjacent detached Georgian town houses almost in Kilburn [32] (see Plate 21). There were probably about ten tenants in each house, but although they were provided with meals, it is not known whether a central kitchen or dining room existed.[33] It is most likely that they were situated in the house where the housekeeper had her office, 72 Priory Road. In 1926, the Society changed its name to the Priory Residential Society Ltd, an action which possibly marked the end of Alice Melvin's involvement. It continued to function as a cooperative home until 1937 when, with profits low and repairs needed, the members resolved to wind up the Society and the houses and land were sold off. The houses at 72 and 74 Priory Road have since been demolished, but the other three are still in existence and are used as private residences.

The reason for Priory Residential Society's short life, 23 years as compared to the 52 years of Melvin Hall, was probably the inconvenient arrangement of the five houses. It would have been possible to have one dining room for all tenants, but it would not have been central, while two or more dining rooms would have decreased the theoretically obtainable economies of scale. The two groups of houses were situated about a quarter of a mile apart, so that communal activities involving all tenants would have been more difficult to organise than at Brent Garden Village, where all houses lay within a few hundred yards of the Lodge, or at Melvin Hall, where most tenants lived in the central building. A further difficulty for tenants of the Priory Road cooperative home was that their accommodation was the oldest of the three societies, and repairs were therefore likely to be necessary.

Between 1909 and 1914, Alice Melvin initiated three friendly societies and the Society for the Promotion of Co-operative Housekeeping and House-Service. She supervised the design of houses and flats which provided accommodation for at least 150 people, and planned the layout of Brent Garden Village. Tantalisingly little is known about Melvin, whose interest in the garden city movement and women's housing led her to invent Melvin Park, the garden city with no housework. The original design of Cedar Court at Brent, where the minimal service area, the 'wash-up', replaced the kitchen, fitted her description of the ideal cooperative home. The evolution of her schemes was halted not due to lack of tenants willing to live in cooperative homes, but because capital was difficult to find. Investors, builders, property owners and landlords were not impressed by a struggling friendly society advocating a revolution in domestic life. Men, in general, were not keen to invest in cooperative housekeeping, mirroring the attitude of working men towards saving money through domestic cooperation. Appeals were made to wealthy women to lend money to the societies, and some money was forthcoming; several women were also involved in running and publicising the societies. These efforts were brought to fruition by Alice Melvin and a small group of friends.

The three schemes which produced housing all succeeded in that they were popular with residents and/or long running. Too few cooperative housekeeping ventures existed to change the status of servants dramatically, particularly in the eyes of non-cooperators with no experience of professionalised domestic work. Melvin certainly managed to prove that the success of cooperative housekeeping was not dependent upon situation within an existing garden city or suburb; a close relationship between housing and the central facilities was more important. The First World War began soon after Priory Residential Society came into being, and Alice Melvin, aged over 60 by the time the war ended, decided to retire from active involvement with the cooperative housekeeping movement.[34] Concern about housing conditions moved from the hardships of middle-class existence towards the priorities of feeding and housing workers. The principles of cooperation and domestic economy were applicable in wartime as well as in peace, but support, as ever, was difficult to find.

8 Communal Living and the War

The reactions of the various factions of the women's movement to the coming of war in August 1914 emphasised their differing perceptions of women's needs. The WSPU rapidly dropped its militant stance in favour of wholehearted support for the war effort, encouraging men to enlist and women to work as non-combatants.[1] The Women's Freedom League (WFL), a less militant offshoot of the WSPU,[2] concentrated on assisting women and children of poor families, as the outbreak of war, combined with earlier hoarding of food, had resulted in an immediate rise in prices. The cost of a loaf of bread almost doubled within a week of the start of the war.[3] The WFL set up the Nine Elms Settlement in south west London, where children were served 1d or ½d dinners of vegetarian soup and large slices of pudding, which they could either eat at the Settlement or take home. The Settlement also distributed cheap or free milk.[4] Sylvia Pankhurst's East London Federation (ELF), originally part of the WSPU but expelled for its active involvement of men and working-class women, opened a series of cheap restaurants in London.[5] The first, a converted pub in Bow, east London, opened at the end of August 1914. 'The Mothers Arms', previously 'The Gunmakers Arms', served two-course meals for adults and children costing 2d and 1d respectively. By October, similar welfare centres had been opened in Poplar, Bromley and Canning Town.[6]

High food prices brought a repetition of earlier calls for communal kitchens to be set up, including an article from Edith Sellers who had first advocated this idea in 1894.[7] Sylvia Pankhurst, writing in August 1914, mentioned the non-profit-making restaurants of Christiania, Norway, when criticising new housing for overlooking the woman's point of view.

> The restaurants might pave the way for the future co-operative house-keeping schemes, for which so many women long today, but which have not hitherto been put into practical use in working class districts.[8]

She was in favour of houses with gardens, rather than flats, as the houses could be grouped around a central area where children would play. She suggested philanthropy as a means of paying for this type of scheme, and a week later a 'Socialist Suffragette' offered to start a fund to buy land for such a venture.[9] Although the ELF worked closely with the labour movement, Pankhurst's ideas on cooperative housekeeping were not endorsed by all working women. A speaker at the Working Women's Conference on Housing, organised by the Women's Labour League in July 1913, commented that 'advanced women' felt that municipal authorities should provide cheap communal laundries. As to cooperation on a larger scale, one woman concluded after the conference: 'I have studied the English character a good bit, and I am convinced that it will be a very long time before any kind of communal housekeeping will appeal to it.'[10]

In contrast to the suspicion with which communal living was regarded by working women, middle-class women and those in positions of responsibility continued to advocate its introduction for households of all classes. The reactions of working-class women and servants to the idea were similar; the lifestyle of middle-class women would improve and they would gain financially, while servants or working-class wives were to give up some elements of privacy and control in return for improved conditions of work and possible financial savings. The impetus to set up new cooperative housing societies had not disappeared with the outbreak of war. The Residential Cooperative, a housing and catering society, was registered in London in 1915, but nothing is known about its activities.[11] Clementina Black, one-time secretary of the Women's Trade Union League, lectured on cooperative housekeeping in June and July 1916, and eventually turned her *Common Cause* articles of the following two months into a book on the same subject.[12] She criticised contemporary housing for its inconvenience, but rejected central kitchens as a remedy for poor domestic service because working women in particular would only patronise them if they were involved in their organisation.[13] She felt that previous cooperative housekeeping experiments had failed through bad management, emphasis on profits and an excess of communality: 'People do not want to pool their lives. They only want to get their food and their service properly organised.'[14] She suggested a quadrangle of 50 two-storey houses, each having eight rooms, centred on a larger building including kitchens and dining hall. The central staff would be organised by a manageress, and residents could eat in the dining hall or in their own homes. Extra benefits would include temporary boarding of pets at the central hall, and staff gardeners looking after personal gardens in the absence of the tenants. Children were welcome, each house retaining its own nursery and nurse. The houses were to be full of labour-saving devices, extra space being created by the replacement of the kitchen by a small scullery.

Black saw the coming of cooperative housekeeping as a means of reforming domestic architecture, the 'prolonged architectural goose-step' of the terrace being replaced by something more imaginative.[15] Probably because she was writing during wartime, she felt it would be unwise to attempt to build cooperative houses at once, preferring to adapt current designs. Although Black's scheme was intended for middle-class residents, she felt that poorer families would benefit most of all from cooperation, but declined to give details of a working-class cooperative home as she had no experience of their style of housekeeping.

Both Clementina Black and Sylvia Pankhurst advocated housing reform as a means of improving the living conditions of both working- and middle-class families, but many other writers felt the problem could be tackled through cooperation on a smaller scale. Some two years after the outbreak of war, *Common Cause* ran a series of articles suggesting cooperative kitchens as a means of combating rising food prices. Simple bulk buying of food would reduce household costs, and delivery of cooked meals from a central kitchen would avoid the necessity of moving house to set up a true cooperative home.[16] One writer, although agreeing that cooperative living could decrease household costs, did not recommend it, as the 'bickerings, backbitings and general dissatisfaction can, unfortunately, be imagined with only too much ease by all who have even limited experience of the life of neighbours in any small town or village'.[17]

Now that many husbands were away from home, married women with children often found themselves short of money and attempting to run large, understaffed homes. They needed to work to support their families, but could not afford nurses or other servants, and often found it necessary to move to smaller homes. Their position was similar to that of single working women 30 years earlier, their small resources and particular needs ruling out much rented accommodation. *The Times* suggested that servicemen's wives should consider cooperative housekeeping, providing they were all of a similar age, upbringing and outlook.[18] A large country house could be taken for a relatively low rent, and each family could have its own sitting room and use of a central dining room. Mrs Diana T. Wilkins was a strong advocate of a similar proposal, writing in *The Englishwoman* and *Common Cause* in support of communal homes for middle-class women. She suggested a large house in north-west London, with access to good schools, and envisaged only a minimum number of servants for the 'rough work', the residents performing all other household tasks with the aid of labour-saving devices. A 'communal mother' would also be paid for supervision of children.[19] She did not see such schemes as continuing after the war, except in the case of widows who would have to carry on working; many women would also return to their previous occupation as servants. Wilkins saw communal living as a sacrifice made necessary by wartime, and indeed felt the crisis might overcome prejudice against a change of lifestyle.[20]

A similar point had been made by Clementina Black in relation to the acceptance of communal living by working-class women. She commented that in pre-war years,

> . . . there were few indications that working women were prepared to make any great change in their housekeeping or to accept any kind of common domestic enterprise. But the last two years have altered their attitude; public kitchens have arisen, and have apparently succeeded; thousands and thousands of women and men have grown accustomed to eat meals in canteens, and hundreds of thousands of women even to living in hostels.[21]

The number of factory canteens had increased from 1915 onwards, reaching 1000 by the end of the war and supplying a million meals a day. This increase was partly a response to the more frequent employment of women; between 1914 and 1918, 800 000 women were recruited into industry.[22] The cheap if unexciting food provided by the canteens was usually welcome, but some women saw the canteens as a paternalistic means of maintaining their efficiency.[23] Food for servicemen was often provided by canteens funded by voluntary subscription, and 'canteening' became a leisure activity for the upper classes.[24] Articles in *The Englishwoman* described a munition workers' canteen and the opening of a community kitchen in Leeds in March 1917.[25] Taking the new factory canteens as examples, Mrs Ernestine Mills made a further call for the setting up of central kitchens for use by working-class women. She felt that a revolution in women's employment was taking place, whose effects would be apparent after the war as many women would not give up their paid work.[26] Central kitchens would help to reduce child mortality in areas where women were overworked, and would be more economic than individual kitchens. Private kitchens had nothing to recommend them 'but a vague sentimentalism' and were simply an excuse for wasting female energy. She dismissed opposition to central cooking as misguided, but her views were unlikely to have been supported by the majority of men:

> It is a popular idea that a man really likes his wife to be a cook, but as a matter of fact, if a man is well fed, he will usually be quite indifferent as to who prepared his food, and, on the other hand, no amount of affection will help him to digest bad cooking.

For almost the first two years of the war, the government did not admit the existence of any problems concerning food supplies or prices, despite complaints in the women's press and accusations of profiteering.[27] Food prices had been rising gradually, being 32 per cent higher in June 1915 than a year earlier, and by September 1916 the cost of living for a working-class family had risen 65 per cent above its 1914 figure. In the summer of 1916 several demonstrations were held to protest against the high cost of living.[28] The government finally acted in late 1916, setting up a Food Department in the Board of Trade, which became the Ministry of Food in December 1916. The first Food Controller attempted to avoid the introduction of rationing by encouraging voluntary restraint, but after his resignation in May 1917, the appointment of Lord Rhondda was soon followed by general rationing.[29] The food situation in the spring of 1917 was so bad that at one point the country had only three to four weeks' supply in stock, and the National War Savings Committee was authorised by the Ministry of Food to conduct a food economy campaign.[30] Food economy lectures and exhibitions were held, and it was recognised that skilled women cooks and administrators would be necessary in the running of the campaign. The National War Savings Committee had been collecting information on the various community kitchens which were already functioning, and eventually, as a result of a decision 'that a policy of a more constructive and lasting nature was needed', the idea of national kitchens evolved.[31]

An experimental kitchen was set up in Westminster Bridge Road, Lambeth, and opened by the Queen in May 1917. Many of those attending the opening were unused to mass public catering, and had to go home and fetch containers for their meals.[32] Apart from works canteens, which were not open to housewives, national kitchens were the first experience of communal cooking for most women who used them. Local authorities were encouraged to start their own kitchens, and in August 1917 the Ministry of Food recommended that members of the Women's Cooperative Guild should be asked to serve on local committees responsible for the administration of national kitchens.[33] Kitchens were slow to appear, however, and the Ministry of Food was criticised for its lack of organisational ability and its refusal to allow women to take on any responsible posts. This was particularly galling as Lord Rhondda had professed himself to be in favour of women's suffrage. In the *Daily Mail*, 'A woman' wrote: 'Now, however, when the conduct of kitchens has become of more importance than ever, and *when paid posts connected with National Kitchens are obtainable*, it is men, not women, to whom these posts are given.'[34] The impression of confusion within the national kitchens bureaucracy was probably correct; the Food Economy Division of the Ministry was responsible for their encouragement and administration, but a separate branch had been established which duplicated its work, and which was 'dignified for personal reasons' by the title National Kitchens Division.[35]

Towards the end of February 1918 a statutory order was made allowing local authorities to establish and maintain national kitchens, the Treasury granting one quarter and lending another quarter of the cost of equipment, the remaining half being allowed as a charge on the rates.[36] The director of the National Kitchens Division, Alderman C. F. Spencer of Halifax, publicised details of his national scheme, which included a limited number of public restaurants to be run in conjunction with the kitchens. Lord Rhondda saw national kitchens as a 'vital necessity', avoiding the

waste of labour, health, material and energy of individual kitchens, but warned that public goodwill was essential to ensure the
success of such a change in eating habits. Spencer

> hoped that the public, without any class distinction, will use
> the national kitchens as freely as they use municipal trams, gas
> and electricity. The kitchens are to be bright and attractive;
> they will be kept supplied with flowers from the parks and
> gramophones and electric pianos will be provided.[37]

A further burst of publicity resulted from the introduction of
Spencer's own invention, the electric kitchen tramcar, in Halifax,
but in general only slow progress was made in setting up a
national network of kitchens.[38] One reason for this was 'public
feeling against any form of co-operative cooking, especially on
the part of women', while another was lack of encouragement
from the Ministry itself.[39] There was dissension within the
National Kitchens Division over the work of its director, who was
accused by his Technical Directors of amateurism and corruption.
The Division's Chief Woman Inspector felt that 'the establishment
of National Kitchens has been blocked in every way', but by this
stage, early 1919, the original reasons for the creation of the
kitchens had been overtaken by the ending of the war in
November 1918.[40]

By the spring of 1918, the Ministry of Food had set up 372
kitchens, 122 in London and Greater London, 250 in the provinces.
Nearly 1000 central kitchens of all types were in existence at the
time of the armistice.[41] Although there had been overwhelming
support for the introduction of national kitchens, and continuing
praise for their provision of cheap, wholesome food,[42] it became
clear by the end of the war that 'Kitchens were not altogether
popular with women'.[43] Marion Phillips, general secretary of the
Women's Labour League and Chief Woman Officer of the Labour
Party commented: 'It was useless to attempt to persuade women
that the Kitchens were to take the place of cooking in the home.
The majority of women preferred to do their own cooking as a
rule and found it cheaper.'[44]

Phillips was a member of the National Kitchens Advisory Committee, as was Mrs C. S. Peel, the writer and expert on domestic
economy. Peel agreed that the average working-class woman
could provide food most cheaply by herself, but pointed out that

middle-class households could save money by eating at restaurants or buying cooked food. She felt that the kitchens fulfilled a need, but never became a necessity: 'It was thought by some of their promoters that national kitchens would endure and become a feature of the nation's life, but that opinion was not based on knowledge of the circumstances of the working people.'[45]

National kitchens had proved a success from an organisational point of view, in providing a reliable source of cheap food, but their customers had apparently not been won over to the principles of communal cooking. Communal living on a larger scale was still outside the experience of most people. Shortages of food were only obvious in 1917, by which time government, local authorities and numerous other organisations were revealing their thinking on reconstruction, the post-war rebuilding or restructuring of society.[46] It had been expected that the war would be short, thus consideration of the nature of post-war society had begun early; the government's Reconstruction Committee was established in March 1916 and replaced by a Ministry of Reconstruction one year later.[47] Lack of previous experience with communal facilities did not prevent many representatives of political parties and other groups from advocating them as part of post-war housing policy. Public response to national kitchens was still uncertain when the chairman of Bradford Health Committee spoke in October 1917 about proposals for ten garden suburbs to be situated on the outskirts of the town. His committee suggested 'the provision of an efficiently staffed communal laundry and cooking kitchen for each village'.[48] They felt that good mothers were a sacred asset to the country and deserved all possible help in the way of central facilities, which were also to include a school, baths and allotments.

Margaret Bondfield, a trade unionist who later became Minister of Labour, was also in favour of domestic cooperation. Her contribution to *Women and the Labour Party*, published in 1919, emphasised the possibilities of saving time through cooperative washhouses and kitchens, nurseries, central heating and electric power in the home. She felt that a reduction of the mother's working day would allow her to use her administrative capacities outside the home.[49] Bondfield had visited Hull House and the Jane Club on her trip to the USA in 1910, and been impressed by the excellent accommodation provided in the cooperative Club.[50]

Marion Phillips, writing in the February 1918 issue of *Labour*

Woman, produced a perceptive article on working-class women and cooperative housekeeping. The article was written before she could assess the reaction of working women to national kitchens, and prior to that experience she viewed communal kitchens favourably:

> There is no reason why, once established, they should not continue and develop after the war is over . . . Given a high standard of cooking such kitchens will very quickly make their way, and all practical women will take advantage of them.[51]

She also emphasised that communal kitchens were to be used in conjunction with individual kitchens, not as a replacement; this was not necessarily uneconomic, for the range frequently heated the living room as well as cooking the meal. Phillips was more than confirmed in her belief that individual kitchens were still needed by the lack of enthusiasm of working women for national kitchens. She suggested that if they were to continue, women should be encouraged to use them as restaurants, or only for occasional meals, which was far from their original function as providers of regular everyday meals.[52]

Phillips felt that cooperative housekeeping did have a part to play in working-class domestic life, but that reform of contemporary housing conditions was necessary before women would be enthusiastic about its introduction. Decent housing, with ample living and bedroom space and a bathroom, all of which could be easily cleaned, was a prerequisite of cooperation. According to Phillips, it was the 'revolutionary ardour' of the working woman which made her anxious for a comfortable cottage, something the middle-class woman already had. Phillips was in favour of extending the cooperative principle into most areas of housekeeping, provided that housing was of a reasonable standard. Apart from the cooperative kitchen, she advocated the small communal washhouse, its advantages of hot water and drying facilities outweighing the lack of privacy and occasional congestion. Even assuming the use of electrical appliances, she still saw working women as spending a considerable amount of time on house-cleaning. Her overall view of cooperative housekeeping was that it might help women to lead more interesting lives, but not simply through their ability to obtain paid work. Her article stressed the point that 'the middle class woman should not in her ignorance force upon the woman who knows, a reform which does not suit the actual conditions'.[53] Phillips' enthusiasm for communal facilities was only slightly diminished by her spell on the National Kitchens Advisory Committee, as in 1920 she was still promoting cooperative food preparation and washing at the Garden Cities and Town Planning Association conference.[54]

The Labour Party manifesto for the general election of December 1918 promised that 'a million new houses' would be built at once by the government, making a 'substantial and permanent improvement' in housing conditions.[55] There was no mention of reform of domestic organisation in the manifesto, and little reference to housing in either the Liberal or Coalition manifestos. Christabel Pankhurst was a candidate in Smethwick, standing for the Women's Party in support of the Coalition, whose own candidate had been withdrawn in her favour. Pankhurst failed to be elected by only 775 votes, and in her election address she said that all new housing schemes should include labour-saving arrangements, 'and also co-operation in the form of central hot water supply, central kitchens and laundries where these are desired by the householders concerned'.[56]

The Women's Party had been formed by Christabel and Mrs Pankhurst when a number of WSPU members objected to the strong anti-German line taken by *Suffragette* (now *Britannia*), and the concentration of WSPU activities on promoting hatred of the Germans.[57] The party came into existence in November 1917, and *Britannia* immediately published its programme for the war 'and after'. This racist and anti-democratic document proposed a system of cooperative housekeeping to relieve married women of the burden of domestic work.[58] The party clearly envisaged schemes on a large scale, with trained staff working in scientifically equipped central kitchens, a hospital, creche, school and laundry. As the party was against worker control of industry, it is doubtful whether their cooperative housekeeping schemes would have been truly cooperative in anything but name.

Britannia continued to print articles on cooperative housekeeping, as *Suffragette* had done before the war; in January 1918 it reproduced an extract from Barry Parker and Raymond Unwin's *The Art of Building a Home*.[59] Shortly after this came a long series by woman architect Annie Hall advocating cooperative housekeeping, which she began by criticising industrial workers for being unproductive and thus increasing the price of building materials.[60] Her plan for a cooperative home was the conventional one of flats and cottages grouped around three sides of a square, each cottage or flat having a sitting room, three bedrooms, bathroom and service room. The latter was to be provided with a gas cooker, sink, dresser and cupboard; meals could be taken at home or in the central dining room. The dresser might have glass doors, 'but this is only practicable where a careful class of tenant is concerned; to do it for others would be a sheer waste of money'.[61] Cupboard space was also provided, but not in excess: 'No cottage cupboard should be large enough to admit of the shelves being used as sleeping berths for children.'[62] The larder, too, was to be small so that there was no temptation to use it for general storage. Hall's cooperative home was intended for poorer tenants, but it was to have laundries, gardens and an internal telephone system. She also suggested a hostel for single people and a children's nursery, important for moulding children's characters. Tenants were to make a small investment in their property, as with other housing societies, to avoid the destruction of self-respect she associated with state-aided housing. She was in favour of planned slum clearance and new housing development, noting that the removal of occupants from slum housing might involve the exertion of force. She criticised the architecture of Letchworth and the garden suburbs for their 'unnecessary fault of incongruity and individual self-assertion'.[63]

Hall's patronising and authoritarian version of a cooperative home was endorsed by the Women's Party, but their argument for the large-scale adoption of cooperative housekeeping had been greeted with some scepticism by the press. *The Globe* agreed that domestic cooperation could produce real economies, 'But whether they will succeed in persuading the actual Mrs Jones to join forces with "that Smith woman" in the flat opposite is another and, we fear, a more difficult problem.'[64] The party made no mention of how it intended to introduce the cooperative housekeeping system, no small matter as it involved total domestic reorganisation. Christabel Pankhurst did not make domestic reform the main platform of her parliamentary campaign in the 1918 election, at which women over 30 could vote for the first time.[65] The Women's Freedom League, while supporting the introduction of communal kitchens, was not intent on such dramatic changes in domestic life. It felt that 'women's knowledge and experience in dealing with the housing question' should be used by means

of the election of representative women to local committees dealing with housing issues.[66]

The Labour Party, through its women's organisation, actually
consulted women about their future housing needs. In autumn
1917 the Women's Labour League (WLL) began a housing
campaign, during which they sold 50 000 copies of a leaflet
entitled 'The Working Woman's House'. The leaflet asked readers
to consider the disadvantages of their present homes, and the
type of home they wished to live in; a plan of a five- to six-
person house was also included as an example of a possible future
home (see Figure 10).[67] Numerous conferences and meetings of a
wide range of women's organisations discussed the ideas contained in the leaflet. The WLL found that working women were
keen to talk about their housing conditions and were interested
in house plans: 'they will go to some trouble to make themselves
familiar with the intricacies of elevations and even with the purely
technical details of the plan.'[68]

The WLL were able to publish the unanimous findings of this
consultation exercise, the first being that women wanted cottages
rather than flats. Houses were to have ample space in which to
bring up a family, were to be easily cleaned with the minimum
of drudgery, and were to have a parlour. A local social centre was
another priority.

The WLL findings were extremely detailed, and mainly related
to the design of a conventional, non-cooperative house. This was
to be expected, as the WLL leaflet had not mentioned cooperative
housekeeping, probably in accordance with Marion Phillips' view
that good housing was the prerequisite of cooperation. Communal
facilities were discussed, with 'democratically governed' laundries
favoured only if a municipal 'bag wash' (laundry service) was not
available.[69] The WLL reported that very few people wanted basic
facilities in their own homes, relying on central services for most
of their needs. The overwhelming majority wanted a house complete in itself, but were aware that cooperation could save money
and labour. Cooperation, however, was to apply solely to consumption:

> Working women who have had experience of the common
> wash-house or the common kitchen have come to the very
> definite conclusion that if co-operation is to work well the
> whole work must be done by highly skilled people, and not
> by providing appliances which each tenant in turn may use.[70]

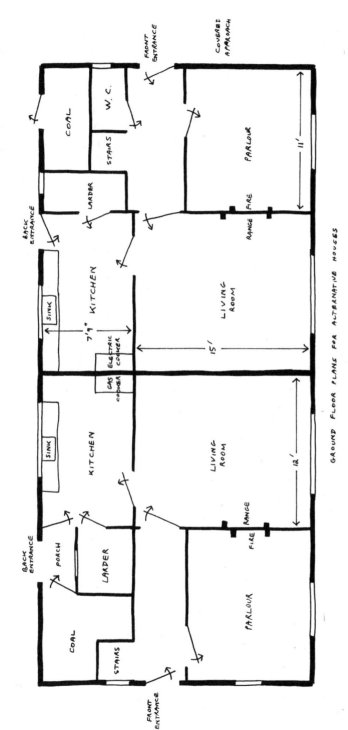

FIGURE 10 *Two versions of ground-floor plans of the working woman's house: on left, with gas cooker, back porch and WC upstairs; on right, with electric cooker, WC downstairs. Both versions had three bedrooms. (Redrawn from A. D. Sanderson Furniss and Marion Phillips, The Working Woman's House, Swarthmore Press, London, 1920, p. 16, by kind permission of the Labour Party Library)*

Thus, the experience of working-class women had led them to reject cooperative housekeeping in favour of socialised domestic work. Few of them were likely to have come across any of the experimental cooperative homes, so that their judgement was based upon the use of centralised facilities which were often poorly designed or situated. The middle-class kitchenless house, of course, had more space than the conventional working-class home.

The WLL found that many women in the labour movement were strongly in favour of siting a communal kitchen in every new housing scheme, for occasional use by housewives and more frequent use by workers who would be away from home at midday. In effect, the request was for a cheap restaurant or take-away food service, mirroring the growth in popularity among the upper and middle classes of 'eating out' in the early years of the twentieth century.[71] Small nursery schools were needed, as well as open play areas and cooperative holiday homes in the country. A system of home helps was suggested, the staff being women who understood 'all the difficulties, the makeshifts and management of the working class family'.[72] Although the cooperative facilities were given detailed consideration, the main weight of the WLL findings was that working women wanted improved versions of the houses they already had; cooperation was most relevant to social life and facilities for children, with the communal kitchen simply providing a cheap and very occasional alternative to home cooking.

One commentator on the WLL exercise applauded the effort to consult women workers, and went on to point out that the wartime experience of young women who had lived in hostels might lead them to view cooperative housekeeping favourably, in comparison with isolated home life.[73] The Scottish Council for Women's Trades had also been discussing housing with working women, and published its report in June 1918.[74] There was some support for communal facilities such as a central washhouse, sewing room, baking oven and recreation room, but on the question of communal kitchens, 'Working class opinion seems to be considerably divided.'[75] The author of the report noted a change in women's attitudes towards communal kitchens, which at first had been regarded 'as an encouragement to idleness on the part of the working class house-mother'. Women had originally felt that family life might be endangered if the wife no longer cooked at home. The report went on to say that this view was no longer held, although it added that communal kitchens were such a recent innovation that any judgement on their popularity was mere speculation.[76] The government adopted a more formal means of obtaining the views of women concerning housing, setting up the Women's Housing Sub-Committee (WHSC) of the Ministry of Reconstruction in late 1917. The committee, formed largely at the instigation of the Women's Labour League,[77] was requested to look from the housewife's point of view at several recent housing schemes, and house plans suggested by the Local Government Board (LGB), which was responsible for local authority housing.[78] They were to make suggestions with reference to the convenience of the housewife, which they did with such vehemence in their First Interim Report that its publication was held up for five months while an internal argument took place over their findings. The committee included Averil Sanderson Furniss, secretary of the Women's Housing Committee of the Labour Party, and Dorothy Peel of the National Kitchens Advisory Committee. Most of the WHSC's work on communal facilities was published in their second report, but the interim report did suggest that a central system of water heating would save fuel and labour.[79] They were also in favour of low housing densities, in order that each house could have its own garden and space was available for common playgrounds attached to large groups of houses.[80] The LGB, in their observations on the report, stated that they 'would desire not to be taken as concurring in the suggestion as to common playgrounds accessible from groups of houses'.[81]

In reply to the WHSC's criticism of the LGB's house plans, the Board accused the committee of disregarding considerations of cost and added that 'The Committee's want of experience in reading plans has, no doubt, been a serious disadvantage to them.'[82] The committee had not simply criticised details of the Board's suggested plans, but had gone further and attacked the housing standards proposed by the Board's memorandum to local authorities issued early in 1918.[83] It felt strongly that a parlour or extra room should be provided, that there should be a bathroom rather than a bath in the scullery, and that storage space should be increased.[84] While the Ministry of Reconstruction and the LGB argued over the publication of the report during the summer of 1918, a committee set up by the LGB in July 1917 and chaired by

Sir John Tudor Walters, a Liberal MP, was working towards the publication of its report on the provision and construction of working-class housing. Relations between the LGB and the Ministry of Reconstruction were not improved by the WHSC's stance on housing standards, and their interim report was never published in full.[85]

Undaunted by the reception given to their first report, the WHSC embarked on a programme of data-gathering in the spring and summer of 1918, including site visits, committee sessions and submissions from interested parties. The committee gave greater emphasis to communal facilities in this second investigation, and visitors to housing schemes were asked particularly to note the provision of playgrounds, open spaces, allotments and other communal arrangements.[86] The Women's Labour League sent in a summary of their collection of working women's views on housing, which, in its section concerning washhouses, neatly expressed the general conflict of opinion over communal facilities. Almost all women preferred to have their own inbuilt washing facilities: 'One or two are in favour of a communal wash house but these are not really working women, being Health Visitors, Midwives, etc.'[87] The majority of submissions to the committee followed this pattern, communal arrangements being advocated by the middle class and rejected by the working class for whom they were intended.

Communal washhouses were particularly unpopular amongst working women. A committee member visiting a garden village in Wrexham asked about the possibility of a communal laundry being erected, and 'gathered that there was a good deal of objection on the part of the tenants to such a plan'.[88] At the Richmond Mothers' Welcome, there was almost unanimous agreement that washing should be done at home, because of the difficulties of combining childcare and food preparation with trips to the laundry or washhouse.[89] Some 27 Camberwell mothers said they did not want a communal kitchen in their area because 'There wouldn't be nothing left for us to do if we hadn't no dinner to cook.'[90] The committee took a great deal of evidence both for and against communal facilities, and in August 1918 four of the members visited Letchworth to see two cooperative housekeeping schemes in operation. Ebenezer Howard conducted the party first to Homesgarth, which they found interesting but not relevant to their inquiry because of its middle-class tenants, and then to

Meadow Way Green. They considered the Green to be a working-class scheme, and saw that tenancies were no longer restricted to single women, as a few families had been allowed to move in. Regarding the shared catering, they 'were told that this system worked very well and prevented grumbling'.[91] The committee had previously seen a pamphlet of Howard's, on 'Domestic Industry as it Might Be'.[92]

Annie Hall, the architect whose articles on cooperative house-keeping had appeared in the Women's Party journal, gave evidence before the committee in July 1918. She told them that communal housing was especially suitable for households with an income of £200 to £500 per year, but was also useful to working-class families. She suggested that each group of houses should be provided with a creche, a nursery school and a central kitchen and restaurant. At the following meeting of the committee, a sub-committee dealing with communal arrangements was set up. It included Averil Sanderson Furniss, and it was originally intended that it should make its report in September, although there is no written record of it doing so.[93] The WHSC investigator and later committee member, Mrs Alwyn Lloyd, visited the munitions village at Gretna in Dumfries, which had been equipped with a variety of central facilities including a kitchen, laundry, cinema and institute. The general design of the village had been carried out by Raymond Unwin, head of the housing branch of the Department of Explosives Supply in the Ministry of Munitions. The resident architect at the site was Courtenay Crickmer, designer of Meadow Way Green, and Mrs Lloyd was impressed with some of his cottages which had previously won an architectural competition at Gidea Park. She did not see the central kitchen, but did visit the washhouses used by women workers living in the hostels.[94] No committee member made a visit to Waterlow Court, as this type of development was not strictly relevant to the investigation, but a submission was received on the subject of accommodation for single women workers. A representative of the Association of Women Clerks and Secretaries wrote to the WHSC, saying 'There is a crying need for more places like Waterlow Court in the Hampstead Garden Suburb.'[95] Her only criticism of the Court was its lack of central heating.

By September 1918 the committee had finished collecting information, to the probable relief of the Ministry of Reconstruction, as the cost of its investigations had been higher than expected.[96]

The Ministry had earlier refused to sanction the issue of 1000 leaflets on housing, giving the WHSC's ideas on points for discussion at meetings of the Women's Cooperative Guild.[97] The committee had also been criticised for its low working-class membership.[98] It published its second and final report in January 1919, the terms of reference having been widened to include a consideration of the difficulties of converting middle-class houses into working-class flats.[99] Although it considered communal arrangements in some detail, none of its main recommendations concerned domestic cooperation but were related to conventional housing standards and the provision of adequate play space.

The committee felt that 'one of the most important results of the war has been to demonstrate the advantages of combination and the wide possibilities of communal life'.[100] In spite of all the evidence from working women in favour of individual washing facilities, the committee wanted to encourage communal washing. It did not recommend either the washhouse or the central laundry, but suggested the bag wash laundry service, an untried scheme which it felt might be run by local authorities.[101] The authorities, cooperatives or private enterprise might also be responsible for some form of communal cooking, as the WHSC doubted that shared kitchens would ever be popular with working women. It suggested that pubs should serve food, thus reminding returning soldiers of 'the sight of the worker and his family sitting under the trees in foreign cafes enjoying a cheap and well-cooked meal. . .'[102] The committee stated that its suggestions concerning communal arrangements were made to provide a basis for experiment. It felt that communal cooking and washing could save labour, but accepted that these arrangements were still so unusual that women's suspicion of them had to be overcome before their introduction was practicable. As the evidence submitted to the committee had shown, working women were not in favour of communal arrangements, but the committee had 'little doubt that the solution of many of the more difficult domestic problems will eventually be found along the lines of co-operation rather than in isolated effort'.[103] It also recommended experiments with central heating systems for groups of houses; Raymond Unwin, in his evidence to the committee, had said that the greatest problem in cottage planning was the provision of hot water and heating systems.[104] Although the LGB had disagreed with the proposal of the WHSC in its interim report for common playgrounds between groups of houses, this recommendation was repeated and enlarged in the final report.

In the introduction to its report, the WHSC welcomed the publication of the report of the Tudor Walters Committee, and emphasised its agreement with two of the Walters Committee statements. The committees both felt that parlours should be provided wherever possible, and that working-class households did not want cooking to be carried out in the living room.[105] The Tudor Walters Report was published in November 1918, in the same week as the armistice, rather overshadowing the WHSC findings which came out two months later.[106] The Tudor Walters Committee was composed mainly of housing and planning experts, including Raymond Unwin, and its report soon became seen as the authoritative work on post-war working-class housing.[107] The only direct contact between the two committees was through Mr E. Leonard, the secretary of the Tudor Walters Committee. He attended a number of meetings of the WHSC during mid-1918, talking in confidence about the provision of sculleries, larders and other relevant features.[108] Leonard was able to tell the WHSC in June 1918 that the LGB had not seen fit to pass on to him (and thus the Tudor Walters Committee), a copy of the WHSC's interim report about which the LGB were pre-varicating.[109] Sir John Tudor Walters would not allow the WHSC to see any evidence given to his committee concerning the house-wife's view of housing, but Leonard did give the WHSC the names of those who had given evidence on this subject.[110] Two of the witnesses were members of the WHSC, Sanderson Furniss and Miss A. Churton, Secretary of the Rural Housing and Sanitation Association, and the third was Marion Phillips. All three were accompanied by working women, and Mrs Pankhurst gave evidence on communal arrangements. Leonard also told the WHSC that his committee was tending towards the view that the bag wash was the only practicable form of laundry provision.

Of the 127 named witnesses seen by the Tudor Walters Committee and its sub-committees, 15 were women, and Courtenay Crickmer was one of those supplying information. In spite of the fact that 'a considerable amount of evidence' was given to the committee on communal services for groups of houses, only seven paragraphs of the report's total of 352 were devoted to the subject. The committee advised the encouragement of experiments in the central supply of hot water and provision of bag wash services, as Leonard had predicted to the WHSC. It did not evince any great enthusiasm for these experiments, and was equally dismissive of communal cooking, which was allocated a single sentence: 'The rapid development of the communal kitchen and messroom may also effect some permanent change in the habits of the people which will also need consideration.'[111] Clearly the committee was not convinced that this 'permanent change' would produce houses of radically different design. It was, however, concerned that wider social, educational and recreational needs should be considered in the planning of new housing schemes.[112]

The Tudor Walters Report recommended a considerable rise in the standard of local authority housing. Post-war houses were to have three bedrooms, a bathroom and a parlour where possible, and sites were to be laid out at a low density on principles earlier expounded by Raymond Unwin, whose influence on the content of the report was greatest of the committee members.[113] Public utility societies were to play a part in the provision of post-war housing, but the bulk of new construction was to be undertaken by the local authorities. The report saw housing societies as being an auxiliary system of provision, although an earlier report to the Ministry of Reconstruction had commended them for the high quality of their house design and their democratic methods of management. Their main problem lay in obtaining sufficient capital, and the societies had suffered from poor central organisation.[114] In the Tudor Walters Report, Unwin's ideas on cooperation and house design were propagated through site plans rather than suggestions of cooperative facilities. Houses were to be grouped round quadrangles or small paths at right angles to the main road.[115] There was no room for idiosyncratic communal schemes in the report, emphasising as it did the standardisation of elements such as doors and windows to reduce construction costs. There were also to be a limited number of basic house plans, which could then be adapted to suit local conditions.[116] Unwin himself chaired the sub-committee responsible for the recommendations on standardisation.[117]

It is strange that the Tudor Walters Report almost ignored the provision of communal facilities, despite the weight of evidence given to the committee on the subject, and the fact that Raymond Unwin had always strongly supported cooperation in housing. Although his views had changed since his early years when he advocated cooperative housing as a means of encouraging communal life and thus socialism, he had always maintained that cooperative housing and shared facilities could bring real advantages. It would appear that the opportunity dramatically to improve the standard of housing provision for a large number of working-class tenants was of greater importance to Unwin than the inclusion of central facilities which might still be in an experimental stage or not universally popular. It would be interesting to know if Marion Phillips' view, that cooperative housekeeping was relevant to working women only after they had been provided with decent housing, was expressed to the committee in her evidence.[118] Wartime developments in industrial standardisation had also been reflected in architectural and town planning theory, the early resignation of Frank Baines from the Tudor Walters Committee showing that diversity and individuality in house design had become outdated. Baines was the architect of Well Hall, a munitions village built at Woolwich in 1915, which used a wide range of materials and achieved a picturesque effect.[119] The move towards standardisation in housing was seen as a result of changes in society; the community was becoming more important than the individual, and good design was seen as functional and efficient.[120] It is interesting that cooperative housekeeping had also been advocated as being the future form of domestic life, the end of the individual household and a means to domestic efficiency. The superficial similarity of these ideas is belied by their opposing bases, voluntary cooperation and imposed standardisation.

The combination of Unwin's enthusiasm for wholesale changes in housing standards and estate planning, combined with general acceptance on the part of the Tudor Walters Committee of the benefits of standardisation, led to the exclusion of facilities which, although useful, might not have been relevant everywhere in the same form. National cooperation, which had been to the fore during the war, was not to be replaced by a national effort to house the war's heroes which could not be diverted into communistic or individualist paths. The Tudor Walters Report must be seen as a great rebuff to advocates of cooperative housekeeping or communal facilities, and a missed opportunity on the part of Raymond Unwin. Unwin's influence and his background of involvement with cooperative housing could have led to a rather different report, where individuality and mutual cooperation were combined with possibilities for the improvement of housing standards. Instead, the contents of the report were adapted and reproduced as the LGB's *Manual on the Preparation of State-aided Housing Schemes* in April 1919.[121] The Minister of Reconstruction had been appointed to the presidency of the LGB in January 1919, and Unwin and the other staff sympathetic to the aims of the Tudor Walters Report had been given posts in the LGB.[122] The views of Unwin and the rest of the committee were thus given legitimation as government housing policy; the LGB's *Manual* contained no mention whatsoever of communal arrangements, although it did continue the Ministry of Reconstruction's interest in the housewife's opinion, saying:

> Local authorities will appreciate the importance of considering the internal arrangements from the point of view of the housewife, and for this purpose they will no doubt obtain the cooperation and advice of competent women.[123]

The July 1919 Housing and Town Planning Act imposed on local authorities the duty of making and carrying out plans for the provision of houses. Schemes submitted to the Ministry of Health (formed from the LGB in June 1919) under this Act could contain 'such incidental, consequential and supplemental provisions . . . as may appear necessary or proper for the purpose of the scheme'.[124] The Act therefore allowed local authorities to provide social centres or other communal facilities if they wished. During the debate on the Bill, only one MP referred to its wider aspects, criticising its lack of consideration of social life as well as housing. The MP, Sir Martin Conway, an art historian and traveller who sat for the Combined English Universities, suggested that villages could have 'a restaurant, or a canteen if you like, where men and their families could feed or drink a cup of tea or even a glass of wine together'.[125] He also felt that facilities such as a creche, library, hall and cinema could be provided. The National Kitchens Division had been very active in persuading the LGB to include the clause concerning supplemental provisions in the Act. The Division's new director, T. G. Jones, felt that the state should be involved with the improvement of facilities for obtaining food; although national kitchens were closing in the wake of the armistice, he felt there was scope for increasing the number of national restaurants in towns and cities.[126]

Neither the Treasury nor the commercial catering organisations

1. Streatham Street 'Model houses for families', the courtyard

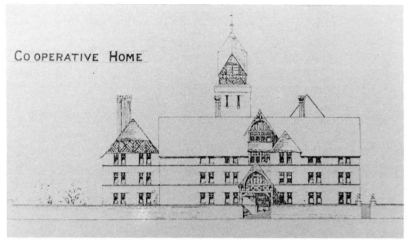

2. Cooperative home designed by E. W. Godwin for Mrs. E. M. King
(*Building News*, vol. 26, 24 April 1874, p. 452)

3. Chenies Street, ladies' residential chambers

5. Nutford House residential club

4. York Street, ladies' residential chambers

6. Queen's Club Gardens

Photo by Gosfold & Co., Hastings.

7. Mrs Daubeny, manageress of the London Distributing Kitchen (*The Lady's Realm*, Feb. 1902, p. 515)

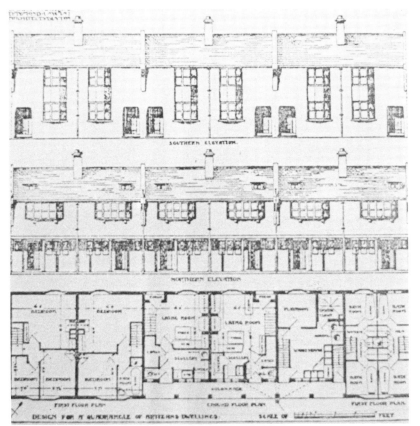

8. Raymond Unwin's design for a quadrangle of artisans' dwellings
(*Raymond Unwin, Cottage Plans and Common Sense*, Fabian Tract No. 109,
Fabian Society, London, March 1902, p. 10; by kind permission of the Fabian
Society)

9. Elmwood Cottages, Letchworth Garden City, by M. H. Baillie Scott (some
alterations have been made to the original design)

10. Homesgarth, Letchworth Garden City, inside the quadrangle (author and *Spare Rib*)

11. The Orchard, Hampstead Garden Suburb, by Parker and Unwin (*Garden Cities and Town Planning*, November 1909, vol. 4, no. 35, p. 248, by kind permission of the Town and Country Planning Association)

Illus. 296.—Group of cottages with a co-operative centre.

12. Raymond Unwin's drawing of a 'group of cottages with a cooperative centre' (Raymond Unwin, *Town Planning in Practice*, Fisher Unwin, London, 1909, p. 381).

13. Waterlow Court, Hampstead Garden Suburb, inside the quadrangle (author and *Spare Rib*)

14. Waterlow Court, outside the quadrangle showing decorative brickwork

15. Pre-First World War picture of the interior of a flat at Waterlow Court (by kind permission of the Hampstead Garden Suburb Archives Trust)

16. Pre-First World War picture of the dining room at Waterlow Court (by kind permission of the Hampstead Garden Suburb Archives Trust)

17. Meadow Way Green North, Letchworth Garden City

18. Mrs Alice Melvin, aged about 60 (taken about 1915; by kind permission of Rosemary Melvin)

19. House in Brent Garden Village, designed by P. Woollatt Home

20. Cedar Court, Brent Garden Village, by Taylor and Huggins

21. Part of the Melvin Cooperative Residential Society (Hampstead) Ltd. property in Priory Road

22. Meadow Way Green South, Letchworth Garden City

23. Guessens Court, Welwyn Garden City, inside the quadrangle

24. St. George's Court, Bournville, Birmingham

were in favour of any extension of the national kitchens scheme. The caterers felt they were already providing all that the population required in terms of cooked food outlets, while the Treasury were opposed to increasing subsidies.[127] The Division's first director saw the Tudor Walters Report as strongly favouring national kitchens.[128] Although this was a great exaggeration, the Division continued to press for the provision of canteens and restaurants in every new housing scheme, and were supported in this aim by a wide range of organisations.[129] The Trade Union Congress, the Conference of Labour Women and over 100 trades and labour councils had passed resolutions supporting the continuation of national kitchens.[130] A magazine article called for kitchens in every street and square, seeing them as a future 'National Institution', but they were still not popular with their working women customers.[131] By the end of 1919, the number of national kitchens had been reduced to 156, of which 129 were also national restaurants.[132] Several local authorities had been unable to find premises for kitchens, and the Treasury refused to sanction discounts on the purchase of ex-Army huts for this purpose, although authorities could buy them cheaply for use in housing.[133] The Treasury continued to oppose all extensions of the kitchens scheme; it had also been against the new Housing Act on grounds of excessive cost.[134] It was eventually decided that the remaining kitchens should be placed under local control, and the Ministry of Food was dissolved in early 1921.[135] The decline of the national kitchens can be attributed to the opposition of the Treasury and the commercial caterers, and their lack of popularity with their customers. The support of labour organisations was not influential enough to expand the aims of government housing policy as outlined in the Tudor Walters Report.

The domination of the LGB by the proponents of the ideas contained in the Tudor Walters Report was one reason for the lack of impact of the WHSC's final report. Its enthusiasm for communal arrangements was ignored in the LGB's 1919 *Manual*, issued only two months after the Ministry of Reconstruction had received the WHSC report. The report arrived following the departure of the Minister of Reconstruction to head the LGB, and the previous poor relations between the two departments may have contributed to the report's failure to produce any perceptible additions to the *Manual*. Unfortunately for the WHSC, by January 1919 their report was too late to have any effect, and due to changes of personnel, was received by the wrong department. The interim report, whose publication had been delayed by the LGB, added to the pressure on the Board to improve their housing standards; their tactics failed eventually, as the LGB's Housing Department was taken over by external appointees.[136] The LGB maintained that the WHSC had not taken cost considerations into account in their interim report, and although this was denied by the Ministry of Reconstruction, the Treasury was clearly against any excessive expenditure on the housing programme which might be incurred through raising standards unduly.[137] The LGB *Manual* suggested that local authorities should consult 'competent women' to obtain the views of the housewife on internal arrangements, and it may be that the professional architects and planners of the LGB's newly-formed Housing Department felt that most of the matters considered by the women's committee were outside the scope of their *Manual*.

The WHSC had first recommended in May 1918 that women should be represented on all public bodies carrying out housing schemes.[138] Several local Women's Advisory Committees were formed, the Bristol committee producing a report in 1919 which agreed with the WHSC's report on the desirability of the bag wash and central heating systems for the provision of hot water to groups of houses. They felt that communal kitchens near the local aircraft factory would be successful, but found no evidence to justify their provision in every new housing scheme.[139] The Ministry of Health issued a circular in December 1919 proposing that women's views on housing schemes should be taken into account by means of public exhibition of plans, the coopting of women on to local authority housing committees, and the setting up of women's advisory committees in all urban districts. The Ministry emphasised that although women's advice on proposed layouts, plans and the internal fittings of houses would be useful, 'nothing should be done which would involve any delay' in the building process.[140] Outside government circles, the Women's Section of the Garden Cities and Town Planning Association had been formed in May 1920, to act as a central information bureau on housing and planning matters for women's organisations, and to provide information for local housing committees. It comprised representatives of 15 women's organisations, one of which was the Women's Freedom League, and was chaired by Lady Emmott, chairperson of the WHSC, with Marion Phillips as vice chairperson. The Fabian Society Women's Group was also a member of the Women's Section.[141]

The Housing Advisory Council (HAC) of the LGB was another organisation in which women participated. It had been set up in April 1919 to provide advice on housing policy, and had originally been intended to be a small committee, meeting frequently to discuss matters such as contracts and standardisation. The Standing Joint Committee of Industrial Women's Organisations was asked to put forward the name of a woman for membership of the HAC, but after a protracted exchange of letters, Marion Phillips, secretary of the Standing Committee, persuaded the LGB to accept two women members. Accordingly Mrs E. Barton (of the Women's Cooperative Guild) and Mrs. Sanderson Furniss joined Lady Emmott on the HAC, all three having been members of the WHSC.[142] The HAC formed a Women's Sub-Committee, and in October 1919 Lady Emmott and Mrs Sanderson Furniss suggested that the Minister of Health should be asked to refer the subject of 'co-operative housing and communal arrangements' to the Sub-Committee. They suggested that the terms of reference might include the consideration of residential clubs for single people, village centres and housing provision for the elderly. Thus the Sub-Committee could continue the work on communal arrangements which had been begun by the WHSC. The chairperson of the Council, Sir John Tudor Walters, agreed to see the Minister on the matter.[143]

Tudor Walters did not contact the Minister, missed two out of the three Council meetings held in 1919, and had its December 1919 meeting postponed as he was busy in the House of Commons. The delay in reaching a decision on the proposal for the Women's Sub-Committee investigation caused Mrs Sanderson Furniss to ask the Council's secretary whether Tudor Walters had the matter in hand; she had

> proposed it on account of representations that had been made to me by a member of the Ministry of Food, and the fact that I am not yet able to give details as to what is being arranged is causing some surprise.[144]

No decision was forthcoming, and the Council was not called

upon to meet again. The standing Joint Committee of Industrial Women's Organisations responded by sending a deputation to see the Minister of Health, Christopher Addison, in June 1920. Addison apologised for 'what seemed to be some oversight' regarding the Women's Sub-Committee investigation, and promised the HAC would deal with the matter without delay. It was five months before the Sub-Committee on Co-operative and Communal Arrangements was finally set up in November 1920, and this further delay persuaded both Barton and Sanderson Furniss to resign their membership of the HAC, with the support of the Standing Committee.[145]

The new Sub-Committee at last met in February 1921, and was so angered by the preceding events that it considered asking the Minister if the Sub-Committee's appointment was merely 'eyewash'. It decided against this, and instead set about changing the subject of its investigation from cooperative and communal arrangements, on the grounds that they

> would be wasting their time in making a detailed report on this subject, as it appears that such schemes would be likely to involve certain additional cost, and the Committee felt that there was no likelihood of any such proposals being considered at the present time.[146]

The Sub-Committee chose to investigate the provision and management of women's hostels, feeling that some effect might be given to its recommendations on this matter. The Sub-Committee, chaired by Lady Emmott and including Dorothy Peel and Henrietta Barnett, produced its short report in May 1921.[147] The report concluded that there was a considerable and probably permanent demand for accommodation for working women, which could be met by the building of large hostels and the conversion of large houses for use as small hostels. Women would be able to rent cubicles or single rooms, or share two-roomed flats, and a restaurant might be provided which would also be open to the public. Henrietta Barnett later said that she had learned a great deal from the evidence of those who came before the Sub-Committee, and the experience had prompted her decision to attempt to establish women's hostels in Hampstead Garden Suburb.[148]

The unsatisfactory nature of women's representation on the Housing Advisory Council was acknowledged by the National

Conference of Labour Women in April 1921. They passed a resolution endorsing the resignations of Mrs Barton and Mrs Sanderson Furniss, and expressing their dissatisfaction with the Ministry of Health's failure to make use of the HAC while submitting to pressure in favour of decreased housing standards.[149] By 1921, the housing programme had been drastically cut back, following the final slump of 1920–1 and the defeats suffered by the labour movement.[150] From mid-1921, local authorities were being advised to build two-bedroom, non-parlour houses.[151] The Sub-Committee on Co-operative and Communal Arrangements was clearly correct in assuming that no money would be available to implement any recommendations it might have made on its original subject of investigation. The cause of the initial prevarication on the part of Tudor Walters and the Minister of Health lies with the composition of the HAC, intended as a small, high-level committee rather than a large advisory body. It appears that once the HAC had been set up, it became too unwieldy and unsuited to its original functions. Tudor Walters had no time for it, and neither he nor Addison was interested in encouraging yet another committee which would report in favour of expensive communal facilities, a subject which the Tudor Walters Report had treated with disdain. Tudor Walters had earlier refused a request from the WHSC to see evidence taken by his committee on topics relevant to the WHSC's investigations.

Recommendations from both the Women's Housing Sub-Committee and the women members of the Housing Advisory Council were ignored or stifled by various departments of government. It had also taken some months before women's skills and expertise were used by the newly formed National Kitchens Division. Although women had gained access to policy-making bodies of government during the war, they had still been denied the power to make policy decisions.[152] Their participation was always of an advisory nature, their recommendations being useful reinforcement for existing or new policy decisions when apt, but carrying no weight when opposing prior decisions. Part of the WHSC's draft interim report was completely suppressed, only a brief summary ever being published. Women appeared to participate more successfully at a local level, where their recommendations on internal arrangements could be fed more directly into the construction process. The highly detailed reports of the WHSC were out of place in the Ministry of Reconstruction, dealing as it did with housing and planning on a large scale. The WHSC had been set up as a result of pressure being brought to bear on the Minister by a women's organisation, and similarly the women's representation on the HAC was increased at the behest of Marion Phillips, secretary of the Standing Committee. The government was anxious for the endorsement of their housing policy by women's organisations, but the powerful group of architects and planners involved with the Tudor Walters Report and its implementation was concerned with issues more complex than those the women's representatives were allowed to consider.

The Tudor Walters Report and the 1919 Housing Act certainly raised housing standards, if only in the short term. As far as can be ascertained, working-class women were very much in favour of these improved standards, and it is hard to see post-war state housing as an imposition of middle-class standards upon the working class, as has recently been argued.[153] Working women would have preferred even higher standards if possible, and if anything was being foisted on to the working class, it was the variety of communal arrangements seen by the middle class as raising the quality of working-class life. The coming of war had certainly altered working women's lives; the number of women in paid work rose by 1 200 000 during the period July 1914 to April 1918, and although women were initially reluctant to take on new jobs, by the end of the war many women had experienced factory canteens, women's hostels or national kitchens.[154] This introduction to domestic organisation was unfortunate for supporters of the cooperative housekeeping movement, as communal arrangements of any sort became strongly identified with wartime circumstances of shortage and imposed collectivism. This was in addition to memories of shared facilities in poorly designed tenements, and was not offset by any wide experience of true cooperative housekeeping experiments.

Within government, communal arrangements only found favour and real support in the Ministry of Food, and probably only in the National Kitchens Division. A wide range of communal schemes was proposed during the war, from the imposed cooperative housekeeping of the Women's Party to the take-away laundries and cooked food services suggested by many working women. At this minimal level, domestic cooperation did not imply any form of communal living, but was more an occasional social and economic asset. True cooperative housekeeping, with its higher social aims, remained the province of the middle and upper classes. Had it not been for the war, the cooperative house-keeping movement, with its increasing number of experimental sites, might have gained strength and eventually built a working-class development. The war brought the imposition of minimal domestic cooperation, which was unpopular with all but a few members of the middle class. The majority of post-war working-class housing was built by the state rather than public utility societies, and with little state support for experimental communal arrangements the only housing available to most people was of conventional design. The war was certainly a setback for the cooperative housekeeping movement. Given the prevailing social and economic conditions of the early years of the century, there were many arguments in favour of domestic cooperation, but the war not only gave many people a taste of cooperation, its after-math brought social and economic changes. If cooperative house-keeping was to succeed in post-war Britain, its aims and methods would have to be adapted to suit a different world.

9 The Movement Declines

The First World War had changed the lives of middle-class women in two ways: it had made available to them opportunities for paid work outside the home, and in many cases it had left them without any domestic help. By 1920, nearly two-thirds of the women who had taken jobs during the war had left them again, and the 'servant problem' became a subject worthy of government consideration.[1] Only a few weeks after the war ended, the Ministry of Reconstruction had set its Women's Advisory Committee to work on the 'Domestic Service Problem'. The Committee reported in March 1919, its main conclusion being that the present system of low-paid, unskilled and inefficient domestic service could be improved by the introduction of training courses, which would encourage women to see domestic service as a skilled occupation.[2] The total number of people employed as servants had decreased by about one-third during the war, but the slump of 1920 resulted in many women returning to domestic service.[3] The general trend in servant numbers between 1881 and 1931 was upward, but because of the increasing population, and in particular the growth of the middle class during the war, the percentage of households with resident servants declined.[4] Expenditure on domestic service only decreased dramatically after the Second World War.[5]

The middle-class housewife's problem with servants was that an efficient, resident servant could not be obtained as cheaply as before the war, if at all. The number of daily maids increased, and a Ministry of Labour report published in October 1923 gave details of several schemes in which servants lived at a centre or hostel and worked at nearby houses.[6] The first English edition of *Good Housekeeping* appeared in 1922 and, with several other magazines aimed at the middle-class homemaker, concentrated on women's place in the home and modern home design.[7] R. Randal Phillips published *The Servantless House* in 1920, suggesting that it was cheaper to buy a range of domestic appliances for £40 than to employ a servant for about the same cost, plus her keep and an allowance for breakages. He felt that servants were 'a mixed blessing, more especially as so few of them are really competent',[8] and emphasised the convenience of electrical appliances and the need for labour-saving design. Electricity had reached almost three-quarters of British households by 1939, and in the 1920s housewives had been offered a wide range of appliances to enhance their homes, from coffee percolators and toasters to cookers and sewing machines.[9] The boom in the sale of electrical appliances came in the 1930s, although manufacturers had been attempting to appeal to women customers since the end of the war.[10] Labour-saving devices were known before the war; they were displayed at the 1910 Ideal Home Exhibition, 'many of them being invented by women for women', but after the war manufacturers made greater efforts to secure women's custom: 'many an elaborate electrical outfit traces its initiation to a trial given to an electric iron. It is really worth while to *give* an iron to every likely consumer.'[11]

Although both the 1919 and 1923 government reports on domestic service advocated the provision of labour-saving equipment in the home, it was noted that

> there is also a curious and quite unreasoning hostility among maids themselves to the use of such appliances, due presumably to the conservatism of which the British race is not infrequently accused.[12]

Immediately after the war, domestic cooperation was suggested as a solution to the difficulties experienced by poorer households. Clementina Black, in a memorandum to the 1919 report on the 'Domestic Service Problem', said

> the best way of economising domestic service would be for a group of householders to establish a common centre for buying, preparing, and distributing food and for providing central heating and hot water.[13]

The Queen commented favourably on her idea, saying that it need involve no loss of privacy for individual families.[14] The coal miners' strike of April 1921 caused the Food Department of the Board of Trade to circulate local authorities on the arrangements for providing cooked food in areas of coal shortage. The remaining 70 national kitchens were to be fully utilised, and others reopened, while families were to be encouraged to combine to cook meals.

The newly formed Emergency Kitchens Committee felt the latter point to be of the 'utmost importance'.[15]

By the early 1920s, communal cooking was increasingly seen as a respectable solution to the problems of middle-class housekeeping. Leonora Eyles looked at the plight of the educated, middle-class wife who had to choose between playing with her children and doing the housework. The ideal house had not yet been built;

> Communal cookery is another solution; perhaps one of the biggest solutions, doing away, as it would, with the dirty kitchen range, the preparation of vegetables, and the tedious food shopping. But there is no machinery for communal cooking yet, and this problem is immediate. . .[16]

There was very little machinery in terms of cooperative housing schemes, but communal cooking equipment certainly existed and had been in use during the war. Many munitions works' canteens used electric cookers, and one London firm had contacted the Women's Housing Sub-Committee to inform them it produced electrical appliances suitable for cooperative living.[17] The postwar revival of restaurants and the spread of eating out to the lower middle classes prompted W. L. George to comment: 'That is the last brick heaved at the old home: thirty years ago, to dine at a restaurant was a rather fast thing to do.'[18] George saw the home of the future as being a flat in a large block, with gas or electric heating, hot meals available from a service lift, easily cleaned furniture and communal day and night nurseries for children. The housewife would be redundant, and all women would take paid work; housekeeping would become a paid trade.[19] H. G. Wells also felt that flats would be the most efficient type of future home, in contrast to the individual house which he saw as 'a cage of needless toil for women'.[20] The modern flat would be supplied with electricity, hot and cold water and storage facilities, and would have access to washhouses and shops. The opposing view was represented in the columns of *Good Housekeeping*, where a response to W. L. George's articles attributed dislike of service flats to the years spent without decent homes during and after the war.

To these same years also may be traced the death of the once popular idea of the 'communal' house. More women today want homes – and with more passion – than ever before. . . Modern woman wants a home worthy of her vacuum cleaner, her rustless steel, her various appliances.[21]

Apart from the state building programme, the early post-war years saw the public utility societies continuing their own attempts to construct new estates and villages. The development plans occasionally made provision for cooperative housing, as in the case of Onslow Garden Village, situated on the slopes of the Hog's Back to the west of Guildford. Its originator was Frederick Litchfield, the assistant managing director of Co-partnership Tenants Limited, who began to interest various Guildford organisations in the idea in May 1918.[22] He brought Ebenezer Howard to Guildford in April 1919 to inspect a prospective site, which Howard thought was suitable, and by February 1920 Onslow Village Limited had become a registered society.[23] The plans for the village were drawn up by Arthur Knapp-Fisher of the London practice Knapp-Fisher, Powell and Russell. Knapp-Fisher, then 32, went on to become vice-president of the RIBA and president of the Architectural Association. There were to be no more than five houses to the acre, leaving room for large gardens. The houses were to be provided with baths and parlours, and were specially designed to be labour-saving. As well as the houses, 200 of which were to be built by September 1921, the prospectus for the village stated:

If it is found desirable, blocks of flats may be constructed for the accommodation of persons wishing to conduct their domestic affairs on a co-operative basis. The chief feature of these flats would be a common dining hall, with hostel servants to attend to the tenants' requirements; and probably a scheme of central heating will be provided.[24]

The first houses were occupied by the end of October 1920, and by May 1921, 60 houses had been erected. Litchfield, chairman of the society, hoped that a block of flats for old people could be built, similar to The Orchard at Hampstead Garden Suburb. Several supporters of the society had connections with the Suburb, and the original scheme for Onslow Garden Village included clubs, an institute and recreation grounds, as planned for Hampstead.[25] In its early years the village was highly successful, just over 300 houses being built in the 1920s, but then building ceased for financial reasons. The cooperative flats had not been included in the part of the plan due for early completion, and were never built. Although they were frequently mentioned in the local press as part of the village's future plans, no design was ever drawn up for them.[26]

Two members of the committee of Onslow Village Limited had a financial interest in Letchworth Garden City, which was already the site of two cooperative housekeeping developments. A third was proposed soon after the war by Ellen Pearsall, who suggested a group of 20 houses catering specifically for families with children. She pointed out that families with children could not use communal dining rooms, adding 'The proposed Pearsall Group is intended specially to meet this need, and will be unique in that the promoters desire children to live there instead of repelling them.'[27] Ellen Pearsall and her husband, Howard Pearsall, had moved to Letchworth from Hampstead, where he had been a local councillor. They were both members of the Fabian Society, and Howard Pearsall became a director of First Garden City Ltd and chairperson of the Howard Cottage Society; Ellen Pearsall was on the board of the latter.[28] A public utility society was formed to carry out the plan for the Pearsall Group, and was registered in October 1919, probably being known as the Garden City Public Utility. It may have been the original intention to build the houses under the auspices of the Howard Cottage Society, in a similar manner to Meadow Way Green, but in January 1920 the Society's board stated that it was taking no further interest in the 'proposed group of cooperative houses' as a public utility society had been formed to deal with the matter.[29] It is unknown whether the death of Howard Pearsall in November 1919 was in any way connected with this decision.

The Pearsall Group was designed by Robert Bennett and Wilson Bidwell, who had both worked for Parker and Unwin at Buxton before setting up their own practice in Letchworth in 1905, where they concentrated on domestic work.[30] Their design (see Figure 11) was very unusual, as the four-bedroom houses had no kitchens at all; there was a pantry, but it was small, and no mention was made of the provision of cooking facilities. The houses had two

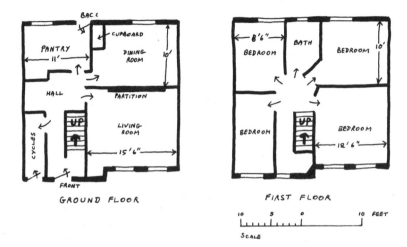

FIGURE 11 *Ground and first-floor plans of a mid-terrace house in a block of six cooperative houses designed by Robert Bennett and Wilson Bidwell for Mrs E. B. Pearsall (redrawn from Garden Cities and Town Planning Magazine, Aug 1920, vol. 10, no. 8, p. 175, by kind permission of* Hugh D. Bidwell and the Town and Country Planning Association)

reception rooms which could be turned into one large room by the removal of a partition. The 20 houses formed a half quadrangle centred on a large block containing the central kitchen and staff accommodation. Two hot meals a day were to be delivered to each house, none of which was more than 100 yards from the central block. All washing up was to be done centrally, and a furnace was to provide hot water for the whole group. The labour-saving design included gas fires, central heating and electric lighting; a children's playground was part of the plan. Ellen Pearsall saw her houses as being suitable for clerical, managerial and professional workers, and calculated that a family could save over £20 per year by living in a Pearsall Group house rather than in an ordinary house with a resident maid. The saving was considerably less if the family chose to employ a daily maid only, and this may have been one reason why the Pearsall Group was never built.

Ellen Pearsall felt that the design of the houses and the central facilities meant that 'the servant difficulty practically disappears', but nothing came of the scheme. The Garden City Public Utility remained in existence throughout the 1920s, with half a dozen members and a small share capital, and was finally wound up in 1936. The design of the Pearsall Group followed the conventional pattern for cooperative homes, but made no concessions to conventional lifestyles with little or no provision for individual cooking. Communal life would have been minimal, with only the children's playground and the tennis court acting as communal areas. The scheme was intended to appeal to those families suffering from the servant problem, but the small financial savings promised were probably not enough to interest investors in the scheme. Possibly the provision of a communal dining room for adults and children might have attracted any remaining enthusiasts for cooperative living; the Pearsall Group included the latest labour-saving devices which in the longer term made the building of cooperative houses less likely.

The first post-war scheme to succeed was Meadow Way Green South, completing the quadrangle of houses and flats stretching across Meadow Way in Letchworth. The south side was a joint venture by Ruth Pym, Miss Dewe and the Howard Cottage Society, as the north side had been. Pym asked the Society to consider completing the Green in June 1920, and by October a number of prospective tenants had been found.[31] Courtenay Crickmer, the architect of the north side, was asked to draw up plans for the south side, and these were produced by February 1921. Crickmer had spent part of the war working as resident architect on the munitions village at Gretna, with its range of communal facilities. No government funding was available for the south side, but the local council agreed to provide about three-quarters of the capital cost, with Pym and Dewe supplying most of the remainder.[32] Delays caused by the difficulties in obtaining funding held up the start of building until mid-1924, but some of the accommodation was let in October 1924 and the scheme was completed in July 1925.[33]

The south side of the quadrangle comprised a communal dining room and kitchen, seven flats and six cottages, five of the flats having two bedrooms and two having three bedrooms (see Plate 22). Crickmer's original design was for three formal, neo-Georgian blocks of flats laid out around a lawned garden with a small pool and a statue.[34] There was a clear difference in style between the north side, with its complex roof line and more decorative appearance, and the severe design for the south side. Crickmer's plans were altered during the three years between the design stage and building, the six cottages being added and many of the neo-Georgian features disappearing, until the result was an austere and less interesting version of the north side. An intermediate drawing for the south side retains several sets of classical columns, but these have vanished from the final design.[35] The housing at Gretna was the first use of simplified design on a large scale, with neo-Georgian decoration, and Crickmer's initial plans for Meadow Way Green South seem to reflect his wartime design experience.[36] The living rooms of all the flats and the communal dining room were south facing, but the corridors and shared staircases were rather gloomy, as Crickmer had managed to squeeze two or three bedrooms, a living room, bathroom and scullery into a small area (see Figure 12). The dining room, situated on the ground floor with the kitchen, was larger than that on the north side, as it had to cater for the tenants of 13 dwellings as opposed to the 10 of the north side.

One reason for the changes in the original plans may have been the need for a more economic design; Crickmer's first design had a large number of staircases, which would have been expensive to build. Barry Parker, a friend of Ruth Pym's, saw the plans before they were presented to the Howard Cottage Society Board. He wrote to the Society's chairperson in support of the completion of the Green, and enclosed an alternative plan with fewer staircases and more dwellings. No mention was made of Parker's suggestion at the Board's following meetings, but the long-term changes in design may have followed Parker's more economical plans.[37]

The average rent for cottages or flats on the south side of the Green was 19 shillings a week, on top of which residents paid for services, gardening and their midday meal.[38] The system of cooperative housekeeping was similar to that followed by the north side, with each tenant taking responsibility for the housekeeping for two weeks at a time. The menu for the coming fortnight was selected by the housekeeper, who aimed to encourage all tenants to take the midday meal; those who opted out paid a small amount towards running costs.[39] Originally a vegetarian meal was also provided, but this became less popular and was finally dropped. The system of weekday meals continued until August 1976, when it was felt that tenants could do their own cooking more economically. Residents moving to the Green in the early 1950s felt that the meal then gave excellent value for

FIRST FLOOR

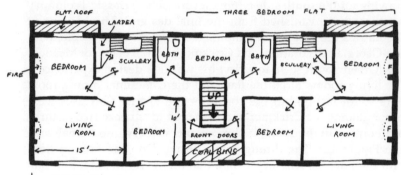

GROUND FLOOR

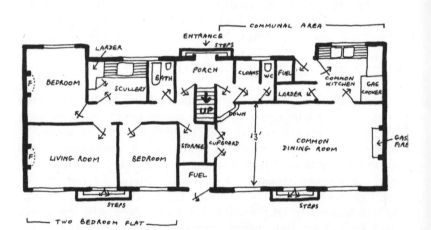

money, although they had been attracted to the Green not by the communal facilities but by its proximity to their workplaces. The cost of the meal was then 1s 3d, according to the scheme's written constitution, which prospective tenants had to agree to abide by. Some families with children lived on the south side, and although the cooperative system worked well both for the families and the single residents, the atmosphere in the dining room was less communal than on the north side. Each house or flat had its own table, and 'you wouldn't dare sit at somebody else's table'. Meals were not social occasions, although the atmosphere was pleasant, with residents chatting as they queued up for service. Several people read books during meals. It is probable that the difference between the collegiate north side and the restaurant-like south side arose because of the preponderance of single tenants on the north side, which had begun as housing for single working women. Families and other residents on the south side treated the meal simply as an opportunity for a cheap meal, and generally did not socialise a great deal.

Although the houses and flats were tightly packed, each had its own garden and privacy was adequate. The communal element of the scheme was seen most clearly in emergencies, when someone was always available to keep an eye on older residents living alone, or to help with minor domestic problems. From the management point of view, Meadow Way Green posed no more problems than any ordinary development, and indeed was always sought after by prospective tenants. The whole quadrangle is still in use, although the south side dining room has now been converted into a flat. The original intention of Ruth Pym and Miss Dewe, the introduction of a form of communal living to Letchworth, proved very successful and endured over half a century. The housing on both sides of the Green has also proved to be popular and adaptable enough to meet modern expectations.

When the First World War ended, Ebenezer Howard was still living in Homesgarth. He and the Garden Cities and Town Planning Association advocated the setting up of a series of new towns after the war, rather than an increase in suburban development. Howard preferred to lead by example instead of continuing with his propaganda work, and in May 1919 he bought the site for the second garden city at Welwyn in Hertfordshire.[40] Welwyn Garden City Ltd was registered in April 1920, and the company set about the development of the town. Despite a poor response from investors and the difficult economic conditions of the early 1920s, by 1940 it was a well-established industrial centre with a population of 18 500.[41] Even in its very early stages, the development company had made clear its intention of encouraging experiments in cooperative housekeeping in the second garden city. Their preliminary announcement in 1919 of the plans for Welwyn referred to cooperative housekeeping and other domestic improvements, and by April 1921 a scheme for 60 cooperative flats and houses was being considered by New Town Housing Ltd.[42] This public utility society had been formed specifically to carry out special housing schemes at Welwyn, and was a subsidiary of the New Town Trust, another public utility which eventually came under the control of Welwyn Garden City Ltd.

New Town Housing's scheme had been drawn up by their own architect, H. Clapham Lander, the cooperative housekeeping enthusiast and designer of Homesgarth. Lander, a council member of the Garden Cities and Town Planning Association, had produced a plan for a central administrative building with two attached wings, each comprising 20 flats. These central buildings were to be surrounded by gardens and tennis courts, and beyond the boundary road were to be 20 detached and semi-detached houses whose residents could use the central facilities (see Figure 13). The flats contained from two to four rooms, and were connected to the common kitchen and dining room by a covered way. Residents of the flats were to have a share in the management of the central services. The basic plan for the new development strongly resembled that of Homesgarth, although the fourth side of the Welwyn quadrangle was less complete than Homesgarth's. Lander had used a combination of flats and houses at Letchworth, a more complex internal arrangement than Welwyn's 40 flats.

Although New Town Housing had stated that they had already secured a site for the proposed cooperative home, nothing further came of the plan until June 1923, when it was presented to the board of the New Town Trust for consideration. A special meeting was convened to discuss the scheme, which now consisted of the 40 flats and central facilities. The board eventually decided to go ahead with the scheme in April 1923 and building began in the following winter, the flats being completed after many delays in January 1925.[43] A woman manager was appointed for the flats,

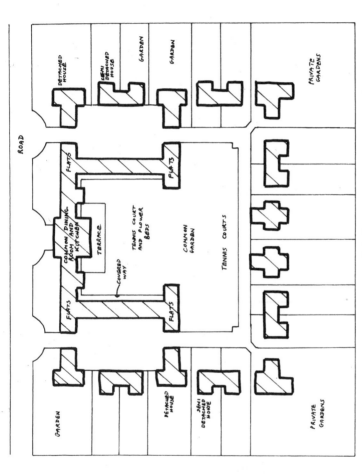

FIGURE 13 *Plan of the original design for Guessens Court, Welwyn Garden City, by H. Clapham Lander (redrawn from New Town Housing Ltd., Welwyn Garden City, April 1921, pp. 4–5, by kind permission of the First Garden City Heritage Museum, Letchworth Garden City)*

which had been named Guessens Court, and by March 12 of the flats were occupied.

The Court was a three-sided quadrangle of flats on two storeys, the quadrangle being completed by the three-storey central facilities block containing the restaurant, kitchen and guest rooms (see Plate 23). The 40 flats each had a living room, bathroom, kitchenette and from one to three bedrooms, access being from a shared staircase. The one-bedroom flats had a considerably smaller living room and bedroom than the larger flats, which were intended for families or groups of friends. Lander's internal planning ensured that no corridor was without natural light from a window or door. The annual rent, which included use of the dining room, varied from £40 for a ground-floor bedsitter to £100 for a first-floor three-bedroom flat, and tenants were required to buy shares in the public utility society.[44] Tenants were also required to spend at least a predetermined minimum sum in the restaurant each week. Maids could be hired by the hour or day, and boot-cleaning and coal-carrying services were provided; the rent covered maintenance of the grounds and use of the tennis courts.

Five years after its opening, it was said of Guessens Court that 'It is fairly well in demand, and just about pays its way.'[45] Several alterations had been made both to the flats and to the central block, while the rent of the largest flats had been reduced by £10 per annum. The restaurant was making a small profit, residents being encouraged to use it by the sale of books of coupons giving a discount on meals.[46] The New Town Trust board decided in 1928 to provide some conventional hotel accommodation in the central block; Welwyn Garden City Development Corporation then took over management of the Court, and the central block became a hotel, although residents of the flats still ate in the communal dining room.[47] In 1970, eight flats became part of the hotel, and the remaining 32 were modernised by the district council and are now used as elderly people's accommodation, a warden living nearby. Guessens Court was successful for a short time in fulfilling its original function, accommodating those 'who desire to be relieved of the burdens of housekeeping', but financial difficulties eventually brought about the change of use of the central block.[48] The Court still retains a communal element, with the provision of a warden service for the residents, and the Court itself provides a pleasant residential environment. Lander's plain design benefits from the use of red tiles and a blue-grey brick in the lower part of the walls, and he also included an entrance archway almost two storeys high. The entrance is flanked by two towers on the outside of the quadrangle, with first-floor balconies, and these unusual details give the Court character and emphasise its calm and enclosure. As in the case of Homesgarth, Lander's design has proved adaptable to modern requirements.

Both Guessens Court and Meadow Way Green South catered for families wishing to cooperate, as did the proposed development at Onslow Garden Village and the Pearsall Group at Letchworth. The Ministry of Health's 1921 report on the provision of women's hostels had emphasised that single working women continued to find great difficulty in obtaining accommodation.[49] Waterlow Court had been built before the First World War as a cooperative home for single working women, and Meadow Way Green North had originally been intended solely for single business and professional women. Several blocks of women's residential chambers had been erected towards the end of the nineteenth century, and after the war efforts to provide decent housing for working women continued. In Liverpool, the Women's Residential Club was opened, having become a registered public utility society in 1924; by 1926 it had 76 members.[50] In Hampstead Garden Suburb, two groups of flats were opened for poorer working women, Queen's Court in 1927 and Emmott Close in 1928. They were not cooperative homes, but bedsitters with shared bathrooms and lavatories.[51]

In Birmingham, George and Elizabeth Cadbury initiated St George's Court, a block of flats for single professional and business women, in 1923. George Cadbury and his brother Richard had moved their factory from central Birmingham into the country, four miles from the city centre at Bournville, in 1879. The model village of Bournville was begun in 1895, and the Bournville Village Trust set up in 1900 in order to improve the housing conditions of Birmingham workers.[52] George Cadbury was one of the first vice-presidents of the Garden City Association, and the first GCA conference was held at Bournville in September 1901. Both George and Elizabeth Cadbury attended the conference; they were both members of the Society of Friends, or Quakers, as were many supporters of the first garden city, including H. Clapham Lander.[53] The Cadburys visited Letchworth in 1905, when Elizabeth presided over a women's housing conference. She had been interested in the problems of women workers for some time, having joined the National Council of Women in 1896.[54] The Society of Friends had always allowed women a strong voice in its affairs, and it may have been their Quaker background combined with Elizabeth's experience of women's housing difficulties which led the Cadburys to form Residential Flats Ltd, the public utility society responsible for St George's Court.

George Cadbury died in October 1922, just before the registration of Residential Flats Ltd in June 1923. Their initial capital of almost £20 000 included a loan from the Trust, now chaired by Elizabeth Cadbury.[55] The Trust's architect, S. Alexander Wilmot, then drew up plans for an open quadrangle of flats to be sited in Bournville, and the block of 32 flats received its first tenants in 1924. Wilmot's red-brick, neo-Georgian quadrangle contained 32 flats, of which four were bedsitters and four had double bedrooms, the rest having single bed recesses (see Plate 24). Each flat in the two-storey block had its own service area, with a sink, larder and facilities for making hot snacks. Bathrooms and toilets were shared, with four or five women using each bathroom. All meals were taken in the ground-floor dining room, which Wilmot had rather strangely sited on the northern, outer side of the quandrangle, overlooking the kitchen yard and the entrances to the flats rather than the inner grass square (see Figure 14). This arrangement did ensure that no living room had a completely northern aspect, however. The kitchen and housekeeper's rooms were situated next to the dining room, and the common room and guest bedrooms were above it. Wilmot's design produced a long, gloomy corridor on each floor, and a first-floor balcony on the opposite side of the corridor to the common room, and therefore less likely to be used. Servants, apart from the lady housekeeper, were accommodated in the attic, in a series of small rooms lit by dormer windows which have now been removed.[56] An annexe consisting of six bedsitters, two bathrooms and a laundry room was added to the Court less than three years after its opening; the bedsitters had proved to be popular because of their low rent.

In its early years, residents paid 15 shillings per week for a bedsitter and 25 shillings per week for a single flat, the rent including rates, some furniture and service.[57] The staff consisted of a lady housekeeper, about four resident maids, a caretaker, two cooks and three or four kitchen assistants. The maids did all the cleaning, including residents' own rooms and bathrooms, would

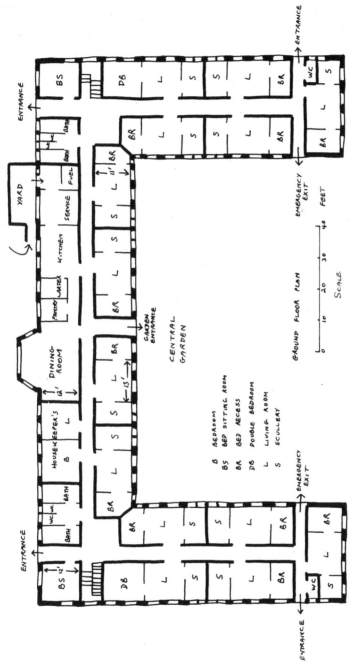

FIGURE 14 *Ground-floor plan of St George's Court, Bournville, by S. Alexander Wilmot (redrawn from plan held by Bournville Village Trust, by kind permission of Bournville Village Trust)*

do ironing and mending, and occasionally served meals out on the lawn. The caretaker brought up coal for residents' fires. One resident who experienced the Court before alterations were made felt the service was 'Excellent . . . You didn't do anything, you had your flat cleaned, all you'd to do was your own personal washing . . . It was really a life of luxury.'[58] Servants appeared to like the Court; staff turnover was low, and there was a greater variety of personal contact than in an ordinary house. The first lady housekeeper appointed to the Court was Miss Georgina Stuart, previously governess to Elizabeth Cadbury's youngest daughter. She stayed for ten years, and 'her social gifts, her artistic taste and friendly approach to others created a happy atmosphere, and made the place a real home for the residents'.[58] The communal atmosphere was encouraged; there were no special seating arrangements in the dining room, everybody normally eating at the two large tables, and the common room was used for card games, meetings and concerts. Residents made friends with those who lived close to them, partly through casual meetings in the corridor on the way to the bathroom or telephone; others were more likely to meet over meals or in the common room.

Elizabeth Cadbury continued to take a great interest in St George's Court, and tried to ensure that residents came from a mixture of professions.[59] Residents were attracted either by the communal dining room, if they disliked or had no time for cooking, or by the prospect of their own flat instead of a hostel bed or lodgings. There was a long waiting list for acceptance at the Court, which had a high reputation locally: 'At one time, if you lived here, in the district, they thought you were Lady Muck. You know, it was quite looked up to.' The Court's governing body was its committee, which was composed of elected representatives of the residents and other interested parties, often connected with the Trust. All residents were encouraged to go to its meetings, but rent payments and repair work were handled by the Trust, not by the Court or Residential Flats. The communal nature of the Court's facilities did not produce any particular management problems for the Trust.

In order to keep the dining room running economically, residents were required to spend a predetermined average sum there each week. Accounts were settled quarterly, and deficits were charged where necessary. This system was unpopular with some residents, although it was possible to spend the minimum amount simply by taking one main meal a day in the dining room. Residents were offered breakfast, lunch, high tea, dinner and Sunday supper, the charges in the early 1950s ranging from breakfast at 8d to dinner at 3 shillings.[60] Although some residents were regarded as difficult to live with, the Court had an extremely low turnover of tenants and the Trust felt it had undoubtedly 'met a very real need'.[61] One resident said of St George's Court in the mid-1950s:

> I thought it was perfect . . . It was ideal for people that were on their own, you see, you could have your privacy, and yet you could be in a community if you wanted, in a way . . . You really had the best of both worlds.

It was a condition of tenancy that residents had to leave on becoming retired or unemployed, and the Court's popularity was reflected in the fact that several retired women managed to retain their flats for long periods by omitting to tell the Trust they had retired. Other residents always colluded in this deception.

By the late 1950s the running costs of the Court were increasing and rents had not risen at the same rate. The standard of service declined and other economies were made, resulting in the accommodation becoming shabby and resembling a hostel rather than a ladies' club. In 1957 it was therefore decided by the Trust and the residents that it would be better to dispense with the dining room and provide all flats with a kitchen, than to maintain the current system at a greatly increased cost. The dining room and common room were converted to flats, and in a further modernisation in 1980 all flats were provided with their own bathrooms. The Court is now used as conventional flat accommodation for men and women, the flats being small and lacking in soundproofing. Wilmot's original plan was not generous in its space standards, so that although modernisation has been possible, the result is a complete loss of the Court's original character. A series of small flats now open on to a dark corridor, with only the grass square inside the quadrangle remaining from the days when the Court was a cooperative home. It is, however, still providing pleasant accommodation for its residents, and was highly successful in fulfilling its initial aims for over 30 years.

Residents of both pre-war and post-war cooperative homes had frequently moved to them because of their convenient location or provision of decent accommodation, rather than specifically to participate in their communal activities. Good accommodation, particularly for single women, had been scarce before the First World War, but there was a great improvement in the housing situation for middle-class households in the late 1920s and 1930s, when private house-building boomed.[62] In spite of cuts in the state housing programme, council houses were being built in numbers far greater than before the war, giving working-class households the option of becoming council tenants rather than renting in the shrinking private sector.[63] Middle-class households found that it was easier to obtain funds for house purchase, and that down payments were small.[64] The 1930s saw an upsurge in sales of domestic electrical appliances for use in homes designed to be labour-saving. The percentage of women working outside the home slowly rose after the war, although many of the new jobs available to women were not well paid.[65] New magazines encouraged women to take more interest in their home life and develop domestic activities into hobbies, rather than emphasising opportunities outside the home.[66] For the increasingly affluent middle-class family, domestic economy was less of a necessity than it had been in pre-war years. New houses were easier to maintain than Victorian homes, and domestic work could be managed by the wife with the aid of electricity and the daily help. The obvious need for communal living had disappeared for this sector of the population, provided the middle-class wife was willing to take on tasks previously performed by servants.

Wifely domesticity did not imply an increase in domestic organisation, and there were still calls for improvements in the efficiency of the home. W. L. George in *Good Housekeeping* of 1923 advocated domestic efficiency, as did Winifred Holtby in 1934, both assuming that increasing numbers of women would undertake paid work:

> There may one day be greater use of co-operation in domestic machinery and planning. There are women who love the snug individualism of their own back-yard, kitchen and parlour. Let them have it. There are others for whom the communal kitchen and restaurant – as in modern luxury flats – the professional cleaner with his electrical equipment, the creche and nursery school, will solve a dozen at present apparently insoluble problems. Men may learn to take a larger share in household work
> . . .[67]

However, the reaction against the forced communality of wartime, and the easy availability of self-contained new housing made the development of middle-class cooperative homes unlikely. Meadow Way Green South and Guessens Court were extensions of pre-war enterprises, Meadow Way Green North having been built in 1914 and Guessens Court being sited in the second garden city. A non-profit-making development such as Brent Garden Village would probably have found difficulty in raising its initial capital, as it could no longer offer the prospect of considerable savings for tenants in the long term; the financial slumps of 1920–1 and 1929 would have discouraged investors from taking risks in unconventional schemes.

Single working women's housing options were gradually improving; although the private rented sector was declining, flats were becoming more numerous, and legislation of 1925 had allowed women full control over their own property.[68] Women who had previously moved to cooperative homes purely to obtain accommodation would be more likely to find self-contained homes elsewhere. Poorer women workers were still in need of good housing, as the Ministry of Health's 1921 report had confirmed, and the housing campaign conducted in 1936 by the Over Thirty Association further illustrated. They produced a pamphlet dealing with the housing situation in London for women earning 35 shillings a week or less, and sent a deputation to the Ministry of Health. The deputation was led by Eleanor Rathbone, Independent MP for the Combined English Universities, who had been involved with the women's movement for many years, and was supported by many women's organisations, including the National Council of Women and the Electrical Association for Women.[69] The aim of the Over Thirty Association was to see single working women recognised as a needy group, eligible for council housing. They suggested that local authorities should build one-room dwellings specifically for single women tenants, who often had to live in inadequate and expensive accommodation and were harassed by landladies. The Ministry's Central Housing Advisory Committee eventually conducted its own perfunctory investigation into the problem, finding little demand from single women for local authority homes. The Association's own survey had shown that where single-person dwellings had been built, waiting lists were long. The reason for the discrepancy probably lay in the fact that single women would not bother to apply to local authorities for accommodation, knowing their needs would have a low priority. The Ministry also doubted whether the women could be defined as working class. It was clear that a demand still existed for homes such as St George's Court and Waterlow Court, but they were unlikely to be profitable as the women themselves could not afford high rents and servants' working conditions gradually improved. High-income middle-class households could still afford several servants, often 'dailies', as wages did not rise during the inter-war years. Highly serviced flats for lower paid women needed servants willing to work long hours, and these were harder to find and more expensive.[70] Only a philanthropic society or trust such as the Bournville Village Trust, with a particular interest in women's housing problems, would have taken on the task of providing decent, inexpensive accommodation for them in the post-war years. Even more highly-paid single women found it difficult to obtain suitable accommodation, as they did not have the financial resources of the middle-class family, yet their status required a high level of personal service. A cooperative home such as St George's Court offered an ideal solution for these women.

The increasing availability of council housing resulted in a general improvement in working-class housing standards, but even by 1935, the Electrical Association for Women (EAW) reported that less than half working-class households had electricity.[71] The EAW found that electric washing machines were popular, as they allowed women to get on with other domestic tasks while the washing was being done, but they also found that hiring charges for electrical appliances were high. They therefore 'suggested that the possibilities of co-operative ownership of certain pieces of apparatus might be explored'.[72] Although there had been no government support for working-class cooperative housekeeping schemes, council flats continued to be built with limited communal facilities, in the tradition of nineteenth-century tenements. The 585 flats erected for the Hackney Borough Council in 1938–40 had a community centre within each quadrangle of flats, containing a hall, clubroom and washhouse with individual washing cubicles and electric washing machines.[73] In Leeds, the Quarry Hill Flats of 1938 were equipped with a central laundry, but the proposed community hall was never built and a swimming pool was removed from the design during the early stages of planning.[74]

One reason for the popularity of flats with local authority architects was the influence of modern movement architecture.[75] Le Corbusier's 1922 Ville Contemporaine was a plan for an elite city, with residential units stacked in blocks provided with hotel service and some communal space.[76] His ideas were ultimately realised in the Unité d'Habitation, built at Marseilles in 1947–52, with its 337 dwellings and integrated shopping arcade, hotel, kindergarten and other communal facilities.[77] The functional aims of Le Corbusier were shared by other modern movement architects in Europe, and in Germany in the 1920s several large working-class estates were built to efficient, labour-saving designs and with communal facilities. The housing was intended to be low rent, light, airy, spacious and functional; both the design and the methods of construction emphasised economy.[78] In Russia, modernists built a 'house-commune' in 1925, a block of flats without kitchens which relied entirely on central servicing. Also in Moscow, another block of flats erected in 1928–9 contained flats with cooking recesses, and was provided with a range of communal facilities; overcrowding of the flats led to their failure.[79]

The ideas of the modern movement reached England mainly through the building of luxury houses and small blocks of private flats, local authorities preferring low-rise estates and traditional styles.[80] Lubetkin's block of flats called Highpoint 1 in north London, built in 1936, were described by Le Corbusier as 'a vertical garden city', residents having the use of a communal tea room, tennis courts, a swimming pool and a garden.[81] Wells Coates' 'minimum' flats built at Hampstead in 1934 contained a bedsitting room, kitchenette and bathroom, and were intended for tenants with incomes above £350 per annum. The services provided included bed-making, shoe-cleaning, laundry collection and window-cleaning, and in its early years meals could be obtained from the staff kitchen, although this service was later reduced.[82] Both Lubetkin's and Coates' flats were examples of socialist planning for workers' housing applied to dwellings for the middle and upper classes.[83] The same functionalist ideas combined with communal facilities were used in highly serviced luxury flats such as Gordon Jeeves' Dolphin Square in Pimlico, with its central sports building and public restaurant.[84] These flats continued the tradition of service flats which did not involve cooperative housekeeping, as there was no commitment from tenants to cooperate; servicing was a purely commercial arrangement.

Modern movement architects were anxious to improve working-class living conditions by providing efficient accommodation of a high standard accompanied by communal facilities. Kensal House, housing association flats built in 1937 in west London, included a social club and nursery school; the architects tried to encourage a village atmosphere with clubs and associations, and felt the school could transform the lives of the children.[85] The aims were similar to those of the philanthropic societies of the nineteenth century which had erected tenements with wash-houses and club rooms. Architects of both working-class and luxury flats in the 1930s applied the same functionalist ideals to their designs. There was support for the idea of the modern flat with communal facilities from the *Daily Worker*, which commented in 1935 that centralised services, including a laundry, creche, kitchen and restaurant were required in high-standard housing accommodation.[86] However, public suspicion of flat-dwelling had not been overcome by the end of the 1930s, although some women's organisations viewed flats favourably as efficient, easily managed homes.[87] The great housing success of the inter-war years was the growth of suburbia, with its millions of self-contained houses and gardens, detested by architects of the modern movement.[88] As housing options for all sections of the population increased in the two decades following the First World War, the economic reasoning behind the advocacy of cooperative housekeeping became less convincing, and advances in house design and the introduction of more efficient domestic appliances made home life simpler. The communal facilities seen by the modern movement as an integral part of working-class life were not always popular, and were most effective when part of luxury housing schemes. Widespread opportunities for households to live independently of one another in decent homes had made the idea of cooperative living seem outmoded. There was no need to make an effort to combine the best of public and private worlds when increased affluence brought the benefits of a comfortable lifestyle without the possible compromises of cooperation. Decent homes were reasonable compensation for the lack of public amenities in suburbia and council estates alike.

As with the First World War, the Second World War eventually brought increases in the number of women employed outside the home, and communal feeding was reintroduced to the public. The conscription of women for war work began in December 1941, and by mid-1943 the proportion of women working was double the figure for 1918. About seven and a half million women were doing paid work by 1943, although this was estimated to be only three-quarters of a million more than would have been the case had pre-war trends continued.[89] Communal feeding began in the blitz, at first as a voluntary response to the emergency, and then in a more organised manner. The London County Council set up 170 Londoners' Meal Service Centres by May 1941, and there were also community kitchens and mobile canteens. The Queen's Messenger Convoys, fleets of vehicles staffed by the Women's Voluntary Service, rushed hot meals to bombed towns. British Restaurants were instigated by the government after the success of the London centres, and were set up by local authorities to provide good, cheap meals. The authorities were guaranteed against loss by the government, but in spite of this, British Restaurants were slow to open, following the pattern of national kitchens in the First World War. Once again, they met opposition from the catering trade. A total of 2160 restaurants had opened by September 1943, and they were found to be very popular.[90] Factory canteens were introduced, as well as free school meals and food supplements for children; the overall effect was an improvement in the general health of the population.[91]

In 1943 the Women's Group on Public Welfare issued a report by their Hygiene Committee on domestic standards and urban life during the early years of the war. The Group, chaired by Margaret Bondfield, had been prompted to consider the matter by the National Federation of Women's Institutes, after women in reception areas for evacuees had protested about the poor health and unpleasant domestic habits of the women and children allotted to them.[92] The Committee reviewed the eating habits of city-dwellers, and commended the local fish and chip shop for providing fresh, wholesome food. 'The lesson of the fish and chip shop is that everyone not only wants, but needs, often imperatively, the possibility of getting meals without having to prepare them.'[93] The Committee went on to suggest that a variety of take-away food services could be sited in the poorer areas of cities, and said of British Restaurants that they had 'made a useful beginning, and it is to be hoped that commercial interests will not be allowed to bring about their abolition after the war'. The

Committee recommended that wartime experience should be used in the setting up of a large-scale system of national restaurants, works canteens and communal cafes and kitchens. In spite of this enthusiasm and the popularity of the British Restaurants, only two years after the ending of the war James Callaghan, later to become Prime Minister, was speaking on behalf of 'the ordinary British housewife' in a House of Commons debate on domestic supplies:

> I read, recently, that something like 190 million meals a year were served in public places, works canteens, and other institutions. That is a lot of meals. The housewife feels – and I am inclined to agree with her – that the emphasis should be turned from the direction of public feeding back to private feeding.[94]

The Parliamentary Secretary to the Ministry of Food, Dr Edith Summerskill, replied that she felt housewives would be dismayed if cafes or canteens were to close, leaving them to provide an extra meal at home.[95] It was 1954 before food rationing finally ended, and although the British Restaurants disappeared, the habit of eating out grew markedly after the war.[96]

Post-war planning began in 1940; the acceptability of social welfare planning had increased, partly as a result of wartime conditions, but although a range of communal facilities was now seen as necessary for new housing developments, there was no lobby for cooperative housekeeping.[97] The individual home had been the basis of pre-war house-building, and had been found to be reasonably efficient as electricity became widely available and domestic appliances more commonly owned. After the war, alternatives to the self-contained home were rarely put forward, and the emphasis in planning for housing needs was on the provision of extra facilities outside the home to ease the housewife's task. The Beveridge Report itself, the basis of the post-war welfare state, suggested that a comprehensive health service should include domestic help for households where the housewife needed hospital treatment, and commented on the difficulty of women's tasks in the home if no communal facilities existed.[98] The Labour government elected in July 1945 had pledged in its manifesto to build labour-saving homes with efficient utility services, and in earlier publicity directed at women had emphasised the independence of the individual home:

your kitchen is the core of your home, your workshop, where you spend much of your time, out of which come the good meals and the clean linen which help to make yours a happy household.[99]

As part of the initial drive to increase the amount of housing accommodation available after the war, the government appealed to families to share their homes with other families. This did not result in any sharing of cooking facilities, however, as the government removed legal barriers preventing the installation of separate kitchens.[100] The centralised planning of the welfare state did not cross the threshold of the family home.

Post-war minimum standards for state house design were set by the Dudley Committee which reported in 1944. The Committee criticised inter-war housing for its lack of provision of club buildings, shops, schools and other amenities, and noted the new concept of the planned community which had emerged between the wars.[101] These 'neighbourhood units' were to be provided with a full range of social amenities to aid the development of community life; the neighbourhood centre might include 'places of worship, the branch-library, a cinema, public house, branch administrative buildings, the necessary clinics, smaller club buildings, and a group of shops'.[102] The Committee favoured houses rather than flats, particularly for families with children, but allowed that some smaller households preferred flats. It felt that the inadequate laundry facilities often provided in flats built between the wars could be improved by the introduction of modern communal laundries. It suggested that prejudice against the communal laundry could be overcome by allocating each tenant a separate washing machine within the laundry for her exclusive use, and increasing the privacy of the whole operation. It also suggested the provision of a creche, and was against the inclusion of utility rooms in flats, hoping 'that the need for separate provision will diminish as communal laundries grow in popularity'.[103]

An investigation of communal laundry facilities conducted in March 1947 for the Ministry of Works found that sharing the facilities caused friction between tenants. The laundries were also disliked because of the need to carry water and washing, and the time spent away from home. The report noted that the bag wash scheme proposed in the Tudor Walters Report had never been put into practice, and concluded that:

> As efficient and cheap laundry services are developed which
> will give real help to the housewife . . . and an adequate piped
> supply of hot water becomes more generally available in the
> home, the value of communal laundry facilities will tend to
> diminish.[104]

The Women's Cooperative Guild, one of the many women's
organisations which had given evidence to the Dudley Committee, agreed that home washing was becoming increasingly important, their 1946 Congress having passed a resolution calling for all
new family houses to be equipped with electric washing
machines, their cost to be included in the rent.[105]

There was some post-war opinion in favour of a more comprehensive range of communal facilities than those outlined in
the Dudley Report, which left the independence of the individual
home unchallenged. At the 1946 Labour Party Conference, housewives were described as becoming an oppressed proletariat, and
one speaker suggested that future housing should be provided with 'communal central kitchens with a hot meals delivery
service, properly staffed nurseries and central play rooms, district
heating centres and even communal sewing centres'.[106] More
importantly, the final report of the New Towns Committee, issued
in July 1946, recommended that consideration should be given to
the provision of amenities such as restaurants and clubrooms
during the planning of groups of dwellings. The Committee had
been impressed by Swedish community houses for families and
single people, and commented that: 'Views differ as to the extent
to which communal facilities of this sort would be acceptable in
Great Britain, but they offer such obvious convenience that they
should be carefully considered.'[107] However, the New Towns Act,
allowing for sites for new towns to be designated and development corporations to be set up, became law only two days after
the report was published, and it appears that the Committee's
recommendation on community houses was ignored. The planning of the first new town at Stevenage was begun even before
the Committee had started its work.[108]

The strongest criticism of the Dudley Report's concept of the
isolated, individual home came from the Reilly Plan, an extension
of Sir Charles Reilly's post-war plan for Birkenhead. Reilly had

been Professor of Architecture at the University of Liverpool, and originated their Department of Civic Design in 1908.[109] His Birkenhead plan included 'Reilly Greens', small village greens which most houses adjoined, while the Reilly Plan carried this idea further, grouping three to five greens around a community centre which contained a restaurant, bar, sports and hobbies areas, library and hall.[110] The Reilly Plan criticised the principle implicit in the Dudley Report that

> the house is the home, the whole home and nothing but the home; that it is right and proper that . . . cooking, eating, washing-up, laundering, study, social intercourse and recreation . . . should take place in the house and nowhere else.[111]

The Plan's alternative was to 'create a physical setting in which spontaneous cooperation between neighbour and neighbour is likely to develop' by linking the private home with semi-public amenities. Family houses situated around the village greens would not contain ordinary kitchens, as the community centre's restaurant provided a meals service, 'a real communal service, and not the same thing as a British Restaurant'. The catering service would supply all meals at low prices, and would be managed by a committee of unpaid residents. Houses would be provided with small electric cookers for emergencies, and the system would leave women free to undertake paid work.[112] The Plan sought to provide an organic link between the individual house and the social amenities, which the Dudley Report had not attempted in its suggestion of reasonable access to amenities within the neighbourhood. The Plan's author felt this arrangement completely ignored 'the universal pre-blitz, inter-blitz and post-blitz phenomenon of frigid isolationism between neighbours in the ordinary street, which is surely a small enough "neighbourhood".'[113]

Although the neighbourhood unit was influential in post-war state housing plans, there was little introduction of shared facilities along the lines of the Reilly Plan. Only Bilston and Dudley councils showed any interest in implementing the details of Reilly's community planning, Dudley beginning an estate on modified 'Reilly green' lines in 1950.[114] The high housing standards set by Aneurin Bevan at the Ministry of Health declined after he had left the Ministry, and the Conservative government of 1951 presided over a further reduction in standards.[115] High-rise flat-building was on the increase from the late 1950s, and although it was government policy to provide a wide range of amenities on estates with flats, these were sometimes omitted on grounds of speed or economy.[116] Three blocks of eleven-storey flats erected in Coventry in 1955 had originally been designed with a communal laundry, but this was withdrawn in favour of equipping all flats with washing machines and drying cabinets; however, these were later lost after negotiations with central government.[117] By the early 1950s, husbands in some working-class homes were beginning to undertake a few domestic duties, and the ownership of domestic appliances was becoming more widespread; by 1961, over one-third of all working-class households owned a washing machine.[118] The declining housing standards of the 1950s eventually provoked the setting up of another committee in 1959 to consider house design; its report, known as the Parker Morris Report, was published in December 1961, and recommended standards for both public and private housing.[119] The Report made no mention whatsoever of communal facilities or shared amenities, except for a reference to children's playspace. Although the committee concentrated on the internal design of dwellings, it took into account the general planning of residential areas and their amenities; in spite of this, its report confirmed the self-contained, individual home as the model for the future.[120] The Parker Morris space and heating standards became mandatory in state housing from January 1969.[121]

In the private sector, post-war housing showed a qualitative improvement in comparison with pre-war speculative building, and the percentage of owner-occupied houses continued to increase.[122] Domestic servants had almost disappeared by 1951, with only 1.2 per cent of households still keeping a resident servant; kitchen planning concentrated on efficiency with the provision of labour-saving devices.[123] The private house of the mid-1960s was medium sized, with four to six rooms, and often with a kitchen smaller than in a council house, although the living area was likely to be larger.[124] Building firms experimented with styles, but not with the self-contained nature of the house itself. It appeared that cooperative homes had disappeared for good, the reasons for their original popularity having been overtaken by improvements in domestic appliances, the increasing cost of servants and a wider choice of housing for both single people and families.

Discussion of associated homes had been taking place for many years before the idea of cooperative housekeeping arrived in England in 1868, and it was to be over a century until its demise when communal dining was abandoned at Meadow Way Green. The reasons behind the rise and decline of cooperative house-keeping, and its influence on house design and the conduct of domestic life, will be discussed in the following chapter. The story of communal living did not end with the building of the final cooperative home in the 1920s, however; cooperative house-keeping had aimed to change the nature of domestic organisation around the turn of the century, and further adaptations of commu-nal living were to arise in the 1960s and 1970s. These new forms of communal living were more relevant to the changed conditions and expectations of the second half of the twentieth century than cooperative housekeeping in its original form, but the aim of reorganising domestic life was exactly the same. The final chapter of the book considers these new communal schemes, and the lessons to be drawn from the entire history of domestic coop-eration.

10 The Rise and Fall of the Cooperative Housekeeping Movement

A total of 15 cooperative housekeeping developments were erected in England between 1874 and 1925, and although the last of their communal functions disappeared in 1976, at least ten of the developments are still in use as housing (see Table 1). Many more developments were proposed,and the principles of cooperative housekeeping provoked much discussion in the press, both of cooperative homes and conventional housekeeping. Earlier chapters have detailed the efforts of pioneers of the cooperative housekeeping movement to propagate their form of domestic revolution, and it remains to assess the impact of cooperative homes on English house design and domestic life. A total of 15 experimental homes built in just over half a century does not immediately appear to constitute any form of revolution.

The basis of the cooperative home was its central dining hall and kitchen, each individual dwelling having only a small kitchenette, unsuitable for cooking large meals. The object of taking part in a cooperative housekeeping experiment was to maintain standards of domestic service without incurring increased costs. Privacy was to be heightened by the removal of the resident domestic servant. The proposed domestic revolution was simply the movement of labour-intensive, hot and smelly cooking out of the individual home and into a central building. Very few of the idea's original advocates in England emphasised the possibilities opened up to women by a reduction in their domestic responsibilities, except to say that wives would be less tired and thus better able to care for their families. In using their cooperative dwellings, both single people and families would extend their occupation of areas previously considered the province of the servants alone. Although kitchenettes were small, they were still adequate to cook snacks; instead of the kitchenless house freeing the housewife or single woman from the burden of supervising cooking, it was more likely to result in her undertaking light

TABLE 1 *English cooperative housekeeping developments*

Date	Development	Site	Mixed/ women	Present use
1874	Stamford Hill	London	M	Unknown
1889	Ladies' Residential Chambers	Chenies Street, Bloomsbury	W	Housing
1889	Sloane Gardens House	Belgravia	W	Unknown
1892	York Street	Marylebone	W	Housing
1899	Fabian house	Canning Town	M	Demolished
1905	Pair of cottages	Letchworth	M	Unknown
1909	Waterlow Court	Hampstead Garden Suburb	W	Housing
1910	Homesgarth	Letchworth	M	Housing
1911	Brent Garden Village	London	M	Housing
1912	Melvin Hall	Golders Green	M	Demolished
1914	Priory Road	Hampstead	M	Housing
1914	Meadow Way Green North	Letchworth	W	Housing
1924	Meadow Way Green South	Letchworth	M	Housing
1924	St George's Court	Bournville, Birmingham	W	Housing
1925	Guessens Court	Welwyn Garden City	M	Housing

cooking tasks more rapidly than would have been the case in homes with non-resident daily servants. In this sense, the kitchen was not removed from the middle-class home but attached to it securely as an integral part, albeit still occupied by the wife alone.[1] Her duties had changed from supervision at all times to occasional preparation.

The removal of the kitchen and resident servant allowed the entire house to be opened up for use by the resident household, the servants' bedrooms and any other accommodation being transferred to the central building. Control over the house by the owner or tenant became total; the daily servant might be encountered at certain set hours, but otherwise, the only point of

contact between occupiers and servants was in the central building, where the servants' own quarters were well hidden. The
dining hall was a more neutral space than the family dining room,
its partial occupation by servants impinging only slightly on the
privacy of the family meal. Servants' and occupiers' living quarters
were completely segregated, the creation of the dining hall defin-
ing the area where prolonged interaction between servant and
household might take place. It was not completely socially neutral,
being owned by the cooperators, but it allowed servants to perform their functions in a space which was not the direct responsibility of the cooperators. Instead of the servant being encouraged
to become part of the household, the relationship was now
indirect and conducted through a housekeeper. This change in
status from household member to employee was accompanied, in
theory, by an improvement in conditions of service. The creation
of the dining room as a neutral space reflects the evolution of the
public street during the nineteenth century, as it became an area
where several functions could be performed with a minimum of
interactions between classes.[2]

The common dining room could also be seen as a symbol of
progress in the organisation of domestic work. Unlike the vast
blocks of catering flats, cooperative developments retained the
small scale of the individual home, even the early ladies' residential flats which were no more than six storeys high. The
growth of the garden city movement and the increase in suburban
house-building provided opportunities for cooperative housekeeping developments on the domestic scale; the attempt to maintain the status quo with respect to service and domestic economy
extended to the design and fabric of the house. It is interesting
to note that Le Corbusier was influenced by the design of Homesgarth, although his apartment blocks were on a much larger scale
and more luxurious.[3] The general design of cooperative homes
also reflected the unchanged division of responsibilities within
the home. Although some theoretical writing on cooperative
housekeeping had emphasised its emancipatory possibilities for
both women tenants and servants, the anglicised adaptation of
the idea resulted in a stress on the purely organisational aspects
of house design within an unaltered social setting. Single women
benefited most from domestic cooperation, as it offered them
an independent, serviced home life which had previously been

unavailable; wives, however, only gained changes in their undiminished domestic duties.

Of all the English writers on cooperative housekeeping, it was only Herbage Edwards, resident in and supporter of Brent Garden Village, who advocated domestic reorganisation as a means to the increased participation of women in paid work outside the home. Few male writers except Edward Carpenter had suggested that men could be expected to undertake even some part of women's domestic duties. In America, the situation was different; Melusina Fay Peirce advocated economic independence for women, whilst Charlotte Perkins Gilman felt that socialised domestic work was a prerequisite of human progress and women's economic independence. More experimental cooperative housing developments took place in America than in England, and although there was no domestic revolution in either country, the difference of approach to the problem of domestic reorganisation can be explained by considering women's status in the nineteenth century.[4] American feminism began early, building on the experience of pioneer women in opening up the west, and later the participation of middle-class women in the anti-slavery cause until the formal founding of the feminist movement in 1848.[5] In England, socialist feminism was strongly advocated in the early years of the nineteenth century, but with the decline of Owenite socialism, feminist reform movements with aims unrelated to socialism became prominent.[6] Although many of the feminist leaders of the British and American anti-slavery movements were in direct contact, British feminism was a generally more moderate force than its American equivalent.[7] American feminists found support in evangelicism, but British churches did not encourage women's active participation; British women were more likely to be attracted to philanthropic reforming activities which did not challenge the social structure.[8]

Women's generally lower status in England as compared to America was reflected in the activities of both wives and women servants. The American constitutional emphasis on liberty quickened the demise of the domestic servant, whereas in England there was no democratic impulse to transform the home; servant labour could be replaced with a wife's labour rather than a technological solution sought.[9] Even in America, when household work was rationalised it was not communalised, although this would have been technically possible.[10] When domestic reorganisation was presented to an English audience as an opportunity for women to become economically independent, as in Charlotte Perkins Gilman's lectures, the idea was derided as having socialist overtones. Its widespread acceptability was ensured only if cooperation could be seen primarily as a means to domestic economy. Women had little capital with which to begin their own experiments in cooperative housing. Most of the nineteenth-century English cooperative homes were built for single working women, a group only marginally involved with conventional home life and thus by definition unable to play the part of the idealised woman of the house. English middle-class wives, used to their domestic role and accepting the existence of servants without question, were not ready or willing to take part in a domestic revolution unsupported by their husbands. The suffrage movement contained some individuals interested in the provision of decent accommodation for single working women, but it was a single-issue movement, working for suffrage and therefore women's independence. Working towards domestic reorganisation before suffrage had been won could even have been seen as a distraction from the main purpose of the movement. With little likelihood of support from most radical middle-class women or conventional middle-class households, the radical form of cooperative housekeeping was rejected as irrelevant, a dilution of the basic theory being used in a travesty of the original intentions as a means of ensuring the continuance of the Victorian middle-class lifestyle into the twentieth century.

Cooperative housekeeping had no application to working-class households when presented simply as a means to domestic economy and increased privacy, as there were no resident servants to remove from the home. Women servants, of course, would be directly affected by the institution of a cooperative housekeeping development, but might have considered it similar to working under hotel conditions. The ideas of Charlotte Perkins Gilman certainly had working-class support, but there was no finance available for housing experiments and many working-class men were against any form of domestic cooperation. Although the suffrage movement had a strong working-class element, there was little evidence that middle-class and working-class women saw strong enough similarities in their domestic lives to act together in an attempt to change male attitudes towards home life. The main point of conflict was the presence of servants in the middle-class household; domestic reorganisation implied a change in status for domestic workers, and the possibility of middle-class women undertaking their own domestic tasks. This rise in status was commended by the advocates of a domestic revolution, but it proved easier to construct new forms of cooperative housing than to change middle-class attitudes towards domestic service. It was the application of technology which finally brought about some changes in the perception of household work.

Of the 15 cooperative housekeeping developments erected around the turn of the century, those intended for single working women had the greatest effect on their tenants' lives, allowing them to take paid work and have a decent home. A middle-class wife in a cooperative dwelling did have more control over its entire area than had been the case when servants were in residence, but the main impact of the introduction of the theory of cooperative housekeeping to England was that it provoked continuing discussion by both men and women on the organisation of the household. Many women felt that an increase in the number of women architects would produce improvements in house design. As the servant problem became important to middle-class households, comments on the inconvenience of contemporary homes were more frequent. In 1888, Mrs Panton strongly suggested 'that female architects for domestic architecture solely would be a great help to all who have to live in houses planned and executed by men who have no idea of comfort. . .'[11] while over 20 years later, the Letchworth resident of a servantless house felt that the planning of labour-saving flats and houses needed women architects: 'As house architects men are a glaring failure. Let them build churches, town halls and theatres, but let women plan our houses.'[12] Women were excluded from the RIBA until 1898, architecture being considered an all-male province, although there were 12 practising women architects in London in 1891. There were also several women interior designers working in the late nineteenth century, both interior design and house design being seen as more appropriate for women.[13] Even by 1921, the census showed only five women architects in London, and none were elected to the RIBA between 1900 and 1922.[14] Lack of official recognition did not, however, prevent women from designing their own houses; in 1845, Harriet Martineau, with no previous architectural experience, planned her own house at Ambleside in the Lake District. She wrote: 'Then came the amusement of planning my house, which I did all myself . . . The whole scheme was fortunate and charming. There is not a single blunder or nuisance in my pretty house.'[15] The weaver Ethel Mairet designed a bungalow in Devon and a house in Sussex for her own use; the bungalow, built in 1912, had plain walls and doors, large windows and built-in storage space. The Sussex house, erected in 1919, contained a double-height weaving room and was built in the arts and crafts style; Mairet produced the original plans for both dwellings.[16]

None of the women involved in designing cooperative homes were qualified architects, all of them acting through qualified male architects to introduce their innovations. Henrietta Barnett insisted that each flat at Waterlow Court should have its own bath, sitting room and bedroom, as well as the shared restaurant and common room. Ruth Pym and Miss Dewe were responsible for the basic plan of the first development at Meadow Way Green, while Alice Melvin planned Brent Garden Village and closely supervised the design of the houses. The first plan for a block of flats in the Village was a clear example of kitchenless dwellings attached to central facilities, but the original plan was later replaced, and Alice Melvin ceased to have any contact with the Village. Plans for several unbuilt cooperative developments were also drawn up by women, including the architect Annie Hall. The discussion of cooperative homes and domestic reorganisation allowed women to enter the public debate on house design, and to suggest changes to conventional plans which might have been completely unacceptable without the theoretical context of cooperation. Although the anglicised version of cooperative housekeeping did nothing to assist the economic independence of married women, it did help single women, and provided a platform for the expression of women's ideas on housing. Women who were not architecturally qualified found they were able to contribute to the process of house design, and thus gain more control over their own living conditions; the publicity these experiments attracted helped to ensure that all women became more critical of house design in general. The original theories of domestic reorganisation were subversive in intention, and although their initial results in England reinforced some aspects of the middle-class lifestyle, they continued to offer the possibility of an alternative lifestyle to those willing to reconsider the conventional home.

The progress of the cooperative housekeeping movement was severely retarded by the social and economic changes which took place during and after the First World War. Before the war, domestic reorganisation had appeared to offer a cost-effective solution to the servant problem and an opportunity for single working women to obtain decent accommodation. The forced communalism of the war years, the difficulty of finding cheap resident servants, the increase of alternative forms of accommodation and the spread of technology into the home made domestic cooperation a less attractive option. Three of cooperative housekeeping's most important publicists, Ebenezer Howard, H. Clapham Lander and Alice Melvin, were active before the war, and although there were three post-war developments, the movement did not adapt to post-war conditions by decreasing its reliance on servants or emphasising the social gains available in cooperative housing developments.

Had there been an attempt by a public utility society to erect a working-class cooperative home before the war, it is likely that funding would have been sought from the Public Works Loan Board, which could lend up to two-thirds of the value of the property for up to 40 years.[17] In the years leading up to the war, state assistance for public utility societies to build on garden city lines was seen by central government as the primary means of improving working-class housing conditions.[18] The societies were not evenly spread throughout the country, and their central accounting was far from exemplary, so that when the post-war housing programme came to be considered in the Ministry of Reconstruction, it was felt that the societies alone could not be expected to erect the large number of houses required.[19]

The need for a crash programme of house-building after the war was stated by a Ministry of Reconstruction advisory panel chaired by Lord Salisbury and including Beatrice Webb and Seebohm Rowntree. The panel estimated that, should the war end, in 1917, a total of 300 000 houses would be required in 1918 to ease the housing shortage.[20] The panel, dominated by Fabians, felt that the local authorities were the only bodies capable of carrying out such a huge building programme successfully, but the Treasury were against the idea as it would involve losses to be born by the Exchequer.[21] The Treasury favoured loan support for the public utility societies, as this lessened the possibility of any ultimate losses. The 1919 Housing and Town Planning Act increased aid to the public utilities and committed the government to bearing losses above the product of a one penny rate on local authority housing programmes, but large authorities had to raise their own capital for housing schemes, and this proved extremely difficult.[22] The Ministry of Health's Housing Committee continued to urge that increased funding be given to public utilities, since the Treasury would profit from this tactic.[23] However, the housing programme, which originally had strong all-party support, was severely reduced in July 1921, due partly to the recommendations of the Cunliffe Report concerning post-war expenditure.[24] The report recommended strict control of public borrowing, and was accepted by the Treasury; although the housing campaign was cut short, it had established the place of local authority housing in national housing provision.

Salisbury's advisory panel had seen the housing programme as a remedy suitable for the post-war situation, 'which may not necessarily be part of an ultimate permanent measure of reform'.[25] Treasury support for public utility societies might have ensured their continued growth after the war had the state housing programme not been undertaken on such a large scale and carried out to such high standards. The societies found it difficult to finance building from their own funds, as they were not exempted from the rent control laws of 1915.[26] The greater availability of local authority housing probably discouraged potential investment in public utility societies on the part of prospective tenants. Although local authorities were allowed to delegate some of their housing activities to the societies, this rarely happened as the authorities were protected from any loss by the 1919 Act, and delegation would have slowed the expansion of their organisations.[27] The possibility of increasing public utility provision after the emergency had been retained under the 1919 Act, but although the number of land and housing societies rose sharply in 1919–20, in the following five years the numbers were static.[28] The war, in provoking the government into beginning a large state housing programme, had also taken the initiative in working-class housing provision from the public utility societies. The societies had Treasury support, but their efforts were not on the same scale

as those of the authorities, and with the decline in their importance went a decline in the likelihood of a working-class cooperative home being built.

The increased wartime provision of communal facilities connected with childcare encouraged discussion within the labour
movement concerning the relative responsibilities of state and
individual household for bringing up children.[29] The Social Democratic Federation was the only party advocating communal childrearing, while the mainstream labour movement preferred to try
to improve state support for the family.[30] The influential Women's
Cooperative Guild concentrated on obtaining a variety of
maternity benefits, and although they were well aware of the
effects of poor housing conditions on health, did not campaign
directly for improved housing provision.[31] Cooperative childcare
facilities, as opposed to better maternity care, were not advocated
by the labour movement in the early twentieth century, and other
communal facilities were accepted only in times of great need (as
with national kitchens) or rejected outright if at all possible (in
the case of washhouses). Communal facilities could be seen as a
threat to the family in a working-class culture centred on home
life.[32] Certain domestic activities had been conducted communally
during the war, but wartime communal provision was not necessarily translated into post-war state aid. Communal feeding, and
thus cooperative housekeeping, were not acceptable as permanent
extensions of the state or other organisations into the home.
Although the wartime and post-war improvements in state support for motherhood resulted in a stream of expert visitors to the
working-class home, they simply replaced the nineteenth-century
philanthropists;[33] the overall privacy of the home was dramatically
increased by the provision of state housing. For working-class
households, any domestic revolution would, as Marion Phillips
put it, take the form of mass provision of comfortable cottages,
not the shared facilities which were so revolutionary to the middle
class.[34]

Women were invited to advise the government on the type of
housing provision required after the First World War, but their
advice was often overlooked or ignored. This occurred because
they were frequently placed on peripheral committees, such as the
Women's Housing Sub-Committee, and their recommendations
involved increased standards and therefore more expense. The

WHSC's findings were echoed by those of the influential Tudor Walters Committee, in slightly watered-down form, but the WHSC's first report fell foul of the LGB, which was attempting to retain its pre-war housing standards. The LGB was able to delay the report's publication because of the impotence of the WHSC within the departmental system. The report was never published in full, and the final WHSC report was overtaken by the publication of the Tudor Walters Report. However, this should not be seen as an attack on women's views on house design, more the results of an interdepartmental feud in which the WHSC became unwittingly involved. State housing standards improved dramatically after the war, women's arguments on design and use of space having been bypassed. The crucial point concerning women's participation on government committees is that their status was lower than that of architects or civil servants; they were required to advise with reference to the 'convenience of the housewife', and were isolated on women's committees, never gaining access to the influential expert committees. The 'user's view' of the home was less important than that of the designer; the arrival of the modern movement was to emphasise this ascendancy of the expert.

Working women themselves were in favour of the comfortable cottage as their ideal future home for the post-war years. The cottage – they felt a family should never have to live in a flat – would be large enough to enable them to bring up a family properly and to live a civilised life; it would have a parlour, separate bathroom, central heating and a supply of hot and cold running water.[35] Decent cottages would have been revolutionary in the context of the expectations of working-class women, although their position as housewives with sole domestic responsibility would have remained unaltered. There was little support for any dramatic change in lifestyle which would have constituted a true domestic revolution; communal facilities were constantly rejected, with their overtones of the supervised, low-status tenements of the past with their poor facilities. In 1931, a London County Council architect commented that communal facilities seemed to be unpopular because

> You are up against the innate desire of the English working man and his wife to have a place of their own . . . You cannot get our folk to take advantage of any communal amenity. The nearest approach we can get to it is a common recreation

ground, or an open space in which all the mothers and children can sit out in the air.[36]

The poor quality of much working-class housing before the First World War was a result of the economics of the house-building industry.[37] Workers needed to live close to their city centre workplaces, but could not afford to pay high rents and often lived in severely overcrowded conditions. The development of the railways and electric tramways brought suburbanisation and the prospect of a home away from the city centre for the better-paid workers. After the turn of the century, the garden city movement offered workers homes in the country and jobs nearby. This is not to say that middle-class norms of good housing were thrust upon working-class tenants, as some critics have suggested.[38] Previous middle-class attempts to design suitable homes for working-class tenants, the model dwelling and the tenement with communal facilities, had been disliked by many of their occupants. Nineteenth-century flats in Yorkshire and Lancashire were never popular, tenants wanting their own front door and being hostile to the appearance of the blocks.[39]

Although the design of workers' houses advocated by the garden city movement and supported by the Tudor Walters Report bore a resemblance to middle-class homes on a smaller scale, they represented the realisation of the comfortable cottage rather than working-class aspirations to a middle-class lifestyle. The English idealisation of rural life by all classes since the seventeenth century has been well documented,[40] and Muthesius commented on the middle- and upper-class predilection for rural life in *The English House* in 1904:

The Englishman hurries up to town for the sole purpose of doing business. In the evening he hastens back to the heart of his family and makes no bones about travelling for up to an hour by railway in order to spend his few hours of leisure as far away as possible from the bustle of the metropolis. In England one does not 'live' in the city, one merely stays there.[41]

The rapid growth of artisan suburbs around the turn of the century mirrored middle-class dislike of city living;[42] post-war local authority housing represented the extension of the opportunity to live in a house with a garden to the poorest section of the population. On the occasion of the presentation to Raymond Unwin of the RIBA's Royal Gold Medal in 1937, he and Barry Parker were described as having 'materialised the Englishman's ideal conception of home as a unit of house and garden combined'.[43] The local authority cottage was a realistic translation into practical, urban terms of the longing for an idealised country life; it provided improved housing conditions for working-class tenants, although neither the comfortable cottage nor real country life presented any challenge to the housewife's sole responsibility for domestic tasks.

The strength of feeling for the individual home, situated in the country or somewhere approximating to it, did nothing to increase the acceptability of the idea of cooperative housekeeping to either the middle or working classes. It is surprising that the idea of domestic reorganisation has persisted in the face of such opposition; although it appealed to the middle class on economic grounds, and for some was a socialistic ideal, a more attractive alternative lifestyle for the working class was represented by the Chartist cottage. It survived because its practical implications were applicable to a variety of circumstances. In its original revolutionary form, women were to be freed from the constraints of purely domestic life, to undertake paid work if they wished. At the same time, improvements were to be made in domestic service and economy. The English tradition of thought on domestic economy concentrated solely on improvements in home life, seeing progress as represented by advances in domestic appliances; women were to retain their domestic responsibilities, although drudgery was to be lessened. Cooperative housekeeping's appeal to conservative thinkers was that of a new method of organising home life; all revolutionary implications were disregarded as irrelevant. Thus as the servant problem was perceived to be increasing by late Victorian households, cooperative housekeeping appeared to be a viable alternative lifestyle. Interest in it declined when the servant problem was diminished and the role of the middle-class wife changed from controller of servants to domestic worker aided by electricity and the daily maid.

The English adaptation of cooperative housekeeping which came closest to accepting the revolutionary implications was its application to the needs of single women workers. Only at one development did residents cooperate to perform domestic work, but the system freed them to take paid work. As these establishments accepted single (including widowed) women only, they did not challenge the division of domestic work within the family home.

The attraction of cooperative housekeeping for the theorists of the garden city movement lay in the prospect of an alternative lifestyle, or even an alternative society, which it presented. The history of utopian thinking and attempts to set up alternative communities stretches back to medieval times.[44] In the nineteenth century, many communities were begun in opposition to the capitalist system, but there were also a series of model communities set up towards the end of the century which reflected the ideals of the new industrial society.[45] The garden city was an attempt to mitigate the worst effects of industrialisation by combining town and country; to its supporters, cooperative housekeeping represented a progressive lifestyle which would liberate both men and women to enjoy the benefits of the new garden cities and suburbs.

Cooperative housekeeping's relationship to home life was always that of a representation of an idealised future, offering the prospect of superficial improvement or complete revolution, depending on the view of any particular advocate. Frustration with contemporary lifestyles perpetually caused discussion of alternatives, in the continuing tradition of utopian thinking. The adaptability of cooperative housekeeping as an idea ensured its survival, but also meant that its full implications could be ignored. Its rise and fall did not bring domestic revolution, but helped to carry forward discussion of the nature of home life and caused the building of homes which were liberating in intent and practice for many of their occupants. Women took the opportunity to put forward their views on house design, and in some cases put their own ideas into practice. The problem of the division of domestic responsibility between men and women remained for future generations to solve; further challenges to conventional home life were to occur in the 1960s, and the final chapter assesses their relationship to the original revolutionary content of cooperative housekeeping.

11 Communal Living Today

Between 1960 and 1982, over five million new homes were built in the United Kingdom, and the proportion of owner-occupied dwellings increased to 59 per cent from just under 50 per cent in 1970.[1] There was a sharp drop in local authority housing starts in 1977, and the decline in public-sector housing activity continued until 1982; the number of housing association dwellings built in 1982 was only just over half the number built in 1978.[2] As housing starts decreased, the total number of households in Britain increased, by over a million between 1971 and 1981, and the average household size dropped from 3.09 people in 1961 to 2.64 in 1982.[3] There has been a concomitant increase in housing provision for single people and the elderly, the number of single-person pensioner households more than doubling in the 20 years before 1982.[4] The Parker Morris Report recommended standards for public and private sector housing, first published in 1961 and made mandatory for public housing in 1969, were withdrawn in April 1981.[5]

Although a 1980 survey found that 63 per cent of women did paid work outside the home, it concluded that:

> While only a minority of women cannot combine a career and children, it is clear that these are rarely considered equally important, since a majority of women feel a home and children is a woman's prime aim and main job and endorse the view that family responsibilities may conflict with having a demanding paid job.[6]

The survey also found that in households where both wife and husband worked outside the home, slightly under one-third of wives and husbands said that the domestic work (excluding child-care) was equally shared, leaving two-thirds of the households where wives did all or most of the domestic work.[7] This finding is not shared by recent time budget analyses, which showed that in 1974–5, men did 35 to 39 minutes of routine domestic work per day, compared with nearly three hours for women with paid jobs and nearly six hours for women without paid jobs. If non-routine domestic tasks such as gardening and decorating are included, then in households where both wife and husband were employed outside the home, husbands did almost half as much domestic work as wives.[8] Earlier surveys have shown that the amount of time spent on domestic work remained fairly stable between the mid–1920s and the 1960s, but in recent years it appears that the time may have decreased due to the advent of more sophisticated domestic appliances; men with full-time paid jobs are also doing more routine domestic work.[9] Women, however, still have the sole or prime responsibility for domestic work in the majority of households.[10] Ownership of some domestic appliances increased dramatically between 1973 and 1982, the percentage of British households with children which possessed deep freezers and tumble driers rising from zero to 65 per cent and 41 per cent respectively. By 1982, 92 per cent of all households with children owned washing machines and 97 per cent vacuum cleaners.[11]

Another side of the affluent and increasingly home-owning society of the 1960s was represented by the underground or alternative society, which flourished between 1967 and 1971 and propagated a mixture of radical politics and new lifestyles.[12] The alternative society was seen, especially by the young, as offering new ways of living outside the conventional structure of the family. Squatting was a manifestation of alternative values, the taking over of empty houses by the homeless, which also provided an opportunity for the conversion of property to suit a wide variety of different communities. Clearly squatting did not offer a long-term answer to housing problems, but experimental squats involving whole London streets showed that shared living and self-management could be successful, some of the shared space being devoted to communal facilities such as workshops, a theatre and a meeting room.[13] The wide range of squatting exercises conducted throughout the 1970s took place in many different building types, although the concentration was on terraced housing; attics and basements were converted into playrooms and living rooms, various groups of squatters opting for more or less communal and private space.[14] 'Community shops, restaurants, bulk buying, creches, workshops and small businesses have all had a chance to exist in squatting communities.'[15] Reasons for squatting could vary from homelessness to the wish to experiment with a new lifestyle, but a squat was rarely more than a temporary home. The commune movement, with its groups of people committed to living together, shared more of the spirit of the cooperative housekeeping movement, which had intended its homes to be both permanent and revolutionary.

A commune has been defined as a group of three or more adults from more than one family or group, with or without children, who have come together for a particular purpose and are committed to living together; commune members share household work and the responsibility for maintaining the home.[16] The commune movement emerged in the mid-1960s and reached its peak in the early 1970s; there were at least 50 communes in existence in Britain in 1970.[17] The object of communal life was to create an alternative to the nuclear family which emphasised mutual care, sharing domestic duties and, in the rural communes, self-sufficiency; commune members saw themselves as living examples of the new society.[18] Although the structure of communes did not necessarily imply the abolition of the sexual division of labour, observers of communes found 'an elaborate and varied array of arrangements designed to disperse conventional male–female divisions of labour'.[19] Communes varied in the degree to which they undertook collective activities, from the extreme of sharing all work and meals in some to the almost conventional arrangements of others whereby only a few peripheral activities were shared.[20] The crucial difficulty which arose when domestic duties were completely shared was the varying degrees of skill of the commune members, particularly in childcare; two observers concluded that even when communes had concentrated on removing sexual divisions in labour, this simply revealed the deeper obstacles to complete equality existing in society.[21] Like the cooperative housekeeping movement the commune movement wished to change society, and one of the hallmarks of both was communal eating, but the commune movement was altogether more radical than cooperative housekeeping. Although the early cooperative housekeepers envisaged a revolution in the position of women, this was to take place within the confines of capitalist society, whereas the commune movement intended to build a wholly new society in which women would not be bound by earlier conventions.

Although many communes and squats were short lived, they

did provide alternative homes, particularly for single people, and acted as examples of new types of accommodation which were later taken up by local authorities and housing associations.[22] In the late 1970s and early 1980s both the public and private sectors began to take new initiatives in the housing of single people, some of which involved the sharing of limited communal facilities within small groups, as in the case of cluster flats. This type of development has been extensively reported elsewhere, as have similar developments for the elderly and mentally handicapped, and they cannot be considered as a form of cooperative house-keeping as they simply involve the use of shared facilities, coop-eration between residents being unnecessary. They are also often intended for a younger, more transient population than the orig-inal cooperative housekeeping developments, which even in the case of the ladies' residential flats were considered as long-term permanent homes.[23]

The Housing Corporation was founded in 1964, its role being expanded in 1974 to take in the provision of funds to housing associations for the building of fair rent accommodation. Any housing association wishing to provide communal facilities in dwellings designed for households of more than one person ('gen-eral family housing') will find that the Corporation's design criteria, on which consideration for funding is based, exclude this type of provision whereby households with otherwise self-contained dwellings cooperate to share some facilities. Common rooms and laundry rooms are only allowable in single-person housing schemes.[24] Correspondence with representatives of the Corporation's regional offices revealed that 'family' schemes con-taining communal facilities would have to be assessed as special cases, since they would lie outside the normal guidelines.[25] Most regions reported no provision of schemes with communal facili-ties, and emphasised their concentration on self-contained dwell-ings, the one exception being the West Region, based at Exeter. This region had a history of involvement with communal ventures, and assessed each case individually, looking particularly at the stability of membership of the group seeking funds. Activity there had centred on requests for funding from groups of young people in the Bristol area wishing to take over old houses and convert them for communal living.[26] Three of these cooperatives or communes are still in existence, and other privately-funded communes are currently working or being planned, one in connection with low energy housing.[27] The attitude of the building societies towards lending money on property with shared facilities is dependent on its marketability. The legal ownership and the structure of the dwelling are important; a loan might be more easily obtained if a shared nursery, for example, was situated in a separate building rather than being an integral part of the structure as a shared kitchen would probably be, thus affecting its future marketability. As with the Housing Corporation, this type of request is so unusual that a building society would have to consider it on its merits as a special case.[28]

There are very few contemporary housing developments for households other than single people which have shared facilities; shared kitchens in particular are very rare. One cooperative funded by the Housing Corporation and situated near Bristol converted a large Victorian house to accommodate four families, who initially shared a kitchen. As the families developed together, they decided to revert to individual kitchens, but to continue sharing other areas such as the laundry and garden. The families felt that they had a greater need for private space than communal space at that stage in the cooperative's existence. It now consists of three families and five single people, living in accommodation midway between a commune and a collective of privatised dwellings; they are converting outbuildings to provide further accommodation, but have not yet found a satisfactory use for certain common areas of the main house, such as the hall, which make up about one-sixth of its total area.[29]

Housing for single-parent families would appear to give great scope for the provision of shared facilities, and even shared accommodation. Erin Pizzey, the founder of Chiswick Women's Aid who has devised a house-sharing scheme for single-parent families, commented: 'When you are on your own with your children what you need for the first few years is imaginative house-sharing schemes that are highly supportive.'[30] In 1981 Gingerbread, the self-help organisation for single-parent families, and the RIBA organised a competition for the design of housing for single-parent families with associated communal facilities. Their intention was to encourage 'innovatory architectural solutions', but they were disappointed with the 108 entries, most of which dealt insensitively with the communal areas. The competition's assessors stated that

Only two entrants were bold enough, or perceptive enough, to attempt the very difficult design problem of a house for sharing. Neither, unfortunately, was a success, and indeed so little is known of the nature of the problem that this was almost bound to be so. Thought needs to be given to what can be shared and what can not; here is a field which requires research for there must be a frequent need for such accommodation.[31]

Nina West Homes is a housing association which has provided accommodation for single-parent families in both new housing developments and conversions, all of which have a day nursery or playroom and sometimes a laundry room attached. All the developments are in London, the first being Fiona House in Leytonstone, which was built in 1972. Its 12 flats were designed in two blocks connected by a playroom, which can be viewed directly from eight of the flats; all the flats are linked by an intercom system so that babysitting can take place without the necessity for the babysitter to leave her or his own flat. The development was also provided with a nursery school which is used by children of the surrounding area as well as those in the flats, which were designed for families with children aged up to five years.[32] Nina West Homes now have nine other developments, making a total of 100 flat places.[33] The exact nature of the playspace varies with each development and the age of the children for which it is designed. In the more recent developments, doors from each flat open on to the play area, and are painted different colours for easy recognition by the children. Women tenants tend to meet in the common play area, which is also used for parties and other communal activities; there are no special management problems in relation to the communal areas. Nina West herself sees the success of her developments as stemming from their small size, all but one consisting of not more than 12 flats. She feels that further communal facilities would not be popular with the single parents, who need private space when they first move into the flats; however, on leaving the flats, two families frequently get together to buy their own house.

Hummingbird Housing Association also provides accommodation for single-parent families, but within the context of a larger development intended for local authority employees and tenants, and single people. Hummingbird's first venture was at Peckham, where 53 flats and houses were built in 1980, and were followed by a further 46, under construction in 1984. The small estate is unusual because of its high level of community provision, consisting of a community centre, laundrette, nursery centre and toy library; a childminding scheme and a holiday playscheme are operated, and a total of 22 staff are employed, including two part-time wardens.[34] The project's original aim was to provide good housing for local workers, thus reducing the high turnover of National Health Service employees in particular. It was funded by the Department of the Environment and the Housing Corporation, amongst many other bodies, a precedent being set when the DOE agreed to pay half the cost of the nursery centre and over half the cost of the community centre. Despite the publicity Hummingbird has received since the estate opened, this precedent has not been taken up by any other agency wishing to provide communal facilities.

Hummingbird's director, Stella Goldman, wanted the project to be large enough to make an impact on its surrounding area, all the communal facilities being available to people living within half a mile of the estate. There is a great deal of subtle and unobtrusive encouragement of contact between tenants, and other users, through the wardens, who purposely have no rent-collecting function, and by the provision of places in which people can meet formally, informally and 'accidentally on purpose'. The community centre houses meetings of single parents, the holiday playscheme, and is hired out for uses ranging from karate to weddings. The toy library also acts as a meeting place for mothers, while accidental contact between people is fostered by the design of the communal facilities. The warden's office is situated on the way to the laundrette, and other communal areas are designed to provide people with a good reason for using them, and thus meeting each other; even the existence of a complex burglar alarm system encourages tenants to meet to arrange keyholding duties. The success of the scheme can be judged by the fact that after four years in use, the houses and flats appear almost new. The yellow brick of the estate, with its red-brick string courses, con-trasts with the grey stone of a Victorian church which intrudes into it. Although the terrace houses and three blocks of flats do not form a quadrangle, together with the communal facilities and the church they successfully enclose the space of the estate, whose footpaths are used by non-residents but which retains its privacy. Stella Goldman commented that capital funding for new developments was far easier to obtain than support for the running costs; the laundrette at Peckham just breaks even, but the nursery costs £60 per child per week, and the holiday playscheme around £15 000 per year. She would like to see the addition of a combined cafe and take-away food service, giving a different type of meeting place to that provided in the community centre, but it would have to be financially viable and create jobs for tenants.

Neither the housing association developments described above nor the Bristol commune have attempted to integrate opportunities for paid work for all tenants or members into their housing, although the Hummingbird estate does provide some employment for tenants. The Seagull Cooperative, a women's housing cooperative which started in May 1976, at first aimed to provide communal housing for women in London, but found that they were prevented from planning a thoroughly communal house conversion, including a workroom, by the application of Parker Morris standards, fire and public health regulations. They eventually decided to try to obtain 'a mixture of types of housing in a local area for women at different stages in their lives with different needs'.[35] A cooperative member commented that:

> *The house and work split is fundamental* . . . Single person housing is so often seen as an extension of transient student residences. You sleep, wash and study in a tiny space . . . There is no space to do other things than prescribed activities. You do those other things *outside the home* – and women with children cannot get out to do them. So workrooms are an essential requirement.[36]

Recently several initiatives have been taken to make it easier for women to undertake paid work outside the home, and to ensure that not all domestic work is performed by women within the home. The 1983 draft alterations to the Greater London Development Plan, in its section on the provision of housing and services with respect to women's needs, states:

Much of the unpaid work of women continues to be carried out in the home and there has been scant attention paid by designers to incorporate communal facilities such as laundries, childcare and other community facilities which would reduce the burden of domestic work ... Public provision of services has not offered women the choice of socialised caring and domestic tasks ... There is however a demand for domestic tasks to be done outside the home.[37]

The Greater London Council has already funded the Westway and Coventry Cross community laundries, the Westway laundry also acting as a social centre.[38] The Norwood Child Care Association in south London began to develop a childcare cooperative in late 1983 which is intended to include 'laundry facilities, the provision of meals, the bulk-buying of food alongside child-care, after-school clubs, childminders' support groups and a family planning clinic'.[39] A cooperative laundry in Leeds has been funded through the local council, and hopes to expand by opening a cafe.[40] Newham Docklands Forum, in their *People's Plan for the Royal Docks*, suggest that the provision of full-time childcare is necessary to 'improve the community life of docklands'; childminders in their area are considering the setting up of a cooperative childcare centre, so that transport, toys and food could be shared.[41] It has even been suggested that the British Restaurant should be revived, not only to provide good food but to act as a centre for the unemployed:

Every community could have a community restaurant, run on a cooperative basis, open from 8am to 10pm. It should be not only a restaurant, but an arts centre, a book exchange shop, an advice and information centre, a place for exchange of skills.[42]

None of these suggestions or new ventures attempts to change the pattern of space within the home, or to develop any form of communal living; they simply mitigate the effects on women of the sexual division of labour. A few modern housing developments in Europe have been designed to include real communal space, shared between families. In Hamburg in 1973, for example, a group of parents and single people designed their own public housing in collaboration with an architect. Their project provided private flats with one or two bedrooms, a living room and in some cases a study, opening on to shared space consisting of living and dining rooms, kitchen and playroom; the whole project accommodated 206 tenants.[43] A Danish housing development of 1974 was built on a village system emphasising neighbourly cooperation, which was achieved by grouping dwellings so that 'every two or four families can, if they like, share their own private court'.[44] Dwellings have shared entrances leading off shared front areas called 'dwelling lanes', which are connected by area lanes to the communal main street and main square, containing the village shop and community centre. The area lanes and main street have been designed to allow residents to erect new communal buildings, such as workshops or playrooms, in them; motor vehicles are kept on the perimeter of the site. Three West German terrace housing developments reported in 1982 all contain communal areas, ranging from internal courtyards, through a communal basement and utility house, to a shared kitchen/living room. In the latter, the lifestyles of the resident families were influenced by the communal area but not restricted, and it could be seen as a basic model of communal living.[45] In contrast to these ventures, in the United States in 1973, land-use zoning laws were used to prevent the introduction of communal living arrangements into one urban area.[46]

In Britain since the late 1970s, women architects have been beginning to suggest alternatives to conventional patterns of domestic space, with their implicit support of the sexual division of labour, and also to define new and non-hierarchical methods of working. Men dramatically outnumber women in the architectural profession, the ratio of male to female architecture students in 1978 being 6 : 1, while in the same year only 5.8 per cent of registered architects were women; 96 per cent of highly paid architectural posts were held by men in 1981.[47] The growth of feminist architectural practice began with the formation of the New Architecture Movement (NAM) in November 1975. The members of NAM, mainly salaried architects, wanted to bring about radical changes in the practice of architecture; feminism began to be more important in the movement from 1977 onwards, and it was hoped that a model design for a communal home could be produced.[48] The Feminism and Architecture Group of NAM received its first commission in 1978 from Clapham Women's Aid, a conversion of five houses into a refuge with a playhouse.[49] By 1980 the Matrix Feminist Design Cooperative, a design and research network, had been formed, to be followed by the Women's Design Service, both London based.[50] Apart from their design work, Matrix have produced an exhibition illustrating the myths of the 'ideal home' and suggesting alternatives to conventional housing.[51] Drawing on their experience of the women's movement, some women architects and students have begun to restructure their methods of working:

> We have developed forms of organization which are designed to encourage all to take part. They are non-hierarchical, intentionally value all contributions, even if tentatively made, and strike hard against mystifications and power playing.[52]

Several recent initiatives have been taken which allow non-architects and planners to obtain some control over the design and building of their own homes. The most publicised of these are Liverpool City Council's housing cooperatives, funded through the Housing Corporation or the DOE. Although the tenant cooperatives employ their own architects, tenants become deeply involved in the design of their homes, each cooperative developing a different working relationship with its architect. Architects have found that

> people soon grasp the complexities of government yardsticks, Building Regulations and space standards, so that, as one put it, 'cost yardstick densities are bandied around as easily as the latest supermarket prices'.[53]

Numerous different designs have been evolved within the cooperatives, some choosing semis, another preferring a series of small courts enclosed by six houses, the courts being seen as 'communal rather than public open spaces, where toddlers can play freely'.[54] In Hackney, local authority refurbishment of the 1939 Lea View estate was carried out in consultation with its tenants. The architects had regular meetings with tenants and held a daily 'open hour' at their site office in order to discover what was really needed. The result was a high degree of tenant satisfaction and costs at most only 5 per cent more than for a simple renovation. One tenant commented: 'It seems like your own little bit of creation. And it just doesn't look like council property.'[55]

Increasing community involvement in architectural and planning decisions has been mirrored by the growth of organisations of professionals working in the community. One of the first projects giving 'community technical aid' was Shelter's Neighbourhood Action Project in Liverpool in 1969, where architects worked with local residents, and which was followed in the 1970s by various other organisations and private practices, including some cooperatives.[56] This activity culminated in the setting up of the Association of Community Technical Aid Centres (ACTAC) in October 1983, with a membership of over 40 organisations. It aims to provide professional advice to those sections of the community which would not normally have access to such services, and 'To increase awareness of the importance of community self-help and user control in the improvement and development of land, buildings and neighbourhoods . . .'[57] The involvement of users in the design process relating to their own homes or community facilities, and subsequently in their management, appears to lead to increased levels of satisfaction on the part of the users, and certainly promotes community control over the immediate environment. However, it has so far not produced any attempts to design homes with shared facilities or unusual arrangements of internal space; apart from problems with building regulations and funding, the individual home may be important as a source of personal fulfilment, a private space 'endowed with qualities absent from shared or public space'.[58] The most probable avenue for the production of housing with communal space is through the work of feminist design groups, possibly using the techniques of flexible building systems or on a small-scale, self-build basis.

In the late 1970s, a conference on women and housing cooperatives reported on the design of homes:

> Flexibility is not only needed externally but internally as well. When we talked about woman-defined architecture, we considered the value of impermanent, adjustable walls to permit scope for changing needs of women and growing children . . . We see the designs of our housing including features that cater for collective childcare.[59]

Flexible housing systems are designed to be responsive to the changing needs of occupants, by enabling alterations in the internal structure to be made within the basic framework of the dwellings.[60] The original idea derives from N. J. Habraken's book *Supports,* and a version of it has been tested on a small north London council estate.[61] PSSHAK (primary support system and house assembly kit) was used for an estate of 45 flats begun in 1976, allowing future tenants to participate in the design of their own homes.[62] Tenants were able to decide on the interior plan of their homes, given the limitations of Parker Morris standards and fittings such as windows and staircases, and this resulted in only two or three of the dwellings having the same design. Although between one-fifth and one-half of the prospective tenants dropped out before completion of the project, the scheme still appears to have been successful, partly because of its pleasant and convenient site.[63] The GLC did not envisage tenants carrying out alterations to the internal structure of their homes themselves, and only intends to make changes if new tenants move into homes on the estate; the original households thus lose all the potential benefits of the system's flexibility. The change to a Conservative administration at County Hall resulted in a decision to turn the estate into a management cooperative, the scheme's architect seeing this as a chance for the tenants to allow changes in the size of flats or to convert a flat into a nursery if a vacancy occurred.[64] Clearly, flexible housing systems have the potential to incorporate communal space at any or all stages of the lives of their occupiers. Occupants, if allowed to make alterations to their homes, will gain increasing control over their own environments and be able to use their creativity within their homes.[65]

Self-build housing has the greatest scope for creative involvement of the occupier, and it has become increasingly popular in the 1980s, with 8000 self-build homes being erected in 1981 and 10 000 the following year; around 1 in 14 new private sector homes is now self-built.[66] Although the usual self-build design is a four-bedroom detached house, semis and a terrace have also been tried. Walter Segal's designs for timber-frame self-build council homes have received much publicity, the Lewisham scheme beginning in 1979 resulting in 14 homes being built by male and female self-builders.[67] Individual choice was allowed greatest freedom during the construction of the interiors; Segal's latest design is for a basic house with 19 variants related to a standard core, self-builders being able to arrange their habitable space around the stairs and service areas of the core.[68] Self-builders in group schemes are often male, but there is 'an all-woman housing estate in Sunderland where a group of five bought the land and supervised the building of five homes without any male interference'.[69] Self-building has mainly resulted in conventional housing, but this need not necessarily be the case; funding through housing associations combined with self-building of innovative designs offers one route towards changing domestic space norms. For those able and willing to consider self-build, it offers a creative alternative to award-winning housing with chronic defects, or estates where

> It is almost as if the existence of the design rules and regulations has in some cases acted as an excuse for the designer to stop thinking about how each individual in each house will use the home and the unbuilt spaces about the home.[70]

The combination of feminist design groups and the increasing number of women learning construction skills indicates that with suitable funding, experiments in changing domestic space arrangements are likely to become more frequent.

Today, most new dwellings, whether in the public or private sector, conversions or new-build, have conventional designs which do not pose any challenge to the traditional division of labour. There are, however, a number of initiatives being taken by community groups, housing associations and local councils which give people the opportunity to make decisions about their own homes and localities, and which take small steps towards the socialisation of domestic work. Although modern housing with communal facilities does exist, there is nothing truly comparable to the original cooperative housekeeping schemes, with their emphasis on cooperation between large numbers of households and their lavish provision of facilities. A few modern households live in communal groups, and many more might wish to do so at certain stages of their development if that choice was possible; however, the rationale for sharing facilities which existed in the early twentieth century does not exist today. Commercial take-away food services and laundrettes are widely available, so unless households opt for the social benefits of communal living and control over their own facilities, cooperation between households need never penetrate inside the individual home.

In spite of outliving their original function, the cooperative homes erected in the early years of this century are still popular places to live. They were designed specifically to combine the individual home with an element of communal living, and although the communal functions themselves have disappeared, the spatial relationship of the buildings remains attractive. Cooperative homes are seen as desirable homes because of their human scale, comfortable, traditional materials, and their easy combination of privacy and community. In none of the developments designed on the quadrangular plan are the sides of the quadrangle more than 75 yards long, and the suburban villas of Brent were situated little further from their communal centre. The materials most often used were brick, tiles and wood, construction being solid enough to withstand future alterations. Space standards were also high in some of the cooperative homes, giving more scope for later conversions. Each household had its own private internal space, and often a private external space; there were also communal internal areas, used only by the occupants, and a large area of communal space, which was actually semi-public but was overseen by all or most of the dwellings. This semi-public area is one of the keys to the lasting success of the cooperative homes as good individual homes. It acts both as a communal meeting place with a pleasant aspect, and as a soft barrier between the cooperative home and the public world. Being open and semi-public, it prevents the dwellings from being totally inward-looking and cut off from their surroundings; some modern housing has drawn criticism because of its 'enclosed, inward-looking clusters of houses'.[71]

The architectural style of the cooperative homes was mainly arts and crafts vernacular, totally different in appearance from the modern movement buildings erected between the wars. The style of the modern movement has not produced a popular domestic architecture in Britain; Mark Girouard commented that 'It has failed almost completely, for instance, to produce . . . images of domesticity with which any large number of people can identify.'[72] Large-scale, system-built housing gives little scope for the personalisation of the home; Amos Rapoport suggests that 'the whole modern movement in architecture can be seen as an attack on users' meaning – the attack on ornaments, on decoration, on "what-nots" in dwellings and "thingamabobs" in the garden . . .'[73] The reaction to modern movement design, which began in the 1970s, has involved a return to traditional materials and forms of architecture.[74] This new direction in architecture has been labelled 'romantic pragmatism', as it attempts to combine a humane style, related to the individual, with modernist rationality.[75] It has also been noted that this type of design bears a close resemblance to Edwardian architecture, with its romanticism and use of natural materials.[76] The triumph of traditional styles over modernism is illustrated by the popularity of a contemporary thatched cottage at the 1984 Ideal Home Exhibition.[77]

The design of the cooperative homes, in a style which is clearly modern in its appeal, shows how communal and private space may be happily integrated. Modern suggestions for the redesign of domestic space often concentrate on shared facilities rather than any form of communal living, or the encouragement of equality in the division of household work through spatial changes.[78] The provision of communal facilities allows the occupier scope to redefine the uses of space within the home, as some activities are removed from the domestic area. This gives the occupier more control over the home, rather than acquiescing to the spatial dictation of the architect. The problem for the architect then becomes one of designing a flexible space, adaptable to a variety of uses, many unforeseen. In its original form, cooperative housekeeping removed almost all domestic labour from the home, leaving only the lightest tasks. The home was thus freed for other activities; this is clearly the extreme position on the scale of cooperative housekeeping schemes, although true communal living goes further and removes barriers between individual homes as well. Cooperative homes can be seen as a step towards increased flexibility of domestic space design, as their internal space was less rigidly defined with respect to activities, and they have proved able successfully to accommodate alterations to their structure. Their architects often worked closely with the future users of the dwellings, thus the following modern quotation, concerned with the need for a new planning ideology, appears to describe exactly the cooperative homes of the early twentieth century: 'Future building must be characterized by the integration of different activities and by an active relationship between people and the built environment.'[79]

The incorporation of new uses of space into the traditional home heralds the crumbling of divisions between home and work, and thus the sexual division of labour. The increase in the number of people without paid work may have already begun to produce changes in the performance of domestic work, but this is as yet uninvestigated.[80] Men without paid work are less likely than men with paid work to have wives who work outside the home, so that although more men are able to spend time in the home, their wives may still be responsible for all domestic work.[81] If the divide between well-paid work done outside the home and domestic or other work done in the home is to be bridged, any work performed in the home must be held to be as important as that performed outside. At present, this is not the case; even highly skilled women data-processors who work at home are paid 'much less than colleagues doing similar work in offices'.[82] A social wage, payable to all individuals irrespective of employment status, is one possible method of encouraging the economic independence of women.[83]

Changes in the design of domestic space can alter people's perceptions of their current and future activities. Conventional domestic space design can act as a reinforcement of the sexual division of labour, but although design changes may help to break down this division, only a dramatic revision of male and female attitudes towards their respective roles can destroy it completely. A prerequisite of free choice between work inside and outside the home, for both women and men, is that domestic work and other work, wherever it is performed, should be seen as equally valuable. The increased use of communal facilities, and the wider acceptance of other lifestyles such as communal living or forms of cooperative housekeeping, will hasten the process of changing responsibilities within the home.

The cooperative housekeeping movement of the late nineteenth and early twentieth centuries showed that it was possible for women to take more control over their environment. In spite of an architectural profession which devalued their contribution and a society in which their interests were held to be solely those of home and family, the ideas of these women resulted in the building of housing which is still in demand today. The movement took in both men and women, with a wide variety of views on politics, the home and women's position in society, but the housing it produced fulfilled their aim of improving the quality of life. The movement enabled the households involved to gain more control over the design and management of their own homes, a process which is continuing today; with some exceptions, neither public nor private sector housing is yet designed to take account of changing lifestyles and to allow potential occupants more control in the design and planning stages, and in the management of public schemes. Cooperative housekeeping in England did not provoke a revolution in the home, but it did present new options to women and accelerate the process by which they were slowly gaining control over their own lives.

Appendix
A Further Note on Cooperative Homes

Designs for cooperative homes continue to be discovered, and rather than disturb the text at a late stage, a brief note of the details is given in this appendix.

1. C. F. A. Voysey, design for Devonshire House, Piccadilly, London, 1923.

   Voysey's design consisted of three 30-storey blocks of flats with communal dining rooms, shops and other services. The tower blocks were medieval in appearance, and would have stood opposite the Green Park underground station. The design was not built. See Simpson, Duncan (1979), *C. F. A. Voysey*, Lund Humphries, London, pp. 134–7; Symonds, Joanna (1976), *C. F. A. Voysey, Catalogue of the Drawings Collection of the RIBA*, D. C. Heath, Farnborough, p. 31.

Notes and References

CHAPTER 1

1. Burnett, John (1980), *A Social History of Housing 1815–1970*, Methuen, London, pp. 58–72.
2. Ibid., p. 75.
3. Poor Law Commissioners (1842), *Report on an Inquiry into the Sanitary Condition of the Labouring Population of Great Britain*, HMSO, London, rep. with introduction by M. W. Flinn (1965), Edinburgh University Press, Edinburgh, p. 141. The report is known as the Chadwick Report.
4. Burnett, *A Social History*, p. 54.
5. Chadwick Report, p. 86.
6. Burnett, *A Social History*, p. 77.
7. For discussion of the variety of house plans, see Muthesius, Stefan (1982), *The English Terraced House*, Yale University Press, New Haven, pp. 101–42.
8. Daunton, M. J. (1983), *House and Home in the Victorian City*, Edward Arnold, London, p. 12.
9. Davidson, Caroline (1982), *A Woman's Work is Never Done*, Chatto and Windus, London, p. 133.
10. Oakley, Ann (1976), *Housewife*, Penguin, Harmondsworth, pp. 34–47.
11. Evans, Tony and Green, Candida Lycett (1982), *English Cottages*, Weidenfeld and Nicholson, London, p. 16.
12. Oakley, *Housewife*, p. 50.
13. Burnett, *A Social History*, pp. 163, 168–73.
14. For changes in domestic technology, see Daunton, *House and Home*, pp. 237–62.
15. Hardy, Dennis (1979), *Alternative Communities in Nineteenth-century England*, Longman, London.
16. Ibid., p. 19.
17. Taylor, Barbara (1983), *Eve and the New Jerusalem*, Virago, London, pp. 37–8.
18. Ibid., pp. 238, 245.
19. Hardy, *Alternative Communities*, p. 44; Taylor, *Eve*, p. 247.
20. *The Economist* (1822), 'To the Working and Other Classes', 2 March, No. 51, pp. 396–9, see p. 396.
21. Darley, Gillian (1978), *Villages of Vision*, Granada, St Albans, p. 161; Combe, Abram (1825), *The Sphere for Joint-stock Companies, with an Account of the Establishment at Orbiston*, Mudie, Edinburgh, rep. Arno Press, NY, 1972, pp. 65–7; Cullen, Alexander (1910), *Adventures in Socialism*, John Smith, Glasgow, rep. Kelley, Clifton, New Jersey, 1972, pp. 226, 291–3; Taylor, *Eve*, p. 248; Hardy, *Alternative Communities*, pp. 36–7.

22. Hodson, William (1838), 'Each for all', *New Moral World*, 25 Aug, no. 200, p. 358; see also Taylor, *Eve*, pp. 253–8; Hardy, *Alternative Communities*, pp. 49–53.

23. Hardy, *Alternative Communities*, pp. 53–8; Taylor, *Eve*, pp. 239, 248–50; One who has whistled at the plough (Alexander Somerville) (1842), 'A Journey to Harmony Hall', *Notes from the Farming Districts*, no. 17, rep. *Cooperative Communities: Plans and Descriptions*, Arno Press, NY, 1972, p. 6.

24. Jones, Lloyd (1841), 'Progress of Social Reform, Queenwood, April 16th', *New Moral World*, 24 April, vol. 9, no. 17, p. 262.

25. Taylor, *Eve*, pp. 249–51.

26. Thompson, Dorothy (1984), *The Chartists*, Temple Smith, London, p. 303.

27. Hardy, *Alternative Communities*, p. 77.

28. Hadfield, Alice Mary (1970), *The Chartist Land Company*, David and Charles, Newton Abbot, p. 35.

29. O'Connor, Feargus (1847), 'To the Members of the Chartist Co-operative Land Company', *Northern Star*, 13 Feb, vol. 10, no. 486, p. 1.

30. Hardy, *Alternative Communities*, pp. 83–105.

31. Armytage, W. H. G. (1961), *Heavens Below*, RKP, London, p. 232.

32. Hadfield, *Chartist Land Company*, p. 189.

33. Thompson, *Chartists*, p. 113.

34. Boyson, Rhodes (1970), *The Ashworth Cotton Enterprise*, Clarendon Press, Oxford; *The Builder* (1863), 'Akroydon, Improved Dwellings for the Working Classes', 14 Feb, vol. 21, no. 1045, pp. 109–17; Lever, W. L. (1902), 'Dwellings Erected at Port Sunlight and Thornton Hough', *The Builder*, 29 March, vol. 82, no. 3086, pp. 312–18; Harvey, W. Alexander (1906), *The Model Village and its Cottages: Bournville*, Batsford, London; Darley, *Villages*, pp. 129, 133–5, 137–45.

35. Burnett, *A Social History*, p. 108.

36. Ibid., pp. 98, 108.

37. Ibid., p. 102.

38. Ibid., p. 204.

39. Pedley, Mrs (1867), *Practical Housekeeping or the Duties of a Housewife*, Routledge, London, p. 1; Caddy, Mrs Florence (1877), *Household Organization*, Chapman and Hall, London, p. 52; Oakley, *Housewife*, p. 49. See also Davidoff, Leonore, L'Esperance, Jean and Newby, Howard (1976), 'Landscape with Figures: Home and Community in English Society', pp. 139–75 in Juliet Mitchell and Ann Oakley (eds), *The Rights and Wrongs of Women*, Penguin, Harmondsworth, pp. 151–9.

40. Branca, Patricia (1975), *Silent Sisterhood*, Croom Helm, London, pp. 47, 54.

41. Pedley, *Practical Housekeeping*, p. 34; Davidoff, Leonore (1976), 'The Rationalization of Housework', pp. 121–51 in Diana Leonard Barker and Sheila Allen (eds), *Dependence and Exploitation in Work and Marriage*, Longman, London, see p. 137.

42. Caddy, *Household*, p. 9.

43. Burnett, *A Social History*, p. 206; Dixon, Roger and Muthesius, Stefan (1978), *Victorian Architecture*, Thames and Hudson, London, p. 69.
44. Burnett, *A Social History*, p. 206; Tarn, J. N. (1974), 'French Flats for the English in Nineteenth-century London', pp. 19–40 in Anthony Sutcliffe (ed.), *Multi-storey Living*, Croom Helm, London, see p. 22; Muthesius, Hermann (1979), *The English House*, Crosby Lockwood Staples, London, first pub. 1904, p. 144.
45. Muthesius, *The English House*, p. 144.
46. Tarn, 'French Flats', p. 38; Burnett, *A Social History*, pp. 206–8.
47. Burnett, *A Social History*, p. 207.
48. King, Anthony (1973), 'Social Process and Urban Form: the Bungalow as an Indicator of Social Trends', *Architectural Association Quarterly*, vol. 5, no. 4, pp. 4–21, see p. 12.
49. For details of Bedford Park, see Bolsterli, Margaret Jones (1977), *The Early Community at Bedford Park*, RKP, London; Darley, *Villages*, pp. 117–21.
50. Marsh, Jan (1982), *Back to the Land*, Quartet, London, p. 173; Bolsterli, *Early Community*, pp. 12, 111.
51. For details of Whiteway, see Hardy, *Alternative Communities*, pp. 201–7; Marsh, *Back*, pp. 107–11; Shaw, Nellie (1935), *Whiteway, a Colony on the Cotswolds*, Daniel, London.
52. Shaw, *Whiteway*, p. 52.
53. Ibid., pp. 54–5, 61.
54. Hardy, *Alternative Communities*, pp. 204–7.

CHAPTER 2

1. Redivivus, Junius (1834), 'Housebuilding and Housekeeping', *Monthly Repository*, vol. 8, Jul/Aug, pp. 485–94, 572–84. 'Junius Redivivus' was William Bridges Adams (1797–1872), an inventor who specialised in machinery concerned with transport, especially railways. He made little money from his inventions. He wrote several political pamphlets around the time of the 1832 Reform Bill, and also wrote various engineering tracts. He later wrote as 'Helix' for the *Westminster Review*. See *Dictionary of National Biography*, vol. 1, pp. 108–9.
2. For example in Davidoff, Leonore (1976), 'The Rationalization of Housework', pp. 121–51 in *Dependence and Exploitation in Work and Marriage*, eds, Barker, Diana Leonard and Allen, Sheila, Longman, London.
3. Taylor, Barbara (1983), *Eve and the New Jerusalem*, Virago, London, p. 79.
4. Morrison, James (1834), 'A Page for the Ladies', *The Pioneer*, 22 March, pp. 262–3. For details on *The Pioneer* and James Morrison, see Taylor, *Eve*, pp. 303–4.
5. Taylor, *Eve*, p. 75.
6. Ibid., p. 96.

7. Helix (1849), 'Human Progress', *Westminster Review*, Oct, vol. 52, no. 1, pp. 1–39. My thanks to Alison Ravetz for this reference. See note 1 above.

8. Gillies, Mary (1847), 'Associated Homes for the Middle Class', *Howitt's Journal*, 15 May, vol. 1, no. 20, pp. 270–3.

9. Gillies, Mary (1847), 'Associated Homes for the Middle Class no. II', *Howitt's Journal*, 17 July, vol. 2, no. 29, pp. 38–41. See also Barmby, Goodwyn (1847), 'United Service Family Associations', *Howitt's Journal*, 19 June, vol. 1, no. 25, pp. 344–5.

10. Tarn, J. N. (1973), *Five per cent Philanthropy*, CUP, Cambridge, pp. 22–3.

11. Poor Law Commissioners (1842), *Inquiry into the Sanitary Condition of the Labouring Population of Great Britain* (Chadwick Report), HMSO, London. Section III; 'The Want of Separate Apartments and Overcrowding of Private Dwellings'.

12. *Illustrated London News*: 23 Feb 1850, vol. 16, no. 414, p. 122, 'The Chartist Estate – Snig's End'; 29 March 1851, vol. 18, no. 476, pp. 253–4, 'The Agapemone'. *Morning Chronicle*, 13 Dec 1842, 'One who has whistled at the plough', 'A Journey to Harmony Hall' (*Notes from the Farming Districts*, No. 17), Ostell, London. Rep: Arno Press, NY, 1972.

13. Tarn, J. N. (1974), 'French Flats for the English in Nineteenth-century London', pp. 19–40 in Anthony Sutcliffe (ed.), *Multi-storey Living*, Croom Helm, London, p. 25.

14. Smith, T. Roger and White, W. H. (1876), 'Model Dwellings for the Rich', *Journal of the Society of Arts*, 31 March, vol. 24, no. 1219, pp. 456–66. See pp. 463–4.

15. Eales, F. E. (1884), 'Houses in Flats', *The Builder*, 8 Mar, vol. 46, no. 2144, pp. 351–3. See p. 351.

16. Martineau, Harriet (1850), 'Associated Homes for Poor Ladies', *The Leader*, 19 Oct, vol. 1, no. 30, p. 711.

17. E. F. L. (1850), *The Ladies' Club Mansion*, E. T. Jeffryes, London. Harriet Martineau Papers, University of Birmingham, HM 1367, dated 16 March 1850.

18. Martineau, Harriet (1983), *Autobiography*, vol. II, Virago, London, p. 228. First pub. Smith, Elder, London, 1877.

19. Callen, Anthea (1980), *Women in the Arts and Crafts Movement 1870–1914*, Astragal Books, London, pp. 42, 171.

20. Martineau, *Autobiography*, vol. II, pp. 225, 306–8. Pichanick, Valerie Kossew (1980), *Harriet Martineau, The Woman and Her Work, 1802–76*, University of Michigan Press, Ann Arbor, p. 139.

21. The plan of Harriet Martineau's house, The Knoll, Ambleside, is in the Harriet Martineau Papers, University of Birmingham, HM 1302. The house still stands. In contrast to Martineau's conventional house design, Catharine Beecher, the American writer on domestic subjects, planned a highly efficient 'Christian' house in 1841. She designed both building and furniture to be lavour-saving, concentrating particularly on storage areas and the kitchen. See Catharine E. Beecher and Harriet Beecher Stowe (1869), *The American*

Woman's Home, J. B. Ford, NY; rep. 1971, Arno Press, NY. The house design was originally published in Beecher's *Treatise on Domestic Economy* in 1841; see Sklar, Kathryn Kish (1973), *Catharine Beecher, A Study in American Domesticity*, Yale University Press, New Haven, pp. 151, 263. Beecher also suggested an improved neighbourhood, to include a common laundry and a bake house 'for all desiring economy of time, labour and money in these directions'. See p. 575 of Catharine E. Beecher (1867), 'A Christian Neighbourhood', *Harper's New Monthly Magazine*, April, vol. 34, pp. 573–84.

22. Martineau, *Autobiography*, vol. II, p. 225.
23. Gillies, Mary (1847), 'Associated Homes', *Howitt's Journal*, 27 March, vol. 1, no. 13, pp. 171–4.
24. Doxsey, Isaac (1868), 'Domestic Co-operation', *The Co-Operator*, Nov 21, vol. 8, no. 173, p. 741.
25. Philergastes (1861), 'Co-operation in Domestic Arrangements', *The Co-Operator*, Oct, vol. 2, no. 17, pp. 65–6.
26. For example, A. C. C. (1860), 'An Equity Village', *The Co-Operator*, Nov, vol. 1, no. 6, pp. 76–7. Women were to be relieved from 'the endless drudgery of their present condition'; machinery would decrease the burden of labour. Also C. (1863), 'Cookery for Working Men', *The Co-Operator*, July, no. 41, p. 22.
27. Backstrom, Philip N. (1974), *Christian Socialism and Co-operation in Victorian England*, Croom Helm, London, p. 143.
28. Ibid., p. 141.
29. *The Co-Operator* (1869), 'Co-operative Housekeeping', 28 Aug, p. 613; Hayden, Dolores (1981), *The Grand Domestic Revolution*, MIT Press, Cambridge, Mass., p. 82.
30. Peirce, Mrs C. F. (1868/9), 'Co-operative Housekeeping', *Atlantic Monthly*, Nov, vol. 22, no. 133, pp. 513–24; Dec, vol. 22, no. 134, pp. 682–97; Jan, vol. 23, no. 135, pp. 29–39; Feb, vol. 23, no. 136, pp. 161–71; Mar, vol. 23, no. 137, pp. 286–99.
31. For details of Peirce's life, see Hayden, *Grand Domestic Revolution*, pp. 67–89, and on her early life, Mitarachi, Sylvia (1980), *Melusina Fay Peirce: Biography of a Feminist*, Bunting Institute Working Paper, Radcliffe College, Cambridge, Mass.
32. Hayden, *Grand Domestic Revolution*, p. 81.
33. Peirce, Mrs C. F. (1870), *Co-operative Housekeeping, Romance in Domestic Economy*, Simpkin, Marshall and Co., London.

CHAPTER 3

1. Pedley, Mrs (1867), *Practical Housekeeping or the Duties of a Home-Wife*, Routledge, London, p. 1.
2. Beeton, Mrs (1861), *The Book of Household Management*, Ward Lock, London. 1869 ed., pub. 1880, p. 1.
3. Branca, Patricia (1975), *Silent Sisterhood*, Croom Helm, London, p. 29.

4. Ibid., p. 47.
5. Prochaska, F. K. (1981), 'Female Philanthropy and Domestic Service in Victorian England', *Bulletin of the Institute of Historical Research*, May, vol. 54, no. 129, pp. 79–85. *See* pp. 79–80.
6. Branca, *Silent Sisterhood*, p. 56.
7. Forty, Adrian (1975), *The Electric Home*, Open University Press, Milton Keynes, p. 41.
8. Ravetz, Alison (1968), 'The Victorian Coal Kitchen and its Reformers', *Victorian Studies*, June, vol. 11, pp. 435–60. See p. 435.
9. Corley, T. A. B. (1966), *Domestic Electrical Appliances*, Cape, London, p. 26; Banham, Reyner (1969), *The Architecture of the Well-tempered Environment*, Architectural Press, London, pp. 58–9.
10. Ravetz, 'The Victorian Coal Kitchen', pp. 459–60.
11. Wiener, Martin J. (1981), *English Culture and the Decline of the Industrial Spirit 1850–1980*, CUP, Cambridge, pp. 30, 157.
12. Ibid., pp. 158–9.
13. Branca, *Silent Sisterhood*, p. 22.
14. Sillitoe, Helen (1933), *A History of the Teaching of Domestic Subjects*, Methuen, London, p. 21.
15. MacCarthy, Fiona (1981), *The Simple Life*, Lund Humphries, London; Marsh, Jan (1982), *Back to the Land*, Quartet, London.
16. *Chamber's Journal of Popular Literature, Science, and Art* (1869), 'Co-operative Housekeeping', 20 March, no. 273, pp. 177–9.
17. Branca, *Silent Sisterhood*, p. 9.
18. Lytton, Edward Bulwer (1870), *The Coming Race*, George Routledge and Sons, London, p. 263.
19. *The Co-Operator* (1869), 'Co-operative Housekeeping', 28 August, p. 613.
20. Hume-Rothery, Mary (1871), 'Co-operative Housekeeping', *The Co-operator and Anti-Vaccinator*, 29 April, pp. 262–3 and vol. 11, no. 302, 13 May, pp. 289–90.
21. Backstrom, Philip N. (1974), *Christian Socialism and Co-operation in Victorian England*, Croom Helm, London, p. 101. *The Co-Operator* had failed in 1871 (see p. 74), in the same year as *Co-operative News* began.
22. E. W. (1872), 'Domestic Co-operation', *Co-operative News*, vol. 2, no. 1, 6 Jan, p. 1.
23. Tarn, J. N. (1973), *Five per cent Philanthropy*, CUP, Cambridge.
24. Curl, James Stevens (1983), *The Life and Work of Henry Roberts 1803–1876*, Phillimore, Chichester, pp. 28, 38.
25. Kerr, R. (1866–7), 'On the Problems of Providing Dwellings for the Poor in Towns', *Transactions of the RIBA*, pp. 36–80. See pp. 50–1, 72.
26. *Building News* (1866). 'Workmen's Dwellings', 5 Jan, vol. 13, pp. 2–3.
27. Tarn, J. N. (1971), *Working-class Housing in 19th Century Britain*, Lund Humphries, London, p. 11.
28. Gaskell, S. Martin (1974), 'A Landscape of Small Houses: the Failure of the Workers' Flat in Lancashire and Yorkshire in the Nineteenth

Century', pp. 88–121 in Anthony Sutcliffe (ed.), *Multi-storey Living*, Croom Helm, London, pp. 88–91.

29. Neale, Edward Vansittart (1872), 'Associated Homes', *Co-operative News*, 27 Jan, vol. 2, no. 4, p. 37.
30. Backstrom, *Christian Socialism*, p. 148.
31. Morrison, W. (1872), 'Associated Homes', *Co-operative News*, 24 Feb, vol. 2, no. 8, p. 85. The Improved Industrial Dwellings Company had been founded in 1863 as a semi-philanthropic company erecting large numbers of self-contained flats. See Tarn, *Working-class Housing*, p. 12. The IIDC was to build one of the early cooperative homes at Hampstead Garden Suburb in 1909.
32. Neale, Edward Vansittart (1880), *Associated Homes: a Lecture*, Macmillan, London.
33. Backstom, *Christian Socialism*, p. 147.
34. Ibid., p. 6.
35. King, Mrs E. M. (1872), 'Work of an International Peace Society, and Woman's Place in it', *Transactions of the National Association for the Promotion of Social Science*, pp. 513–14.
36. *Crockford's Clerical Directory* (1860), Crockford's, London. See entry for Moss King, Critchill Rectory, Blandford, Dorset. My thanks to the Venerable Geoffrey Walton, Archdeacon of Dorset, for help with information on Mrs King.
37. King, Mrs E. M. (1874), 'Confederated Homes and Cooperative Housekeeping', *Report of the British Association for the Advancement of Science*, 43rd meeting, Bradford, Sept 1873, John Murray, London, pp. 195–6.
38. *The Times* (1873), 'Cooperative Housekeeping', 24 Sept, p. 7.
39. King, E. M. (1873), 'Co-operative Housekeeping', *Contemporary Review*, Dec, vol. 23, pp. 66–91.
40. Ibid., p.77.
41. Ibid., p. 81.
42. Strasser, Susan (1982), *Never Done*, Pantheon, NY, p. 163.
43. Oakley, Ann (1982), *Subject Women*, Fontana, Glasgow, p. 182.
44. Census of England and Wales, 1871 (1873), vol. III, *Population Abstracts*, C872, HMSO, London.
45. Strasser, *Never Done*, pp. 166–7.
46. Davidoff, Leonore (1974), 'Mastered for Life: Servant and Wife in Victorian and Edwardian England', *Journal of Social History*, Summer, vol. 7, no. 4, pp. 406–28. See p. 411.
47. 'Confederated Homes and Co-operative Housekeeping' (1873), *Englishwoman's Review of Social and Industrial Questions*, Oct, no. 16, pp. 313–15; article abridged from *Daily News*. The Housewife (1873), 'Co-operative Households', *The Queen*, 4 Oct, p. 268.
48. Letter dated 23 March 1855 from Lydia Becker to her aunt. Fawcett Library, Autograph letter collection, vol. 28, The Becker letters, part A, no. 2003.
49. Lydia Becker's family diary. Fawcett Library, Autograph letter collection, vol. 8; see entries 7 Nov 1873 – 11 Dec 1873, and 17 Sept 1873.

50. Becker, Lydia E. (1867), 'Female Suffrage', *Contemporary Review*, vol. 4, pp. 307–16; see p. 313.
51. Rosen, Andrew (1974), *Rise up, Women!*, RKP, London, pp. 8–10.
52. King, E. M. (1874), 'Co-operative Housekeeping', *Building News*, 24 April, vol. 26, pp. 452–3, 459–60.
53. Harbron, Dudley (1949), *The Conscious Stone*, Latimer House, London, pp. 95–7.
54. Aslin, Elizabeth (1969), *The Aesthetic Movement*, Elek, London, p. 63; Dixon, Roger and Muthesius, Stefan (1978), *Victorian Architecture*, Thames and Hudson, London, p. 27.
55. Harbron, *Conscious Stone*, pp. 97–8; *Women and Work* (1874), 'Industrial and Educational Bureau', 6 June, no. 1, p. 5.
56. Newton, Stella Mary (1974), *Health, Art and Reason*, John Murray, London, p. 106. The lecture was later issued as a pamphlet.
57. *Englishwoman's Review* (1881), 'National Dress Society', 15 June, vol. 12, no. 98, p. 272. See also King, E. M. (1881), 'Dress Reform', *The Sanitary Record*, 15 June, vol. 2 (NS), pp. 443–4.
58. Rational Dress Association (1883), *Catalogue of the Exhibition of the Rational Dress Association*, 1883, Princes Hall, Piccadilly, W. Wyman, London; rep. 1978, Garland Publishing, NY. See pp. 4, 12–13.
59. Becker, Lydia E. (1888), 'On Stays and Dress Reform', *The Sanitary Record*, 15 Oct, vol. 10 (NS), pp. 149–51.
60. King, E. M. (1875), 'The Science of Domestic Economy', *Transactions of the National Association for the Promotion of Social Science*, Glasgow meeting, 1874, Longmans, Green, London, pp. 948–9.
61. Hayden, Dolores (1981), *The Grand Domestic Revolution*, MIT Press, Cambridge, Mass., p. 82.
62. Ramsay, Elizabeth, P. (1875), 'Co-operative Housekeeping', *Englishwoman's Review of Social and Industrial Questions*, Oct, vol. 6, no. 30, pp. 435–43.
63. Oakley, *Subject Women*, pp. 146–7.
64. Higgs, Edward, (1983), 'Domestic Servants and Households in Victorian England', *Social History*, May, vol. 8, no. 2, pp. 201–10. See p. 205.
65. Ibid, p. 202.
66. Marwick, Arthur (1967), *The Deluge*, Penguin, Harmondsworth, pp. 97, 327.
67. Prochaska, 'Female Philanthropy', p. 85.
68. Ibid., pp. 82–3; Higgs, 'Domestic Servants', p. 207.
69. Redivivus, Junius (1834), 'Housebuilding and Housekeeping', *Monthly Repository*, Jul/Aug, vol. 8, pp. 485–94, 572–84.
70. Lytton, *The Coming Race*, p. 263.
71. Englander, Dr Sigmund (1875), 'A New System of Dwelling for the Working Classes', *Transactions of the National Association for the Promotion of Social Science*, pp. 715–16.
72. Morfit, Marie, C. C. (1876), 'On Co-operative Housekeeping', *Transactions of the National Association for the Promotion of Social Science*, pp. 618–19.

73. Mrs Beeton, *Book of Household Management*, p. 7; Branca, *Silent Sisterhood*, p. 54.
74. Hall, Edwin T. (1874), 'Flats – British and Foreign', pp. 81–103 in W. Shaw Sparrow (ed.), *Flats, Urban Houses and Cottage Homes*, Hodder and Stoughton, London, p. 85.
75. Perks, Sydney (1905), *Residential Flats of all Classes*, Batsford, London, p. 161. Plans of Queen Anne's Mansions are between pp. 158–9.
76. Tarn, J. N. (1974), 'French Flats for the English in Nineteenth-century London', pp. 19–40 in Anthony Sutcliffe (ed.), *Multi-storey Living*, Croom Helm, London, p. 27.
77. *The Builder* (1877), 'Queen Anne's Mansions and Milton's Garden', 2 June, vol. 35, no. 1791, p. 556; *The Builder* (1875), 'Queen Anne's Mansions, Westminster', 16 Oct, vol. 33, no. 1706, p. 924.
78. Perks, *Residential Flats*, p. 161.
79. Tarn, 'French Flats', p. 38.
80. Fisher, Roswell (1877), 'The Practical Side of Cooperative House-keeping', *Nineteenth Century*, Sept, no. 7, pp. 283–91.
81. Webster, Augusta (1877), 'Co-operative Housekeeping', *The Examiner*, 6 and 13 Oct, pp. 1257–8, 1291–2; also in *A Housewife's Opinions*, (1879), Macmillan, London, pp. 6–15.
82. Ibid., p. 11.
83. Ibid., p. 15.
84. Dixon and Muthesius, *Victorian Architecture*, p. 27.
85. Stevenson, J. J. (1880), *House Architecture*, Macmillan, London, vol. 2, p. 113.
86. Stamp, Gavin (1980), *The English House 1860–1914*, International Architect/Building Centre Trust, London, pp. 22–3.

CHAPTER 4

1. Branca, Patricia (1975), *Silent Sisterhood*, Croom Helm, London, p. 54.
2. Prochaska, F. K. (1980), *Women and Philanthropy in Nineteenth-century England*, OUP, London, p. 6.
3. *Census of England and Wales, 1871* (1873), vol. III, *Population Abstracts*, C872, HMSO, London.
4. *The Lancet*, 30 March 1867, p. 401, quoted in Harrison, Brian (1981), 'Women's Health and the Women's Movement in Britain: 1840–1940', pp. 15–71 in Charles Webster (ed.), *Biology, Medicine and Society 1840–1940*. CUP, Cambridge. See p. 20.
5. Greg, W. R. (1862), 'Why are Women Redundant', *National Review*, April, as quoted in Rosen, Andrew (1974), *Rise up, Women!*, RKP, London, pp. 4–5.
6. *Englishwoman's Review* (1899), 15 April, vol. 30, pp. 133–4.
7. *Census of England and Wales, 1881* (1883), vol. III, C3722, Table 6, HMSO, London; *Census of England and Wales, 1901* (1903), Summary Table, C1523, Table 36, HMSO, London.

8. Matthews, Jacquie (1983), 'Barbara Bodichon: Integrity in Diversity', pp. 90–123 in Dale Spender (ed.), *Feminist Theorists*, The Women's Press, London. See p. 111.
9. Prochaska, *Women and Philanthropy*, p. 228.
10. Callen, Anthea (1980), *Women in the Arts and Crafts Movement 1870–1914*, Astragal Books, London, pp. 8–9.
11. Davidoff, Leonore and Hall, Catherine (1983), 'The Architecture of Public and Private Life', pp. 327–45 in Derek Fraser and Anthony Sutcliffe (eds), *The Pursuit of Urban History*, Edward Arnold, London, pp. 343–4.
12. *Women and Work* (1874), 'Industrial and Educational Bureau', 6 June, no 1, p. 5.
13. Wells, H. G. (1980), *Ann Veronica*, Virago, London (first pub. 1909) p. 87.
14. Feilding, Lady Mary (1887), 'Help without Charity for Gentlewomen, by Money Invested in Flats and Producing Fair Interest', *Work and Leisure*, Sept, vol. 12, no. 9, pp. 236–7.
15. Feilding, Lady Mary (1887), 'Homes or Flats for Ladies', *The Queen*, 10 Dec, p. 752.
16. Ibid.
17. Feilding, Lady Mary (1887), 'How Associated Dwellings may be Carried Out', *Work and Leisure*, Nov, vol. 12, no. 11, pp. 287–9. See p. 289.
18. Esperance (1886), 'The Pfündes Haus Freiburg', *Englishwoman's Review*, 15 Nov, vol. 17, no. 163, pp. 482–6; *Work and Leisure* (1887), letter, Jan, vol. 12, no. 1, p. 28.
19. *Work and Leisure* (1887), 'A Castle in the Air', Sept, vol. 12, no. 9, pp. 231–5.
20. Twining, Louisa (1887), 'A Castle in the Air', *Work and Leisure*, Oct, vol. 12, no. 10, pp. 283–4; Twining writes that she has been advocating the advantages of associated homes for over 25 years, the obstacles being the independence and 'insularity' of English women, and the high cost of buildings and land in London. A. G. G. (1887), 'Argument for Associated Dwellings for Gentlewomen', *Work and Leisure*, Nov, vol. 12, no. 11, pp. 286–7; Feilding, Lady Mary (1887), *Work and Leisure*, 'How Associated Dwellings may be Carried Out', Nov, vol. 12, no. 11, pp. 287–9.
21. *Work and Leisure* (1888), 'A Castle in the Air', Jan, vol. 13, no. 1, pp. 1–4.
22. *Stock Exchange Official Yearbook* (1954), Thomas Skinner, London, p. 2994. The Ladies' Dwellings Co. Ltd changed its name to Sloane Gardens House, Ltd in 1934, and later became Sloane Securities Ltd.
23. See Chapter 2, note 16.
24. Holcombe, Lee (1983), *Wives and Property*, Martin Robertson, Oxford, p. 218.
25. Ibid., p. 219.
26. Rosen, *Rise up, Women!*, p. 12.
27. *Englishwoman's Review* (1889), 'Ladies' Residential Chambers', 15 June, vol. 20, no. 193, pp. 271–3 (reprinted from *The Queen*); see also

M. B. (1889), 'Dwellings for Working Gentlewomen', *The Queen*, 13 April, vol. 85, no. 2207, p. 503.

28. *The Builder* (1889), 'The Ladies' Residential Chambers, Chenies Street', 9 Nov, vol. 57, no. 2440, pp. 332–3.
29. *Englishwoman's Review*, 'Ladies' Residential Chambers', 15 June, p. 272.
30. Ibid.
31. The chambers are now used as flats by Camden Council. A Miss Black was one of the original residents, staying one year only, but it is impossible to say whether this was Clementina Black. See Post Office London Directory, 1890 onwards.
32. *Work and Leisure* (1889), 'The Ladies Dwellings Company, Limited', July, vol. 14, no. 7, pp. 171–2.
33. *Work and Leisure*, 'A Castle in the Air', Sept.
34. *Englishwoman's Review* (1888), 'The Ladies' Dwellings Company', 15 Aug, vol. 19, no. 183, pp. 344–7.
35. *Work and Leisure* (1889), 'Sloane Gardens House', Nov, vol. 14, no. 11, pp. 285–8.
36. *The Queen* (1892), 'Homes without Housekeeping', 14 May, vol. 91, no. 2368, p. 815.
37. Old maid (1897), 'Ladies' Dwellings', *The Queen*, 4 Oct, vol. 88, no. 2284, p. 507; Audley (1893), 'Ladies' Residential Clubs', *The Queen*, 20 May, vol. 93, no. 2421, p. 846.
38. *The Queen* (1895), 'A Club for Professional Women', 7 Sept, vol. 98, no. 2541, p. 435.
39. *Work and Leisure* (1889), 'Sloane Gardens House', April, vol. 14, no. 4, pp. 87–8. See p. 88.
40. Perks, Sydney (1905), *Residential Flats of all Classes*, Batsford, London, p. 158. The York Street Chambers still exist, the plaque giving their name and date of building clearly visible on the Wyndham Street side.
41. Hobhouse, Emily (1900), 'Women Workers: How they Live, How they Wish to Live', *Nineteenth Century*, March, vol. 47, no. 277, pp. 471–84. Hobhouse later exposed the use of concentration camps by the British in the Boer War. See Pakenham, Thomas (1982), *The Boer War*, Futura, London, p. 503ff. For work with Women's Industrial Council, see Fisher, John (1971), *That Miss Hobhouse*, Secker and Warburg, London, p. 67; Fry, A. Ruth (1929), *Emily Hobhouse*, Cape, London, p. 62.
42. *Building News* (1901), 'New Brabazon House, Pimlico, SW', 14 June, vol. 80, no. 2423, pp. 797, 820; 94 rooms, common dining hall. *The Architect* (1904), 'Lady Brabazon's Home for Gentlewomen', 19 Feb, vol. 71, p. 128; accommodation for 84. *Building News* (1905), 'St George's House, Vincent Square', 18 Aug, vol. 89, no. 2641, p. 218; rooms for 50 professional ladies. *Building News* (1905), 'Hopkinson House, Vauxhall Bridge Road, SW', 22 Dec, vol. 89, no. 2659, p. 875; residential flats for ladies, architect, R. S. Ayling (who also designed Lady Brabazon's Home for Gentlewomen).
43. *Building News* (1915), 'Home for Educated Women Workers, Nutford

House, Brown Street and Nutford Place, W', 8 Sept, vol. 109, no. 3166, pp. 260, 264–5, 275; *The Builder* (1916), 'Nutford House, W', 5 May, vol. 110, no. 3822, p. 341. Nutford House is now used as a hall of residence by the University of London.

44. Higgs, Mary and Hayward, Edward E. (1910), *Where shall she Live?*, P. S. King, London, pp. 180–1.

CHAPTER 5

1. Muthesius, Stefan (1982), *The English Terraced House*, Yale University Press, New Haven, p. 51.
2. Oliver, Paul, Davis, Ian and Bentley, Ian (1981), *Dunroamin*, Barrie and Jenkins, London, p. 60.
3. Oakley, Ann (1982), *Subject Women*, Fontana, Glasgow, p. 183; White, Cynthia L. (1970), *Women's Magazines 1693–1968*, Michael Joseph, London.
4. Dyhouse, Carol (1977), 'Good Wives and Little Mothers: Social Anxieties and the Schoolgirls' Curriculum, 1890–1920', *Oxford Review of Education*, vol. 3, no. 1, pp. 21–35.
5. Sillitoe, Helen (1933), *A History of the Teaching of Domestic Subjects*, Methuen, London, p. 60.
6. Johnson, H. T. (1889), 'Cooking by Co-operation – a Suggestion', *Englishwoman's Review*, 15 August, vol. 20, no. 195, pp. 346–8.
7. Johnson, H. T. (1889), 'Cooking by Co-operation', *Englishwoman's Review*, 14 Sept, vol. 20, no. 196, pp. 398–400.
8. *The Queen* (1889), 'Distributive Kitchens', 29 April, vol. 105, no. 2731, pp. 725–6.
9. M. B. (1899), 'A Distributive Kitchen', *The Queen*, 8 April, vol. 105, no. 2728, p. 606.
10. Kenealy, Annesley (1902), 'Travelling Kitchens and Co-operative Housekeeping', *The Lady's Realm*, Feb, vol. 11, pp. 513–20.
11. Burnett, John (1968), *Plenty and Want*, Penguin, Harmondsworth, pp. 235–6, quotes Mrs J. E. Panton (1888), *From Kitchen to Garret*, Ward and Downey, London, p. 19 as allowing £2 per week to keep 'Angelina, Edwin and the model maid' in comfort. See Burnett, op. cit., p. 237 for food prices at the turn of century.
12. Wolff, Captain M. P. (1884), *Food for the Million*, Sampson Low, Marston, Searle and Rivington, London.
13. Strange, Dr (1889), 'Co-operative Cooking, by a "Society for Supplying the Poor with Cheap and Wholesome Cooked Food"', *The Sanitary Record*, 15 Oct, vol. 11 (NS), p. 154.
14. Sellers, Edith (1894), 'The People's Kitchens in Vienna', *Nineteenth Century*, Nov, vol. 36, no. 213, pp. 744–53.
15. Sellers, Edith (1895), 'How to Organise a People's Kitchen in London', *Nineteenth Century*, March, vol. 37, no. 217, pp. 409–20.
16. Sellers, Edith (1914), 'Experiments in Cheap Catering', *Nineteenth Century and After*, Nov, vol. 76, no. 453, pp. 1123–37. See pp. 1136–7.

17. Rowntree, Joseph and Sherwell, Arthur (1901), *British 'Gothenburg' Experiments and Public-house Trusts*, Hodder and Stoughton, London, p. 4.
18. The Fox and Pelican pub at Grayshott, Hampshire, was a similar refreshment house, opened by the Grayshott and District Refreshment Association in August 1899. The pub sign was designed and painted by Walter Crane, and George Bernard Shaw presented a small library of books. The pub was taken over by Gales Brewery in the late 1950s, and still exists today. See Smith, J. H. (1978), *Grayshott, The Story of a Hampshire Village*, Petersfield Bookshop, Petersfield, Hants., Cp. 7.
19. Liddington, Jill and Norris, Jill (1978), *One Hand Tied Behind Us*, Virago, London, p. 40.
20. Webb, Catherine (1927), *The Woman with the Basket*, Women's Cooperative Guild, London, p. 21. The quotation is taken from the December 1921 *Woman's Outlook*.
21. Ibid., pp. 23–4.
22. Gaffin, Jean and Thoms, David (1983), *Caring and Sharing*, Cooperative Union, Manchester, p. 6, quoting from M. L. Davies (1904), *The Women's Cooperative Guild, 1883–1904*, Kirkby Lonsdale.
23. Webb, Catherine (1893), 'Co-operation as applied to Domestic Work', May, sheet produced for Women's Cooperative Guild annual meeting, Leicester, 13–15 June; BLPES, Women's Cooperative Guild collection, vol. 1, item 7, folio 11.
24. Women's Cooperative Guild (n.d.~1899), *Cooperative Housekeeping*, Popular Paper no. 27, Women's Cooperative Guild, Nottingham; BLPES, Women's Cooperative Guild collection, vol. 1, item 53, folio 165. Guild Winter circular, Sept 1894, shows Mrs Adams willing to lecture on 'Cooperative Homes and Small Incomes'; vol. 1, item 9, folio 13. Guild Winter circular Aug 1895 shows Miss Bamford willing to lecture on 'Associated Homes'; vol. 1, item 10, folio 15.
25. Davies, Margaret Llewelyn (1900), *A Co-operative Colony*, Women's Cooperative Guild, Kirkby, Lonsdale.
26. Knight, Mrs (1900), *Coffee and Cooked Meat Shops*, Women's Cooperative Guild, Nottingham.
27. Webb, Catherine (1927), *The Woman with the Basket*, p. 59.
28. Tarn, John Nelson (1973), *Five per cent Philanthropy*, CUP, Cambridge, Cp. 6.
29. Laurance, Jeremy (1983), 'Paternalism that Works? – Toynbee Hall at 100', *New Society*, 9 June, vol. 64, no. 1073, pp. 388–9. There were 600 settlements worldwide by 1900.
30. Barnett, Henrietta O. (1918), *Canon Barnett, His Life, Work, and Friends*, John Murray, London, vol. II, p. 41.
31. Ibid., p. 233.
32. Ibid., p. 234.
33. Addams, Jane (1961), *Twenty Years at Hull-House*, Signet, NY, p. 74; first pub. 1910.
34. Hayden, Dolores (1981), *The Grand Domestic Revolution*, MIT Press, Cambridge, Mass., pp. 164–9.

35. Barnett, Henrietta O., *Canon Barnett*, vol. I, p. 216.
36. Ibid., p. 28.
37. Hardy, Dennis (1979), *Alternative Communities in Nineteenth–century England*, Longmans, London, pp. 78–81.
38. Hill, Octavia (1883), 'Common Sense and the Dwellings of the Poor, I Improvements now Practicable', *Nineteenth Century*, Dec, vol. 14, no. 82, pp. 925–33. See p. 933.
39. Morris, William (1884), 'The Housing of the Poor', *Justice*, 19 July, vol. 1, no. 27, pp. 4–5. See p. 4.
40. Ibid., pp. 4–5.
41. Ibid., p. 5.
42. Morris, May (1936), *William Morris, Artist, Writer, Socialist*, Blackwell, Oxford, vol. II, p. 129.
43. Thompson, Paul (1977), *The Work of William Morris*, Quartet, London, p. 48.
44. Morris, William (1915), *Collected Works of William Morris*, Longmans Green, London, vol. 23, p. 22.
45. Briggs, Asa (ed.) (1962), *William Morris, Selected Writings and Designs*, Penguin, Harmondsworth, p. 176.
46. Ibid., pp. 176–7.
47. Morris, William (1970), *News from Nowhere*, ed. James Redmond, RKP, London, first pub. 1890, pp. 6, 34, 51–2, 86.
48. Thompson, Paul, *The Work of William Morris*, p. 48.
49. Callen, Anthea (1980), *Women in the Arts and Crafts Movement 1870–1914*, Astragal Books, London, p. 215.
50. Marshall, Peter (1962), 'A British Sensation', pp. 86–118 in Sylvia E. Bowman *et al.*, *Edward Bellamy Abroad*, Twayne Publishers, NY. See p. 87.
51. Lipow, Arthur (1982), *Authoritarian Socialism in America*, University of California Press, Berkeley, p. 24.
52. Bellamy, Edward (1982), *Looking Backward*, Penguin, Harmondsworth (first pub. 1888) p. 96.
53. Ibid., p. 126.
54. Bowman, Sylvia E. (1979), *The Year 2000, A Critical Biography of Edward Bellamy*, Octagon Books, NY, p. 291.
55. Bellamy, Edward, *Looking Backward*, pp. 184–6.
56. Marshall, Peter, *A British Sensation*, p. 96.
57. Redmond, James (1970), 'Introduction', pp. xi–xl in William Morris, *News from Nowhere*, RKP, London. See pp. xxxvi–xxxvii.
58. Morris, William, *News from Nowhere*, p. 55.
59. Marshall, Peter, *A British Sensation*, p. 96ff.
60. MacCarthy, Fiona (1981), *The Simple Life*, Lund Humphries, London, p. 9.
61. Ibid., p. 13; Rowbotham, Sheila and Weeks, Jeffrey (1977), *Socialism and the New Life*, Pluto Press, London, p. 44.
62. Marsh, Jan (1982), *Back to the Land*, Quartet, London, p. 124.
63. Kropotkin, Peter (1974), *Fields, Factories and Workshops Tomorrow*, Allen and Unwin, London, pp. 151–2.
64. For fuller explanation of the theoretical background to the 'back to

the land' movement, see Hardy, Dennis, *Alternative Communities*, pp. 78–83 and Marsh, Jan, *Back to the Land*, p. 8–23.

65. Marsh, Jan, *Back to the Land*, p. 19.
66. Rowbotham and Weeks, *Socialism and the New Life*, p.41; MacCarthy, Fiona, *The Simple Life*, p. 11.
67. Carpenter, Edward (1914), *Love's Coming-of-age*, Methuen, London (first pub. 1896) p. 59.
68. Ibid.
69. Ibid., p. 85.
70. Blatchford, Robert (1976), *Merrie England*, Journeyman Press, London (first pub. 1893) foreword.
71. Ibid., p. 17.
72. Liddington and Norris, *One Hand Tied*, p. 119.
73. Blatchford, Robert, *Merrie England*, p. 20.
74. Lichtheim, George (1975), *A Short History of Socialism*, Fontana, Glasgow, pp. 200, 202.
75. Hobsbawm, E. J. (1964), *Labouring Men*, Weidenfeld and Nicholson, London, pp. 250–71.
76. Cannadine, David (1982), 'Utopia Limited', *London Review of Books*, 15 July–4 Aug, pp. 20–1. See p. 20.
77. Britain, Ian (1982), *Fabianism and Culture*, CUP, Cambridge, p. 202.
78. Lane, Ann J. (1983), 'Charlotte Perkins Gilman: The Personal is Political', pp. 203–17 in Dale Spender (ed.), *Feminist Theorists*, Women's Press, London. See p. 208.
79. Hill, Mary A. (1980), *Charlotte Perkins Gilman, The Making of a Radical Feminist 1860–1896*, Temple University Press, Philadelphia, p. 284.
80. Gilman, Charlotte Perkins (1935), *The Living of Charlotte Perkins Gilman*, D. Appleton-Century Company, NY, p. 203.
81. Rowbotham and Weeks, *Socialism and the New Life*, p. 103.
82. Gilman, *The Living*, p. 209.
83. *Fabian News* (1896), Sept, vol. 6, no. 7, p. 30.
84. Hayden, *The Grand Domestic Revolution*, p. 188.
85. Gilman, *The Living*, pp. 233–7.
86. Gilman, Charlotte Perkins (1898), *Women and Economics*, Unwin, London. All references to this work are from the 6th edition, pub. 1908, Putnam's Sons, London.
87. Ibid., p. 67.
88. Ibid., p. 120.
89. Ibid., p. 210.
90. Ibid., p. 245.
91. Ibid., pp. 245–6.
92. Ibid., p. 242.
93. Ibid., pp. 314–15.
94. Gilman, *The Living*, p. 26.
95. Hill, *Charlotte Perkins Gilman*, p. 201.
96. Gilman, *The Living*, p. 230.
97. *Woodhull and Claflin's Weekly*, (1870), 'Sixteenth Amendment: Independence vs. Dependence: Which?', 25 June, p. 5.

98. Weimann, Jeanne Madeline (1981), *The Fair Women*, Academy Chicago, Chicago, pp. 539–40.

99. Putnam, J. P. (1980), 'The Apartment-house', *American Architect and Building News*, vol. 27, no. 732, 4 Jan, pp. 3–5; Hayden, *The Grand Domestic Revolution*, pp. 189–94.

100. S.D.S. (1899), 'Review: Women and Economics, C. P. Stetson', *Fabian News*, Nov, vol. 9, no. 9, pp. 35–6.

101. *Englishwoman's Review* (1899), 'Review: Women and Economics', 16 Oct, vol. 30, no. 243, pp. 272–4.

102. *The Humanitarian* (1899), 'Review: Women and Economics', Dec, vol. 15, no. 6, pp. 449–52. See p. 452.

103. Gilman, *The Living*, p. 260.

104. Diary of Beatrice Webb, 9 April 1924, typescript pp. 43–4; it should be added that she had been attempting to work when a guest in a country house used by the Labour Party, and had not been wholly successful due to the demands of social life. Britain, *Fabianism and Culture*, p. 141.

105. *Fabian News* (1899), May, vol. 9, no. 3, p. 12. Interested parties were told to apply to Percy Alden of Mansfield House, East London, for terms. The site of the cooperative home at 87 Barking Road, Canning Town is now occupied by shops and a garage.

106. McEwen, D. (n.d., probably pre-1914), Preliminary memorandum for The Associated Dwellings Company (Limited), London; collection of Nuffield College Library, Fabian Archives, E119/2. Daniel McEwen joined the Fabian Society in 1890.

107. Muthesius, Hermann (1979), *The English House*, Crosby Lockwood Staples, London (first pub. 1904/5) p. 146.

108. Ibid.

109. Ibid., p. 145.

110. Chew, Doris Nield (1982), *The Life and Writings of Ada Nield Chew*, Virago, London, p. 54.

111. Robertson, Priscilla (1982), *An Experience of Women*, Temple University Press, Philadelphia, p. 149; Duelli-Klein, Renate (1983), 'Hedwig Dohm: Passionate Theorist', pp. 165–83 in Dale Spender (ed.), *Feminist Theorists*, Women's Press, London. See pp. 169–70, 181.

112. Berneri, Marie Louise (1950), *Journey through Utopia*, RKP, London, pp. 281, 287–9.

113. Further details of housing in industrial villages are given in Chapter 1. See also Darley, Gillian (1978), *Villages of Vision*, Granada, St Albans, pp. 122–36; Meakin, Budgett (1905), *Model Factories and Villages*, Fisher Unwin, London.

114. Toynbee, Polly (1971), *A Working Life*, Hodder and Stoughton, London, p. 112; Darley, *Villages of Vision*, p. 140–4.

115. Harvey, W. Alexander (1906), *The Model Village and its Cottages*, Batsford, London, p. 5; Darley, *Villages of Vision*, pp. 137–40.

116. Meakin, *Model Factories*.

117. Cadbury, George (1900), 'Bournville Estate: Important Statement by Mr George Cadbury', *Birmingham News*, 10 Feb, vol. 41, no. 1042, p. 7.

118. Howard, Ebenezer (1965), *Garden Cities of Tomorrow*, Faber and Faber, London. See preface by F. J. Osborn, pp. 18–19.

119. Fishman, Robert (1982), *Urban Utopias in the Twentieth Century*, MIT Press, Cambridge, Mass., p. 32.

120. Macfadyen, Dugald (1933), *Sir Ebenezer Howard and the Town Planning Movement*, Manchester University Press, Manchester, p. 20; Fishman, *Urban Utopias*, p. 33.

121. Macfadyen, *Sir Ebenezer Howard*, p. 21.

122. Ibid., p. 20; Marsh, *Back to the Land*, p. 224.

123. Howard, E. (1983), 'Summary of E. Howard's Proposals for a Home Colony', *Nationalization News*, Feb, vol. 3, pp. 20–1.

124. Howard, *Garden Cities*, p. 9.

125. Ibid., pp. 78–9.

126. Ibid., p. 54.

127. Hertfordshire County Record Office (HCRO), Howard Papers, D/EHoF1, manuscript first draft of 'Tomorrow' (n.d.~ 1892).

128. HCRO, Howard Papers, D/EHoF3, early draft of 'Tomorrow' (~1892).

129. *Fabian News* (1898), 'Review', Dec, vol. 8, no. 10, p. 39.

130. Fishman, *Urban Utopias*, pp. 56–7.

131. HCRO, Howard Papers, D/EHoF3, lecture to Fabian Society, (1901), 11 Aug.

132. Fishman, *Urban Utopias*, pp. 57–60 gives a good account of these events.

133. Lander, H. C. (1901), 'The Advantages of Co-operative Dwellings', pp. 61–8 in The Garden City Conference at Bournville 1901, *Report of Proceedings*, Garden City Association, London.

134. Garden City Conference, p. 80; Keable, Gladys (1963), *To-morrow Slowly Comes*, Town and Country Planning Association, London.

135. British Architectural Library, FRIBA nomination papers for H. C. Lander, no. 1554, 1914; Nuffield College Library, Fabian Archives, F85/1, p. 74. Sheppard, F. W. (ed.) (1970), *Survey of London*, vol. 36, *The Parish of St Paul, Covent Garden*, Athlone Press, London, p. 140.

136. Johnson, Kenneth (1976), *The Book of Letchworth*, Barracuda Books, Chesham, Bucks, p. 46; Lander, H. C. (1900), 'Consideration of Practical Difficulties as regards Building', pp. 27–31 in *Fabian Tract* no. 101, Fabian Society, London, April. See p. 31. The paper was originally given at the Fabian Society Housing Conference, London, 1 March 1900 (see Nuffield College Library, Fabian Archives, G48/1, item 2). Lander also gave a paper on 'Building Difficulties' on 15 Dec 1899; see *Fabian News* (1899), Dec, vol. 9, no. 10, p. 38.

137. Personal details on H. C. Lander taken from letter written by C. H. Sparks, April 1955 to the RIBA *Journal*; letter held by BAL, H. C. Lander biography file.

138. Lander, 'The Advantages of Co-operative Dwellings', p. 62; the Garden City Association later published the paper as Garden City Tract no. 7.

139. Ibid., p. 64.

140. See Chapter 3, note 60.

141. Unwin, Raymond (1901), 'On the Building of Houses in the Garden

City', pp. 69–74 in Garden City Conference, *Report of Proceedings*. See p. 70.

142. Ibid., p. 72.
143. Miller, Mervyn (1981), 'Raymond Unwin 1863–1940', pp. 72–102 in Gordon E. Cherry (ed.), *Pioneers in British Planning*, Architectural Press, London. See p. 73. Much of the detail on Unwin's early career comes from Miller. See also Miller, Mervyn K. (1981), 'To Speak of Planning is to Speak of Unwin', unpub. PhD thesis, University of Birmingham.
144. Rowbotham and Weeks, *Socialism and the New Life*, p. 50.
145. Unwin, Raymond (1889), 'Sutton Hall', *Commonweal*, 15 June, p. 160.
146. Rowbotham and Weeks, *Socialism and the New Life*, p. 57
147. Miller, 'To Speak of Planning', p. 74.
148. For details of the growth of the arts and crafts movement, see Naylor, Gillian (1971), *The Arts and Crafts Movement*, Studio Vista, London; Davey, Peter (1980), *Arts and Crafts Architecture*, Architectural Press, London; Callen, *Women in the Arts and Crafts Movement*.
149. Taylor, Nicholas (1980), 'The Houses of Parker and Unwin', pp. 11–26 in *Barry Parker and Raymond Unwin: Architects*, Catalogue of exhibition, Architectural Association, London. See pp. 13–15.
150. Parker, Barry and Unwin, Raymond (1901), *The Art of Building a Home*, Longmans, Green, London. See Chapter 7, 'Of Cooperation in Building', Raymond Unwin.
151. Ibid., p. 94.
152. Ibid., pp. 101–2.
153. Ibid., p. 104.
154. Swenarton, Mark (1981), *Homes Fit for Heroes*, Heinemann Educational, London, pp. 22–3.
155. Unwin, Raymond (1902), 'Cottage Plans and Common Sense', *Fabian Tract* no. 109, March, Fabian Society, London.
156. Ibid., p. 15.
157. *The Builder* (1901), 'Report of Meeting', 9 Nov, vol. 81, no. 3066, pp. 403–4. See p. 404.
158. Unwin, 'On the Building of Houses in the Garden City', p. 72.
159. Miller, 'Raymond Unwin', p. 81; Fishman, *Urban Utopias*, pp. 62–3.
160. Darley, *Villages of Vision*, p. 117–21; Bolsterli, Margaret Jones (1977), *The Early Community at Bedford Park*, RKP, London.
161. Johnson, Bernard (1977), *Brentham, Ealing's Garden Suburb*, Brentham Society, London.

CHAPTER 6

1. The original First Garden City plan by Barry Parker and Raymond Unwin, 1904, is held by First Garden City Museum, Letchworth (FGCM).
2. Miller, Mervyn (1979), 'Garden City Influence on the Evolution of

Housing Policy', *Local Government Studies*, Nov/Dec, vol. 5, no. 6, pp. 5–22. See p. 10.

3. Miller, Mervyn (1979), 'Letchworth Revisited – Cheap Cottages from 1905', *Housing Outlook*, no. 4, pp. 10–14. See p. 10.

4. Parker, Barry and Unwin, Raymond (1905), 'The Cheap Cottage: What is Really Needed', *The Garden City*, July, vol. 1, no. 4, pp. 55–8. See p. 55.

5. Kornwolf, James D. (1972), *M. H. Baillie Scott and the Arts and Crafts Movement*, Johns Hopkins, Baltimore, pp. 7, 115.

6. Scott, M. H. Baillie (1894-5), 'An Ideal Suburban House', *The Studio*, vol. 4, pp. 127–32.

7. Taylor, Nicholas (1980), 'The Houses of Parker and Unwin', pp. 11–26 in *Barry Parker and Raymond Unwin: Architects*, Catalogue of exhibition, Architectural Association, London. See p. 15.

8. Scott, M. H. Baillie (1906), *Houses and Gardens*, Newnes, London, pp. 102–3.

9. Dyson, H. Kempton (1905), *Cheap Cottages and the Exhibition at Letchworth*, vol. 18, pt I, Sept, pp. 108–15, pt II, Oct, pp. 154–69. See pp. 109, 158, 165. See also Weaver, Lawrence (1913), *The 'Country Life' Book of Cottages*, Country Life, London, pp. 31–2.

10. *The Book of the Cheap Cottages Exhibition* (1905), County Gentleman and Land and Water, London, p. 91.

11. Scott, *Houses and Gardens*, pp. 102–3; Elder-Duncan (1913), *Country Cottages and Week-end Homes*, Cassell, London, p. 62.

12. Elder-Duncan, *Country Cottages*, p. 63 (first pub. 1906). See correspondence between Howard Cottage Society Ltd and First Garden City Ltd, held by Howard Cottage Society; letter dated 13 July 1914 from FGC on subject of Meadow Way Green, mentions party door as in Dr Ledward's two cottages by Baillie Scott, built in Norton Way North, 1905. See also Letchworth Street Directory, 1907.

13. Howard, Ebenezer (1905), Paper read before Mansion House Housing Council, 11 July, Mansion House, London; HCRO D/EHoF3.

14. Phipson, Evacustes A. (1905), 'Why not Associated Homes?', *The Garden City*, July, vol. 1, no. 4, p. 64.

15. Wells, H. G. (1905), 'A Modern Utopia', *Fortnightly Review*, Feb, vol. 77, no. 458, pp. 366–80; Wells, H. G. (n.d.), *A Modern Utopia*, Odhams Press, London, pp. 417–18.

16. Wells, H. G. (1905), 'Utopianisms 1, The Garden Cities', *Daily Mail*, 18 March, p. 4.

17. Wells, H. G. (1905), 'Utopianisms 2, A Cottage in a Garden', *Daily Mail*, 30 March, p. 4.

18. Wells, H. G. (1905), 'Joint Households', *Daily Mail*, 25 May, p. 6.

19. Wells, H. G. (1905), 'A Woman's Day in Utopia', *Daily Mail*, 7 June, p. 4. See also Wells, H. G. (1905), 'State Babies', *Daily Mail*, 20 April, p. 4.

20. Gilman, Charlotte Perkins (1903), *The Home, its Work and Influence*, McClure, Phillips, NY; rep. Source Book Press, NY, 1970.

21. *Fabian News* (1905), Advertisement for Gilman lectures, Feb, vol. 15, no. 2, p. 8. The lectures were 'on different aspects of the Woman's

Question' and cost one guinea for the whole course, or 4 shillings each.

22. *Daily News* (1905), 'The Servant Difficulty', 21 Feb. Press cuttings describing the Gilman lecture tour of 1905 are to be found in the Charlotte Perkins Gilman Papers, Schlesinger Library, box 23, folder 289.

23. *Morning Leader* (1905), 'Servant Girl Problem', 21 Feb; *Daily Mirror* (1905), 'Houses that could be Run without Servants', 22 Feb; *Daily Mirror* (1905), 'Getting Rid of Servants', 22 Feb; *Daily News* (1905), 'Doom of the Kitchen', 22 Feb; A.M.B. (1905), *Society Pictorial*, 'A Mad Notion', 4 March; Marguerite (1905), 'Domestic Reform', *Sunday School Chronicle*, 2 March. The *Daily Express, Daily Mail, Aberdeen Free Press, Daily Telegraph, Manchester Dispatch, Birmingham Mail, Sheffield Telegraph* and *Newcastle Evening Mail* were among other newspapers reporting Gilman's lectures in Feb/Mar 1905.

24. Gilman, Charlotte Perkins (1935), *The Living of Charlotte Perkins Gilman*, D. Appleton-Century Company, NY, p. 301. H. G. Wells and C. P. Gilman corresponded with each other; letters dated July 1906 and June 1908 are to be found in Charlotte Perkins Gilman Papers, Schlesinger Library, box 12, folder 150. One subject mentioned is Wells' attitude to women.

25. Miller, Mervyn (1978), *Letchworth Garden City 1903–1978*, catalogue of exhibition at First Garden City Museum, North Hertfordshire District Council, pp. 46–9.

26. Crane, Walter (1905), 'Co-operative Housekeeping', *The Garden City*, July, vol. 1, no. 4, p. 59.

27. Crane, Walter (1907), *An Artist's Reminiscences*, Methuen, London, pp. 258, 367–8.

28. Crane, Walter (1905), *Ideals in Art*, George Bell, London, pp. 115–17.

29. BAL, FRIBA nomination papers for Lionel F. Crane, no. 1764, 1921.

30. Crane, *Ideals*, pp. vii, 114–15, 117.

31. Proposed experiment in house grouping for the purpose of common kitchen arrangements, to be tried in 'Garden City' (1904), Macdonald, Hampstead. FGCM, BL 442.

32. Howard, Ebenezer (1906), 'Co-operative Housekeeping', *Daily Mail*, 18 Aug, p. 7; reprinted in *The Garden City* (1906), NS vol. 1, no. 8, Sept, pp. 170–1. See also *Fabian News* (1906), Sept, vol. 16, no. 10, p. 37 for notice of Lander's participation in scheme.

33. Howard, Ebenezer (n.d. post-1909), 'Cooperative Housekeeping, Applying the Principle to a Working-class Scheme'; FGCM, BL 442.

34. Howard, Ebenezer (1907), 'Letchworth Co-operative Houses', *The Garden City*, Oct, vol. 2, pp. 436–8. See also p. 434.

35. Letchworth Co-operative Houses Ltd (1911), *Prospectus*, Letchworth; FGCM, BL 443. Minutes of First Garden City Ltd, 2 July 1980, 1 Oct 1908, 11 Nov 1909, 24 Nov 1910; held by Letchworth Garden City Corporation, with thanks to Doreen Cadwallader for obtaining this information.

36. Bremner, C. S. (1911), 'Cooperative Housing at Letchworth', *Pall Mall Gazette*, 29 Nov.

37. Howard, E. (1910), 'Cooperative Housekeeping' (opening day speech at Homesgarth), 20 Nov, ms., HCRO, D/EHoF3; Letchworth Cooperative Houses Ltd (1910), Letter to shareholders, 5 Oct, FGCM, BL444; *The Builder* (1903), 'Ingram House, Stockwell', 12 Sept, vol. 85, no. 3162, pp. 272–3.

38. *Bristol Mercury* (1909), 'A Communal House', 28 June, FGCM, 1908/9 cuttings, p. 177.

39. Letter from C. H. Sparks, April 1955 to the RIBA *Journal*; letter held by BAL, H. C. Lander biography file.

40. *Westminster Gazette* (1910), 'Mistress and Maid', 24 Nov; report, 28 Nov; FGCM, cuttings 1910, pp. 82–3.

41. Lander, H. Clapham (1911), 'Associated Homes', *Garden Cities and Town Planning*, NS vol. 1, no. 3, April, pp. 62, 71–2.

42. Howard, Ebenezer (1913), 'A New Way of Housekeeping', *Daily Mail*, 27 March, p. 4. See also *Garden Cities and Town Planning* (1913), April, NS vol. 3, no. 4, p. 88.

43. Howard, Ebenezer (n.d.~1913), 'Cooperative Housekeeping and the New Finance', ms., HCRO, D/EHoF10.

44. Brex, Twells (1913), 'Privacy of the New Housekeeping', *Daily Mail*. 3 April, p. 6.

45. Letter from Lucy Carr Shaw to Ebenezer Howard, 3 March 1913, HCRO, D/EHoF25; Chappelow, Allan (1961), *Shaw the Villager and Human Being*, Charles Skilton, London, pp. 184–5. Lucy Carr Shaw was the sister of George Bernard Shaw.

46. Howard, Ebenezer (n.d. post-1909), 'Cooperative Housekeeping, Applying the Principle to a Working-class Scheme'; FGCM, BL 442.

47. Howard, Ebenezer (1913), 'A New Outlet for Woman's Energy', *Garden Cities and Town Planning Magazine*, June, vol. 3, pp. 152–9. See p. 158. Typescript of article in HCRO, D/EHoF10.

48. Gilman, *The Living*, pp. 301–2.

49. *Fabian News* (1913), July, vol. 24, no. 8, p. 59.

50. Interview with Doris Nield Chew, daughter of Ada Nield Chew, quoted in Liddington, Jill and Norris, Jill (1978), *One Hand Tied Behind Us*, Virago, London, p. 236; Chew, Doris Nield (1982), *Ada Nield Chew*, Virago, London, pp. 42, 54.

51. See, for instance, Chew, Ada Nield (1911), 'All in the Day's Work: 1, Mrs. Turpin', *The Englishwoman*, July, vol. 11, no. 31, pp. 39–48; Haslam, James (1910), 'Life in a Lancashire Factory Home', *The Englishwoman*, June, vol. 6, no. 17, pp. 210–20; Fraser, Helen (1913), 'The Women's Home of Glasgow', *The Englishwoman*, Dec, vol. 20, no. 60, pp. 257–61.

52. Enid (1911), 'The Lady at the Round Table', *The Referee*, 28 May; FGCM, cuttings 1911, p. 278.

53. George, W. L. (1913), *Woman and Tomorrow*, Jenkins, London, p. 89.

54. Marguerite (1911), 'Cooperative Kitchens', *Sunday School Chronicle*; FGCM, cuttings 1911, p. 164.

55. Mumford, Lewis C. (1914), 'Community Cooking', *The Forum*, July, vol. 52, pp. 95–9; Hayden, Dolores (1981), *The Grand Domestic Revolution*, MIT Press, Cambridge, Mass., p. 336.

56. Purdom, C. B. (1913), *The Garden City*, Dent, London, p. 103. In later years, Purdom referred to Homesgarth only briefly, as 'interesting'; see (1925), *The Building of Satellite Towns*, Dent, London, p. 64. See also Hayden, *The Grand Domestic Revolution*, p. 336.
57. Bremner, C. S. (1911), 'Co-operative Housing at Letchworth', *Pall Mall Gazette*, 29 Nov.
58. *Architects' and Builders' Journal* (1911), 'Kitchenless Dwellings', 29 Nov.
59. Ambler, Jones (1902), 'Artisans' Dwellings from the Private Point of View', *The Builder*, 17 May, pp. 495–7.
60. Howard, Ebenezer, 'A New Way of Housekeeping', p. 4.
61. Interviews with Ken Spinks and Miss K. M. Kaye, Letchworth, 14 Nov 1983. Towards the end of the Second World War, communal meals were eaten in the evening on weekdays and at midday at weekends.
62. The housewife (1873), 'Co-operative Households', *The Queen*, 4 Oct, p. 268.
63. Green, Brigid Grafton (1977), *Hampstead Garden Suburb 1907–1977*, Hampstead Garden Suburb Residents Association, p. 6; Barnett, Henrietta O. (1905), 'A Garden Suburb at Hampstead', *Contemporary Review*, Feb, vol. 87, pp. 231–7. A full account of the origin and development of Hampstead Garden Suburb can be found in Green, *Hampstead Garden Suburb* and Slack, Kathleen M. (1982), *Henrietta's Dream*, Slack, London.
64. Barnett, Henrietta (1918), *Canon Barnett, His Life, Work, and Friends*, John Murray, London, vol. 2, p. 313; Barnett, *A Garden Suburb*, p. 235.
65. Green, *Hampstead Garden Suburb*, p. 11.
66. Ibid., pp. 10–11.
67. *Garden Cities and Town Planning* (1909), 'Co-partnership Homes for the Aged at Hampstead Garden Suburb', Nov, vol. 4, no. 35, pp. 248–9. Sadly the Orchard was demolished in 1970, after years of neglect, and replaced by dull modern flats.
68. Miller, Mervyn (1981), 'Raymond Unwin 1863–1940', pp. 72–102 in Gordon E. Cherry (ed.), *Pioneers in British Planning*, Architectural Press, London. See p. 85.
69. Unwin, Raymond (1909), *Town Planning in Practice*, Fisher Unwin, London, p. 382.
70. Ibid., p. 381.
71. Ibid., p. 383. See also Unwin, Raymond (1909), 'Co-operative Architecture', *The City*, (pub. Letchworth), Nov, pp. 249–55.
72. Green, *Hampstead Garden Suburb*, p. 11.
73. Barnett, Dame Henrietta (1928), *The Story of the Growth of the Hampstead Garden Suburb 1907–1928*, HGS Trust, London, p. 20.
74. Ibid.
75. Tarn, John Nelson (1968), 'The Improved Industrial Dwellings Company', *Transactions of the London and Middlesex Archaeological Society*, vol. 22, pp. 43–59.
76. Barnett, *The Story of HGS*, p. 20; Slack, *Henrietta's Dream*, p. 96.

77. Barnett, *The Story of HGS*, p. 21. Records of the IIDC's administration of Waterlow Court have been lost or destroyed; personal communication to author, Mount Provincial Developments Ltd, 20 Sept 1983.
78. Scott, M. H. Baille (1906), *Houses and Gardens*, Newnes, London, pp. 116–18; Scott, M. H. Baillie and Beresford, A. Edgar (1933), *Houses and Gardens*, Architecture Illustrated, London, p. 276; Kornwolf, James D. (1972), M. H. Baillie Scott, list of works, no. 85.
79. Scott, M. H. Baillie (1909), 'Ideals in Building, False and True', pp. 139–51 in T. Raffles Davison (ed.), *The Arts Connected with Building*, Batsford, London. See p. 150.
80. Scott, M. H. Baillie (1911), 'Mr Baillie Scott on the Modern Home', *Garden Cities and Town Planning*, Sept, NS vol. 1, no. 8, pp. 199–200.
81. Scott, and Beresford, *Houses and Gardens*, p. 257. Waterlow Court was illustrated in numerous magazines, including: 'Waterlow Court (1909), *British Architect*, 9 July, pp. 19–22; 'The Hampstead Garden Suburb and its Architecture' (1912), *The Builder*, 30 Aug, vol. 103, no. 3630, pp. 250–6, see p. 255; 'The Builder (1909), 10 July, vol. 97, no. 3466, p. 48. Stickley, Gustav (1909), 'Rapid Growth of the Garden City Movement, which promises to reorganise social conditions all over the world', *The Craftsman*, Dec, vol. 17, no. 3, pp. 296–310. See p. 309. The plans of Waterlow Court are held by Hampstead Garden Suburb Archives Trust. See also Kornwolf, M. H. Baillie Scott, list of works no. 122 and pp. 312–16.
82. Lloyd, T. Alwyn (1909), 'The Associated Homes at Hampstead Garden Suburb', *Garden Cities and Town Planning*, Nov, NS vol. 4, no. 35, p. 246; Longhurst, Esther (1909), 'How can I Earn a Living?', *Woman Worker*, 8 Sept, vol. 4, no. 10, p. 235.
83. Information on early life at Waterlow Court from interviews with Miss C. Bury and Miss Bessie Wright, 7 July 1983, Golders Green and Hampstead Garden Suburb.
84. Scott and Beresford, *Houses and Gardens*, p. 1.
85. Lady Phyllis (1908), 'Flats for Working Ladies', *The Bystander*, 16 Dec.
86. *Guardian*, 9 Dec 1908.
87. Dawson, Julia (1909), 'Our Woman's Letter', *Clarion*, 16 July; FGCM cuttings 1908/9, p. 192. Julia Dawson was the pseudonym of Mrs D. J. Myddleton-Worrall; see Liddington and Norris, *One Hand Tied*, p. 275. Articles supporting Waterlow Court: *The Sphere* (1909), 'About Woman's Sphere and Interests', 17 July, p. iv; *Evening News* (1909), 'Lonely Girls', 1 July; *Daily News* (1909), 'Bachelor Girls' Flats', 1 July.
88. Barnett, *The Story of HGS*, pp. 73–4. Information from Brigid Grafton Green, Hampstead Garden Suburb Archives Trust archivist.
89. *The Common Cause* (1909), 'Institute for Domestic Service', 17 June, p. 126.
90. Somervell, E. L. (1909), 'Suffragist Ideals', *National Review*, March, vol. 53, no. 313, pp. 139–48; Onslow, Lady Madeleine (1909), 'The Tactics of War', *The Englishwoman*, Oct, vol. 3, no. 9, pp. 256–66;

Somervell, E. L. (1909), 'The Open Letter', *Women and Economics, The Englishwoman,* Dec, vol. 4, no. 11, pp. 162–4; A woman worker (1910), 'Live and Let Live', *The Englishwoman,* Jan, vol. 4, no. 12, pp. 266–72. See p. 271.

91. Hamilton, Cicely (1981), *Marriage as a Trade,* Women's Press, London (first pub. 1909), p. 27.

92. Anon. (1903), *Christopolis,* S. W. Partridge, London, p. 49.

93. Owen, Edwards (1908), *Nutopia or Nineteen-twenty-one,* Henry J. Drane, London, p. 66.

94. *Englishwoman's Review of Social and Industrial Questions* (1903), 'Co-operative Cooking', 15 Oct, vol. 34, no. 259, pp. 267–8; Austin, Gertrude (1911), 'The Rothschild Tenement Houses in Paris', *The Englishwoman,* Nov, vol. 12, no. 35, pp. 188–95.

95. Information on the lives of Miss R. I. Pym and Miss S. E. Dewe, and the history of Meadow Way Green, obtained from interviews with Miss V. Exton, Mr McBride, Mr and Mrs Woollons, 29 June 1983, Letchworth; Ken Spinks, Margaret Pooley, Elaine Tickle, Miss K. M. Kaye, 14 November 1983, Letchworth.

96. *Letchworth Citizen* (1938), 'Members Show their Gratitude', 18 Nov.

97. Mervyn, Miller (1979), 'The Howard Cottage Society', *Housing Outlook,* Summer, no. 5, pp. 13–16,. See p. 14.

98. Minutes of the Board of the Howard Cottage Society, 5 May 1914 and 31 July 1914.

99. Correspondence between Howard Cottage Society and the Public Works Loan Board, 30 June 1914–29 July 1914; held by Howard Cottage Society.

100. Letter from Howard Cottage Society to First Garden City Ltd, 22 May 1914; held by Howard Cottage Society.

101. Correspondence between Howard Cottage Society and First Garden City Ltd, 22 May 1914 to 30 July 1914; held by Howard Cottage Society.

102. Obituary, C. M. Crickmer (1971), *Building,* 5 Feb, vol. 220, p. 6/46.

103. Purdom, *The Building of Satellite Towns,* p. 65.

104. Letchworth Settlement Annual Report 1935–1936, The Settlement, Letchworth, p. 4; *Letchworth Citizen* (1946), 'Death of Former Warden of Settlement', 6 Aug, pp. 1, 5.

105. Purdom, *The Building of Satellite Towns,* p. 65.

106. Purdom, C. B. (1949), *The Building of Satellite Towns,* Dent, London, p. 63.

107. *Letchworth Citizen,* 'Death of Former Warden of Settlement', 6 Aug, p. 5.

108. Letter from C. P. Gilman to Miss Seruya, 15 Adam Street, London, dated 30 March 1913, Fawcett Library, autograph letter collection, vol. 3, part B; Gilman was annoyed to be considered exclusively as a 'socialist' or 'suffragist'. *Daily News,* 15 May 1913, reports that Gilman was a guest of Mr and Mrs Fisher Unwin when in London, where she met well-known suffragists.

109. Chew, Ada Nield (1914), 'The Problem of the Married Working

Woman', *Common Cause*, 6 March, rep. pp. 230–4 in Chew, Doris Nield, *Ada Nield Chew*. See p. 233.

110. Liddington and Norris, *One Hand Tied*, pp. 236–7.

111. S.B. (1911), 'The Burden of Housework', *Votes for Women*, 7 April, p. 442.

112. Rosen, Andrew (1974), *Rise Up, Women!*, RKP, London, pp. 174–5.

113. Howard, Ebenezer (1913), 'A New Outlet for Women's Energy', *The Suffragette*, pt I, 29 Aug, vol. 1, no. 47, p. 799, pt II, 5 Sept, vol. 1, no. 47, p. 815.

114. Pankhurst, Christabel (1913), 'Married Women's Health', *The Suffragette*, 5 Dec, vol. 2, no. 60, p. 169.

115. Pankhurst, Christabel (1913), 'The Burden of Poverty', *The Suffragette*, 26 Dec, vol. 2, no. 63, p. 245.

116. Thompson, Paul (1977), *The Edwardians*, Granada, St Albans, p. 245.

117. Rosen, *Rise Up, Women!*, p. 70; Liddington and Norris, *One Hand Tied*, pp. 206–7.

118. Culpin, Ewart G. (1913), *The Garden City Movement Up-to-date*, Garden Cities and Town Planning Association, London, lists 54 garden city schemes; see also Abercrombie, Patrick (1910), 'A Comparative Review of Examples of Modern Town Planning and "Garden City" Schemes in England', *Town Planning Review*, April, vol. 1, no. 1, pp.18–38 and July, vol. 1, no. 2, pp.111–28.

119. Robinson, David N. (1981), *The Book of the Lincolnshire Coastline*, Barracuda, Buckingham, pp. 85–6, 96–7; personal communication from David N. Robinson, 23 July 1983.

CHAPTER 7

1. *The Standard* (1911), 'Domestic Drudgery', 15 Nov.

2. Alice Melvin lived at 63 Princes Avenue, Finchley in 1910. The house still exists, each pair of terraced houses attempting to masquerade as a semi-detached.

3. *Daily Mail* (1910), 'The Co-operative Kitchen', 24 Aug.

4. Details of Brent Garden Village (Finchley) from reports of the Chief Registrar of Friendly Societies for the year ending 31 December 1910, Part B, *Industrial and Provident Societies* (1911), HMSO, London; see reg. no. 5073. Files on the Society have been destroyed. *Birmingham Post* (1910), 'New Garden Suburb for London', 11 Aug.

5. E. L. (1910), 'Co-operative Housekeeping', *Health and Home*, 25 Aug.

6. *Town Planning Review* (1911), 'The Brent Garden Village: A New Departure', Jan, vol. 1, no. 4, pp. 340–1; M.D. (1910), 'Co-operative Housekeeping', *Daily Mail*, 1 Sept, p. 9.

7. *Town Planning Review*, 'The Brent Garden Village', p. 341; *Christian Commonwealth* (1910), 'The Brent Garden Village', 24 Aug. See also *Pall Mall Gazette* (1910), 'Co-operative Housekeeping', 5 Sept; *Daily News* (1910), 'Brent Garden Village', 5 Sept; *The Standard* (1910),

'Brent Garden Village', 5 Sept; *Christian Commonwealth* (1910), 'Brent Garden Village', 7 Sept.

8. Gilman, Charlotte Perkins (1898), *Women and Economics*, Unwin, London, p. 243; see Chap 5, p. 70 above.
9. *The Times* (1911), 'A Kitchenless House', 14 Nov, p. 7.
10. *Daily Express* (1911), 'Paradise for Wives', 16 Nov.
11. *Leeds Mercury* (1911), 'Kitchenless Houses', 16 Nov; *Daily Telegraph* (1911), 'Topics of the Hour', 18 Nov; *Daily Sketch* (1911), 'First Houses without Kitchens: Residents dine at a Central Hall', 16 Nov, p. 16.
12. Meredith, M. (1911), 'Housing of Educated Women Workers', *The Englishwoman*, Feb, vol. 9, no. 26, pp. 159–64; see p. 162. See also Benoit-Levy, Georges (1911), *La cité-jardin*, Cités-jardins de France, Paris, vol. 3, pp. 65–6.
13. Kelly's Finchley Directory 1914–15.
14. Cedar Court plans, and plans of other village housing by P. Woollatt Home, held by London Borough of Barnet, Borough Engineer and Surveyor's Department, Finchley. See plan no. 3211 for Cedar Court. The area of the original Brent Garden Village consists of Finchley Way, Hamilton Way, The Drive and part of Brent Way, London N3.
15. Davin, Anna (1982), 'Foreword', pp. ix–xxiv in Chew, Doris Nield, *Ada Nield Chew*, Virago, London. See pp. xix–xx; *The Freewoman* showed the breadth of feminist debate, and was published from Nov 1911 until Oct 1912.
16. Low, B. (1912), 'Two Practical Suggestions', *The Freewoman*, 15 Feb, vol. 1, no. 13, p. 252; Starling, B. W. F. (1912), 'Cooperative House-keeping', *The Freewoman*, 22 Feb, vol. 1, no. 14, p. 273; Chapman, Dorothy (1912), 'Group-houses', *The Freewoman*, 29 Feb, vol. 1, no. 15, p. 291; Edwards, A. Herbage (1912), 'Group Houses', *The Freewoman*, 7 March, vol. 1, no. 16, p. 312. Edwards probably lived at Fernbank, one of the first Woollatt Home houses to be built (the plans were approved in July 1911); it stood almost opposite the Lodge, and still exists today.
17. Minutes of meeting of Fabian Women's Group, 17 June 1913, Nuffield College Library, Fabian Archives, H25. *Fabian News* (1913), Report of Mrs Herbage Edwards' address on 'The Reorganisation of Domestic Work', July, p. 62.
18. *The Standard* (1911), 'Domestic Drudgery', 15 Nov; *The Standard* (1911), 'No Housework', 16 Nov, p. 4; Melvin, Alice (1912), 'Abolition of Domestic Drudgery by Co-operative Housekeeping', *The Free-woman*, 11 April, vol. 1, no. 21, pp. 410–12.
19. Melvin, Alice (1912), 'Cooperative Housekeeping and the Domestic Worker', *The Freewoman*, 4 April, vol. 1, no. 20, pp. 386–7; Melvin, 'Abolition'.
20. Melvin, 'Co-operative Housekeeping', p. 386.
21. Melvin, 'Abolition', p. 410.
22. *The Standard*, 'Domestic Drudgery'; *The Standard*, 'No Housework', p. 4. Lovegrove, 1878–1951, was made a Fellow of the RIBA in 1916, and wrote *The Life, Work and Influence of John Vanbrugh, 1663–1726*,

Pewtress, London, 1902. See *The Builder* (1951), 'Obituary', 28 Sept, p. 432.

23. *The Standard*, 'No Housework', p. 4.
24. Rogers, F. W. (1911), 'Towards Better Co-operative Housing', *Garden Cities and Town Planning*, June, NS vol. 1, no. 5, p. 131; Culpin, Ewart G. (1913), *The Garden City Movement Up-to-date*, Garden Cities and Town Planning Association, London, p. 60.
25. *The Standard*, 'No Housework', p. 4. The town planning scheme for Ruislip approved in 1914 made no mention of Melvin Park or any similar development.
26. Oliver, Kathlyn (1912), 'Cooperative Housekeeping', *The Freewoman*, 20 June, vol. 2, no. 31, p. 98 (see also reply from Alice Melvin); Oliver, Kathlyn (1912), 'Cooperative Housekeeping', *The Freewoman*, 4 July, vol. 2, no. 3, p. 137.
27. *The Standard*, 'Domestic Drudgery'; *The Standard*, 'No Housework', p. 4.
28. File on Melvin Hall Co-operative Housekeeping and Service Society (Golders Green) Limited held by Registry of Friendly Societies, reg. no. 5472R Middx. See also Kelly's Finchley Directory 1913–14.
29. Kelly's Finchley Directory 1914–15. Melvin Hall was situated on the north side of Golders Green Road, between Princes Park Avenue and Highfield Road. All information on the recent history of Melvin Hall is from personal communications with Mr John Rogers, last chairman of the Melvin Hall Society, 27 July 1983 and 17 August 1983.
30. *Daily News* (1912), 'A New Arcadia', 12 Feb.
31. Records of the Priory Residential Society Ltd, reg. no. 5757R, are held by the PRO, FS 17/246.
32. Post Office London Directory, 1915.
33. The Society owned 26, 28, 30, 72 and 74 Priory Road; see Post Office London Directory, 1915. In 1926, there were 55 members, and by 1935 there were 50; see Report of the Chief Registrar of Friendly Societies for the year 1926.
34. Information on Alice Melvin has now been provided by her granddaughter, Rosemary Melvin. Alice Melvin was born Alice Mary Dover on 15 February 1865, the eldest child of a ladies' maid and a cabinet-maker. She married George William Melvin, a fellow Sunday School teacher, in 1879 and their first two children both died when very young. Alice Melvin attributed their deaths to poor housing conditions, and this appears to be the start of her interest in housing problems. By 1903–4, she was running a boarding house for young men in London, where 'she was an excellent housekeeper, a good cook and a devoted mother'. Her connection with Brent Garden Village ended when other members of the management committee decided to sell the houses rather than renting them. Her first husband died in 1919, and shortly afterwards she married Harry Bone. Alice Melvin lived until the age of 90, 'and to the end of her days was quite a formidable person to engage in an argument'. From personal communication with Rosemary Melvin, 21 October 1984.

CHAPTER 8

1. Rosen, Andrew (1974), *Rise Up, Women!*, RKP, London, pp. 248–51; Marwick, Arthur (1977), *Women at War 1914–1918*, Fontana, Glasgow, pp. 30–2.
2. Rosen, *Rise Up*, p. 92; the WFL was formed in 1907.
3. Marwick, *Women*, p. 34.
4. Ibid., pp. 33–4; Leaflet (n.d.) describing the Women's Freedom League Settlement, 1 Everett Street, Nine Elms Lane, London, S.W. held by the Imperial War Museum Library, Women's Section, SUF 9/8.
5. Rosen, *Rise Up*, pp. 217, 223.
6. *Woman's Dreadnought* (1914), 'Our "Cost Price" Restaurants', 12 Sept, no. 26, p. 101; Workers' Suffrage Federation (1916), *Report of Social Work in 1915*, Workers' Suffrage Federation, London, p. 3, held by Imperial War Museum Library, Women's Section, SUF 8/1; Marwick, *Women*, p. 34.
7. Sellars, Edith (1914), 'Experiments in Cheap Catering', *Nineteenth Century and After*, Nov, vol. 76, no. 453, pp. 1123–37; see above, Chap. 5, p. 60.
8. Pankhurst, E. Sylvia (1914), 'How to Meet Hardship', *Woman's Dreadnought*, 22 Aug, no. 23, p. 90.
9. *Woman's Dreadnought* (1914), 'Cottages', 29 Aug, no. 24, p. 93.
10. *Labour Woman* (1913), 'Houses Utopian and How to Get Them, A Report of the Working Women's Conference on Housing held on 30 May 1913', July, vol. 1, no. 3, pp. 33–7, see p. 35; Turner, Kate C. (1913), 'The Housing Question', *Labour Woman*, Aug, vol. 1, no. 4, p. 55.
11. The Residential Cooperative, 14 Victoria Street, Westminster was registered with the Registry of Friendly Societies in 1915 and dissolved in 1925. Its reg. no. was 5939, and its records have been destroyed.
12. Black, Clementina (1918), *A New Way of Housekeeping*, Collins, London.
13. Ibid., pp. 45–6.
14. Ibid., p. 55.
15. Ibid., p. 100.
16. Powell, Mrs Owen (1916), 'Cooperative Housekeeping', *Common Cause*, 30 June, vol. 8, no. 377, p. 150; Esdaile, Mrs Katherine (1916), 'Cooperative Kitchens', *Common Cause*, 7 July, vol. 8, no. 378, pp. 167–8; see also *Common Cause* (1915), 'A House that does its Own Work', 26 Nov. vol. 7, no. 346, pp. 435–6.
17. Esdaile, 'Cooperative Kitchens', p. 167.
18. *The Times* (1916), 'Cooperative Homes', 31 May, p. 5.
19. Wilkins, Diana T. (1916), 'Communal Housekeeping', *The Englishwoman*, Dec, vol. 32, no. 96, pp. 222–6.
20. Wilkins, Diana T. (1917), 'A Housing Problem', *Common Cause*, 16 Feb, vol. 8, no. 410, pp. 593–4; see also Wilkins, D. I. (1917), 'Some

Housing Suggestions for Professional Women', *Common Cause*, 22 June, vol. 9, no. 428, p. 136.

21. Black, *A New Way*, p. 111.
22. Marwick, Arthur (1967), *The Deluge*, Penguin, Harmondsworth, p. 122; Marwick, *Women*, pp. 73, 166; Burnett, John (1968), *Plenty and Want*, Penguin, Harmondsworth, p. 278.
23. Marwick, *Deluge*, p. 123.
24. Ibid., p. 157.
25. Walshe, Eileen, (1915), 'A Munitions Workers' Canteen', *The Englishwoman*, Oct, vol. 28, no. 82, pp. 29–35; Davies, E. Chivers (1917), 'Communal Kitchens', *The Englishwoman*, May, vol. 34, no. 101, pp. 89–100. See also Ford, Emily (1917), *Common Cause*, 20 Apr, vol. 9, no. 419, p. 11.
26. Mills, Mrs Ernestine (1916), 'Real Food Economy', *The Englishwoman*, May, vol. 30, no. 89, pp. 151–8.
27. Burnett, *Plenty*, pp. 273–4.
28. Marwick, *Deluge*, pp. 133–5.
29. Burnett, *Plenty*, pp. 274–6; Peel, Mrs C. S. (1929), *How We Lived Then 1914–1918*, Bodley Head, London, pp. 73–8.
30. Burnett, *Plenty*, p. 275; Imperial War Museum Library, Women's Section, FOOD 3.1/12.
31. Imperial War Museum Library, Women's Section, FOOD 3.1/12.
32. Peel, *How We Lived*, p. 84.
33. Webb, Catherine (1927), *The Woman with the Basket*, Women's Cooperative Guild, London, p. 139.
34. A woman (1918), 'Where are the Kitchens', *Daily Mail*, 16 Feb.
35. Beveridge, Sir William H. (1928), *British Food Control*, OUP, London, p. 66.
36. The National Kitchens Order, 1918, no. 223.
37. *The Times* (1918), 'National Kitchens', 5 Feb, p. 9.
38. On the electric kitchen tramcar, see *Daily Mirror*, 27 April 1918; *Electrical Times*, 25 April 1918 and *Yorkshire Post*, 26 April 1918. The tramcar was so popular police had to regulate the crowd. See Labour Party archives (LP), Consumers' Council, CC/NK 52–54. On progress of national kitchens, see LP, Consumers' Council, CC/NK 98, Memorandum on national kitchens and restaurants, n.d., approx. Sept 1918.
39. LP, Consumers' Council, CC/NK 98 and CC NK/103, paper by Jesse Argyle on national kitchens with distributing depots, 5 Oct 1918.
40. LP, Consumers' Council: CC/NK 113, letter to Sir Alan Anderson from Technical Directors, National Kitchens Division, 1 Jan 1919; CC/NK 118, letter from Miss E. Ball to Marion Phillips, 13 Jan 1919. Spencer resigned due to 'pressure of work' on 29 Jan 1919, see CC/NK 259.
41. *Municipal Journal* (1918), 29 March, p. 355; Cox, R. Hippesley (1918), 'Village Kitchens', *The Englishwoman*, Nov, vol. 40, no. 119, pp. 65–7.
42. For example Turner, C. (1918), 'National Kitchens and National Health', *The Englishwoman*, Sept, vol. 39, no. 117, pp. 97–101.

43. LP, Consumers' Council, CC/NK 328, Minutes of the National Kitchens Advisory Committee, 15 Oct 1919, quotation from Marion Phillips.
44. Ibid.
45. Peel, *How We Lived*, p. 85.
46. Marwick, *Deluge*, p. 205.
47. Ibid., p. 258; Swenarton, Mark (1981), *Homes Fit for Heroes*, Heinemann Educational Books, London, p. 67.
48. Smith, E. J. (1917), 'Ten Gardens Suburbs for Bradford', *Garden Cities and Town Planning*, Oct, NS vol. 7, no. 3, pp. 53–5, see p. 55.
49. Bondfield, Margaret G. (1919), 'Women as Domestic Workers', pp. 66–73 in Marion Phillips (ed.), *Women and the Labour Party*, Headley Brothers, London. See p. 71.
50. Bondfield, Margaret (1949), *A Life's Work*, Hutchinson, London, pp. 110–12.
51. Phillips, Marion (1918), 'Co-operative Housekeeping and Housing Reform', *The Labour Woman*, Feb, vol. 5, no. 22, pp. 255–6. See p. 255.
52. LP, Consumers' Council, CC/NK 328, Minutes of the National Kitchens Advisory Committee, 15 Oct 1919.
53. Phillips, 'Co-operative Housekeeping', p. 256.
54. *Labour Woman* (1920), 'Women at Olympia', March, vol. 8, no. 3, pp. 36–7. See p. 37.
55. Craig, F. W. S. (1975), *British General Election Manifestos 1900–1974*, Macmillan, London, p. 31.
56. Pankhurst, Christabel (1918), 'Miss Pankhurst's Election Address', *Britannia*, 13 Dec, vol. 7, no. 26, p. 229; Rosen, *Rise Up*, p. 269.
57. Rosen, *Rise Up*, pp. 252–4.
58. Pankhurst, Emmeline, Pankhurst, Christabel, Kenney, Annie and Drummond, Flora (1917), 'The Women's Party', *Britannia*, 2 Nov, vol. 6, no. 22, pp. 171–2.
59. Unwin, Raymond and Parker, Barry (1918), 'Co-operative Housekeeping', *Britannia*, 11 Jan, vol. 6, no. 31, p. 246.
60. Hall, Annie (1918), 'Co-operative Housekeeping', *Britannia*, 22 Feb, vol. 6, no. 37, pp. 327, 336. See p. 327. Series continued: vol. 6, pp. 345, 361, 367, 379, 410, 412, 420–1, 428, 435, 442–3, 466, 477, 492, 494 and vol. 7, pp. 2, 9, 14, 20, 38, 42.
61. Ibid., p. 410.
62. Ibid., p. 412.
63. Ibid., p. 9.
64. Reprint of leading article from *The Globe*, 'The Women's Plan', in *Britannia* (1917), 9 Nov, vol. 6, no. 23, p. 179. See also *Britannia* (1917), 23 Nov, vol. 6, no. 25, p. 197.
65. Rosen, *Rise Up*, p. 269.
66. *The Vote* (1918), 1 Mar, p. 162.
67. Furniss, A. D. Sanderson (1919), 'The Working Woman's House', pp. 74–85 in Marion Phillips (ed.), *Women and the Labour Party*, Headley Brothers, London; Furniss, A. D. Sanderson and Phillips,

Marion (1920), *The Working Woman's House*, Swarthmore Press, London.
68. Furniss and Phillips, *Working Woman's House*, p. 22.
69. Ibid., p. 34.
70. Ibid., pp. 49–50.
71. Burnett, *Plenty*, pp. 229, 294.
72. Furniss and Phillips, *Working Woman's House*, p. 63.
73. Crawford, V. M. (1919), 'Some Points in the Housing Problem', *The Catholic Citizen*, 15 May, vol. 5, no. 5, pp. 35–6.
74. Irwin, Margaret H. (1918), 'Industrial Housing from the Housewife's Point of View', Scottish Council for Women's Trades, Glasgow, held by Imperial War Museum Library, Women's Section, EMP 46/5.
75. Ibid., p. 18.
76. Ibid., p. 24.
77. Swenarton, *Homes Fit*, p. 91.
78. Women's Housing Sub-Committee, Ministry of Reconstruction (1918), *First Interim Report*, Cd. 9166, HMSO, London, p. 3.
79. Cd. 9166, para. 13.
80. Cd. 9166, para. 21.
81. PRO RECO 1/624, Notes of the Local Government Board on the First Interim Report of the Women's Housing Sub-Committee of the Advisory Council of the Ministry of Reconstruction, 27 Aug 1918, p. 3. Also PRO RECO 1/631, WH 97.
82. Ibid., p. 6; see Swenarton, *Homes Fit*, pp. 90–2, for details of the fate of Cd. 9166.
83. Local Government Board (1917), Memorandum for the Use of Local Authorities with respect to the Provision and Arrangement of Houses for the Working Classes.
84. Cd. 9166, p. 2.
85. Swenarton, *Homes Fit*, p. 92; PRO RECO 1/624.
86. PRO RECO 1/631, WH 8.
87. PRO RECO 1/631, WH 71, Report of Enquiry Conducted by the Women in the Labour Party, 19 June 1918, p. 5.
88. PRO RECO 1/631, WH 46, Report on Wrexham and Queensferry Garden Villages, 24 May 1918, Miss M. D. Jones.
89. PRO RECO 1/631 WH 96, Notes of Discussion at the Richmond Mothers' Welcome, 18 Aug 1918, J. O. Stewart.
90. PRO RECO 1/631, WH 38, Report of meeting held by Miss Maud Bell at Camberwell, n.d., probably May 1918; see also PRO RECO 1/631 WH 32, and papers in PRO RECO 1/633.
91. PRO RECO 1/631, WH 92, Visit to Letchworth Garden City, 1 Aug 1918.
92. PRO RECO 1/631, WH 19, Ebenezer Howard, Domestic industry as it might be. This pamphlet is not present in the PRO file, although listed there. D. Hayden (1976), 'Collectivizing the Domestic Workspace', *Lotus International*, Summer, no. 12, pp. 72–89, see p. 83, states that the pamphlet was published in 1906.
93. PRO RECO 1/630, Minutes of the meetings of the Women's Housing Sub-Committee, 27th meeting July 1918, and 28th meeting, 15 July

1918. See also PRO RECO 1/631, WH 100, List of members of sub-committees.

94. PRO RECO 1/631, WH 70, Gretna Green and East Riggs, Dumfries, n.d. 1918, pp. 2, 5; Swenarton, *Homes Fit*, pp. 58, 62.

95. PRO RECO 1/633, Letter from Eleanor Fitz-Gerald to WHSC, 21 June 1918.

96. PRO RECO 1/631, WH 102, Note from Miss E. M. Waley, secretary to the committee, to the WHSC, n.d., Sept 1918.

97. PRO RECO 1/627, Summary of points for discussion at WHSC meetings.

98. PRO RECO 1/627, Appointments to WHSC, approx. Sept 1918.

99. Women's Housing Sub-Committee, Ministry of Reconstruction (1919), *Final Report*, Cd. 9232, HMSO, London.

100. Cd. 9232, para 73.

101. Ibid., paras 20, 67–9.

102. Ibid., paras 70–1.

103. Ibid., para 66.

104. Ibid., para 6; PRO RECO 1/631, WH 93, Interview with Mr Raymond Unwin, 29 July 1918.

105. Cd. 9232, para 1.

106. Local Government Boards for England and Wales and Scotland (1918), Report of the Committee appointed by the President of the Local Government Board and the Secretary for Scotland to consider questions of building construction in connection with the provision of dwellings for the working classes in England and Wales, and Scotland, and report upon methods of securing economy and despatch in the provision of such dwellings, Cd. 9191, HMSO, London. Known as the Tudor Walters Report.

107. Swenarton, *Homes Fit*, p. 93.

108. PRO RECO 1/630, Minutes of Women's Housing Sub-Committee meetings.

109. PRO RECO 1/631, Interview with Mr Leonard, 20 June 1918.

110. Ibid.

110. Tudor Walters Report, paras 166–172, 351.

112. Ibid., para 53.

113. For detailed analysis of Raymond Unwin's influence on the Tudor Walters Report, see Swenarton, *Homes Fit*, pp. 92–108.

114. PRO RECO 1/482, Ministry of Reconstruction, Report by Mr Bryce Leicester on Public Utility Societies and Housing, Dec 1917.

115. Cd. 9191, para 58.

116. Ibid., paras 188, 191–2.

117. Swenarton, *Homes Fit*, p. 105.

118. The evidence taken by the Tudor Walters Committee is not available at the PRO; personal search, and personal communication with Mervyn Miller, 4 May 1983.

119. Pepper, Simon and Swenarton, Mark (1978), 'Home Front: Garden Suburbs for Munition Workers', *Architectural Review*, June, vol. 163, no. 976, pp. 366–75. See pp. 368–9. Swenarton, *Homes Fit*, p. 93.

120. Pepper, Simon and Swenarton, Mark (1980), 'Neo-Georgian Maison-type', *Architectural Review*, Aug, vol. 168, no. 1002, pp. 87–92.
121. Local Government Board (1919), *Manual on the Preparation of State-aided Housing Schemes*, HMSO, London.
122. Swenarton, *Homes Fit*, pp. 53, 110. Unwin had been seconded to the Ministry of Munitions from the LGB in 1915.
123. LGB, *Manual*, para 35.
124. Public General Acts 1919, p. 95; Merrett, Stephen (1979), *State Housing in Britain*, RKP, London, pp. 35, 309.
125. Hansard, Parliamentary Debates, Commons, vol. 144, 8 Apr 1919, cols 1915–1916.
126. LP, Consumers' Council, CC/NK 275, National Kitchens Division report by T. G. Jones, 21 March 1919; CC/NK 318 National Kitchens Advisory Committe, 12 March 1919.
127. LP, Consumers' Council, CC/NK 131, Report on National Kitchens by Charles Spencer, n.d. mid-Jan 1919; CC/NK 306, T. G. Jones to Marion Phillips, 27 Nov 1919.
128. LP, Consumers' Council, CC/NK 131, Report on National Kitchens by Charles Spencer, n.d. mid-Jan 1919.
129. LP, Consumers' Council, CC/NK 133, Memorandum on National Kitchens and restaurants, Marion Phillips, late-Jan 1919; CC/NK 144, Houses of the future, W. E. Whyte, n.d. mid-Jan 1919.
130. LP, Consumers' Council, CC/NK 281, Letter from Marion Phillips to Mr Syrett, Ministry of Food, 3 Apr 1919; CC/NK 306, T. G. Jones to Marion Phillips, 27 Nov 1919.
131. Head, V. J. F. (1919), 'National Restaurants', *The Catholic Citizen*, 15 Oct, vol. 5, no. 10, pp. 80–1. See also Turner, C. (1919), 'Women and the Future of the National Kitchens', *The Englishwoman*, Dec, vol. 44, no. 132, pp. 161–9.
132. LP, Consumers' Council, CC/NK 308, Report for Consumers' Council, 17 Dec 1919.
133. LP, Consumers' Council, CC/NK 306, T. G. Jones to Marion Phillips, 27 Nov 1919.
134. LP, Consumers' Council CC/NK 329, National Kitchens Advisory Committee minutes, 26 Nov 1919; Swenarton, *Homes Fit*, p. 80.
135. LP, Consumers' Council, CC/NK 316, National Kitchens Advisory Committee, 3 March 1919.
136. Swenarton, *Homes Fit*, p. 110.
137. PRO RECO 1/624, Correspondence concerning WHSC Interim Report, Comments by Captain Reiss, 28 June 1918; Swenarton, *Homes Fit*, p. 80.
138. PRO RECO 1/625, Representation of women on housing schemes, 24 May 1918.
139. *Housing* (1919), 'Women's Views', 2 Aug, vol. 1, no. 2, p. 21.
140. Furniss and Phillips, *Working Woman's House*, p. 77; *Housing* (1920), 'Women's Advisory Committees', 5 Jan, vol. 1, no. 13, p. 171.
141. *Garden Cities and Town Planning* (1920), June, vol. 10, no. 6, p. 140; *Garden Cities and Town Planning* (1921), March, vol. 11, no. 3, p. 73.
142. PRO HLG 52/871, Housing Advisory Council.

143. PRO HLG 52/871, HAC minutes, 8 Oct 1919.
144. PRO HLG 52/871, Letter from Mrs Sanderson Furniss to J. C. Wrigley, 8 Dec 1919.
145. PRO HLG 52/871, Correspondence with Minister of Health, April 1920–February 1921; Webb, Catherine (1927), *The Woman with the Basket*, Women's Co-operative Guild, London, pp. 140–1.
146. PRO HLG 52/871, Internal memorandum by J. C. Wrigley to Mr Forber, 11 February 1921.
147. Ministry of Health (1921), *Report of the Sub-Committee of the Housing Advisory Council on Co-operative and Communal Arrangements*, HMSO, London.
148. Barnett, Dame Henrietta (1928), *The Story of the Growth of the Hampstead Garden Suburb 1907–1928*, Hampstead Garden Suburb Trust, London, p. 71. Two hostels were opened in the suburb, Queen's Court in 1927 and Emmott Close in 1928.
149. PRO HLG 52/871, Letter from Marion Phillips to Sir Alfred Mond, 15 June 1921.
150. Swenarton, *Homes Fit*, pp. 130–3; Merrett, Stephen (1979), *State Housing in Britain*, RKP, London, pp. 40–1.
151. Swenarton, *Homes Fit*, p. 161.
152. See Abrams, Philip (1963), 'The Failure of Social Reform: 1918 – 1920', *Past and Present*, April, pp. 43–64. Abrams seems to confuse access to policy-making bodies with real power, at least in respect of housing policy; see pp. 61–2.
153. Sutcliffe, Anthony (1984), 'Anglo-French Perspectives on the Creation and Experience of the Domestic Environment', *Planning History Bulletin*, vol. 6, no. 1, pp. 18–32; see pp. 21–2.
154. Board of Trade, Industrial (War Inquiries) Branch (1918), *Report on the Increased Employment of Women during the War*, Cd. 9164, xiv 767, HMSO, London, p. 2; Marwick, Arthur (1982), 'Women's Fightback on the Home Front', *Times Higher Education Supplement*, 10 Sept, no. 514, pp. 11–12, see p. 11.

CHAPTER 9

1. Marwick, Arthur (1977), *Women at War 1914–1918*, Fontana, Glasgow, p. 162.
2. Ministry of Reconstruction (1919), *Report of the Women's Advisory Committee on the Domestic Service Problem*, Cmd. 67, HMSO, London, pp. 2, 4.
3. Marwick, Arthur (1967), *The Deluge*, Penguin, Harmondsworth, p. 327.
4. Ibid., pp. 326–7; Political and Economic Planning (1945), *The Market for Household Appliances*; PEP, London, p. 25.
5. Stone, Richard and Rowe, D. A. (1966), *The Measurement of Consumers' Expenditure and Behaviour in the United Kingdom 1920–1938*, CUP, Cambridge, p. 27.

6. Ministry of Labour (1923), *Report of the Committee appointed to Enquire into the Present Conditions as to the Supply of Female Domestic Servants*, HMSO, London, p. 41; (1945), PEP *The Market*, p. 26.
7. White, Cynthia, L. (1970), *Women's Magazines 1693–1968*, Michael Joseph, London, p. 103; Beaumann, Nicola (1983), *A Very Great Profession*, Virago, London, p. 109.
8. Phillips, R. Randal (1923), *The Servantless House*, Country Life, London (first ed. 1920), pp. 9, 147.
9. Forty, Adrian (1975), *The Electric Home*, Open University Press, Milton Keynes, p. 42; Whyte, Adam Gowans (1922), *The All-electric Age*, Constable, London.
10. Stone and Rowe, *The Measurement*, p. 21.
11. M.A. (1910), 'Science versus Drudgery', *The Englishwoman*, May, vol, 6, no. 16, pp. 97–8, see p. 97; *Electrical Review* (1919), 'Domestic Electrical Appliances', 20 June, vol. 84, no. 2169, pp. 715–17, see. p. 717. See also *The Electrician* (1920), 'The Ideal Home Exhibition at Olympia', 13 Feb, vol. 84, no. 2178, pp. 170–1.
12. Cmd. 67, p. 28; Ministry of Labour (1923), *Report*, p. 9.
13. Cmd. 67, p. 33.
14. *The Queen*, (1919), 'Of Interest to All Women', 29 March, vol. 145, no. 3770, pp. 368–9.
15. Sillitoe, Helen (1933), *A History of the Teaching of Domestic Subjects*, Methuen, London, pp. 216–17.
16. Eyles, Leonora (1923), 'What is a Woman to Do?', *Good Housekeeping*, Nov, vol. 4, no. 3, pp. 35, 120, 122-3, see p. 122. See also Eyles, Margaret Leonora (1922), *The Woman in the Little House*, Grant Richards, London, pp. 123–6.
17. Whyte, *All-electric*, p. 183; PRO RECO 1/633, Letter to WHSC from R. A Lister and Co., 1 July 1918.
18. George, W. L. (1923), 'What is a Home?', *Good Housekeeping*, July, vol. 3, no. 5, pp. 11–12, 80, see p. 80; Burnett, John (1968), *Plenty and Want*, Penguin, Harmondsworth, pp. 294–6.
19. George, W. L. (1923), 'No Housewives, No Homes', *Good Housekeeping*, Aug, vol. 3, no. 6, pp. 9–10, 72.
20. Wells, H. G. (1924), 'Mr Wheatley's "Little House"', *Westminster Gazette*, 16 Aug, no. 9701, pp. 1, 3.
21. Seymour, Beatrice Kean (1924), 'The Houses Men Build for Us', *Good Housekeeping*, April, vol. 5, no. 2, pp. 182, 184, 186–7. See pp. 182, 187.
22. Onslow Village Limited, Minute Books, May 1918.
23. Ibid., 12 April and 2 March 1920. The society's registration number was 7638.
24. Onslow Village Limited, (1920), Prospectus and descriptive booklet, Guildford, p. 10, held by Guildford Muniment Room, TG 808/1; see also *Housing* (1921), 'Onslow Garden Village', 3 Jan, vol. 2, no. 39, p. 191.
25. Guildford Muniment Room, Press Cuttings 1911–21, Book 173/225/5; *The Times* (1920), 'Guildford Garden Suburb Scheme', 26 Feb;

Surrey Weekly Press (1920), 'Onslow Village', 27 Feb; *Surrey Advertiser and County Times* (1920), 'Chat with Mr Litchfield', 6 Mar.

26. Personal communication with W. F. Nurse, Secretary, Onslow Village Limited, 19 May 1983; *Garden Cities and Town Planning Magazine* (1920), 'Onslow Garden Village', Dec, vol. 10, no. 12, pp. 243–5; *Surrey Times* (1920), 'The Onslow Village,' 10 April. See also *The Builder* (1920), 'Onslow Garden Village', 24 Dec, vol. 119, no. 4064, pp. 722–3; *British Builder* (1921), 'Houses for Manual Workers – and Others', Feb, pp. 233–4. The village still exists, the society having started building again after 1945; the houses are hidden behind high hedges in a warren of narrow roads.

27. Pearsall, E. B. (1920), 'Co-operative Houses at Letchworth', *Garden Cities and Town Planning Magazine*, Aug, vol. 10, no. 8, pp. 174–5.

28. *Fabian News* (1894) Mar, vol. 4, no. 1, p. 4; Miller, Mervyn (1979), 'The Howard Cottage Society', *Housing Outlook*, Summer, no. 5, pp. 13–16.

29. Minutes of the Board of Howard Cottage Society, 13 Jan 1920. The Garden City Public Utility's registration number was 7283.

30. RIBA biography files; Miller, Mervyn (1978), *Letchworth Garden City 1903–1978*, North Hertfordshire District Council, p. 74.

31. Minutes of the Board of the Howard Cottage Society, 2 June 1920 and 13 October 1920.

32. Minutes of the Board of the Howard Cottage Society, 18 October 1923, 29 Jan 1924 and 26 June 1924.

33. Minutes of the Board of the Howard Cottage Society, 16 October 1924 and 2 July 1925.

34. *The Builder* (1921), 'Proposed Flats, Meadow Way Green, Letchworth', 15 July, vol. 121, no. 4093, pp. 75, 76f.

35. Design for a block of flats, Meadow Way, 23 Apr 1921 by C. M. Crickmer and Allen Foxley, BAL Drawings Collection, RAN 10/L/12.

36. Swenarton, Mark (1981), *Homes Fit for Heroes*, Heinemann Educational Books, London, pp. 60–1.

37. Letter from Barry Parker to Bolton Smart, 18 Jan 1921, Howard Cottage Society records.

38. Purdom, C. B. (1925), *The Building of Satellite Towns*, Dent, London, p. 65.

39. Information on Meadow Way Green South from interviews with Mr McBride and Mr and Mrs Woollons, 29 June 1983, and Miss K. M. Kaye, 14 November 1983, Letchworth. See also Meadow Way Green Co-operative Housing Scheme Constitution.

40. Hebbert, Michael (1981), 'Frederic Osborn 1885–1978', pp. 177–202 in Gordon E. Cherry (ed.), *Pioneers in British Planning*, Architectural Press, London, pp. 179–80; Macfadyen, Dugald (1933), *Sir Ebenezer Howard and the Town Planning Movement*, Manchester University Press, Manchester, pp. 100–1.

41. Schaffer, Frank (1972), *The New Town Story*, Granada, London, pp. 23–4.

42. A scheme for a second garden city, 25 Sept 1919, p. 5, with letter

from F. J. Osborn, 4 Oct 1919, PRO HLG 49/8; also held by FGCM. New Town Housing Ltd, descriptive pamphlet, April 1921, pp. 3–5, FGCM.

43. Minutes of the Board of New Town Trust, 16 March 1923–18 Dec 1924, HCRO, D/E Ff B33.

44. Purdom, *Building of Satellite Towns*, pp. 180–1.

45. Welwyn Garden City Limited (1929), Notes on the objects, general character, and organisation of the undertaking, Dec, HCRO, D/ EEs B 66.

46. Minutes of the Board of New Town Trust, 26 July 1928–28 Nov 1929, HCRO, D/ EFf B33.

47. Minutes of the Board of New Town Trust, 20 Sept 1928, HCRO, D/ EFf B33; personal communication with M. R. Hughes, 16 June 1983; information supplied by Welwyn Hatfield District Council, 6 Oct 1983. The Hotel is now called The Garden.

48. Purdom, *Building of Satellite Towns*, p. 181.

49. Ministry of Health (1921), *Report of the Sub-Committee of the Housing Advisory Council on Co-operative and Communal Arrangements*, HMSO, London. See above, Chap. 8, p. 154.

50. Report of the Chief Registrar of Friendly Societies for the year 1926, Part 3, *Industrial and Provident Societies* (1927), HMSO, London. The Women's Residential Club was located at 24 North John Street, Liverpool; its registration no. was 9799.

51. Both groups of flats were managed by the United Women's Homes Association. See Slack, Kathleen M. (1982), *Henrietta's Dream*, Slack, London, pp. 97–8 and Green, Brigid Grafton (1977), *Hampstead Garden Suburb 1907–1977*, Hampstead Garden Suburb Residents Association, p. 16.

52. Darley, Gillian (1978), *Villages of Vision*, Granada, St Albans, p. 139; Scott, Richenda (1955), *Elizabeth Cadbury 1858–1951*, Harrap, London, p. 91.

53. Scott, *Elizabeth Cadbury*, p. 94; letter from C. H. Sparks to the editor, *RIBA Journal*, April 1955, held by BAL, H. Clapham Lander biography file.

54. Scott, *Cadbury*, pp. 82, 94.

55. Ibid., p. 135; Bournville Village Trust (1928), *Bournville Housing*, BVT, Birmingham, p. 37.

56. S. Alexander Wilmot's plan of St George's Court is held by Bournville Village Trust. Information on life at the Court and its management from interviews with Mr Ken Pegg (ex-general manager, BVT), 24 January 1984 and Miss L. Tetley (resident, St George's Court), 4 May 1984; Bournville.

57. BVT, *Bournville Housing*, p. 37.

58. *Birmingham News* (approx. 1940/1), Memorial service to Miss Georgina Stuart, 19 June. My thanks to Jane Sutton of BVT for this reference.

59. Scott, *Cadbury*, pp. 135, 137.

60. Leaflets giving tariff for St George's Court, held by BVT.

61. The Bournville Village Trust 1900–1955 (1955), BVT, Birmingham, p.

31. See also *Garden Cities and Town Planning* (1925), 'Public Utility Societies at Bournville', July, vol. 15, no. 7, pp. 160–5. See p. 162.

62. Merrett, Stephen (1979), *State Housing in Britain*, RKP, London, p. 51.

63. Ibid., pp. 52, 61; Daunton, M. J. (1983), *House and Home in the Victorian City*, Edward Arnold, London, p. 294.

64. Merrett, *State Housing*, p. 52.

65. Stevenson, John (1984), *British Society 1914–45*, Penguin, Harmondsworth, pp. 170, 175, 184–5; Oakley, Ann (1982), *Subject Women*, Fontana, Glasgow, pp. 146–7.

66. Stevenson, *British Society*, pp. 400–1.

67. Holtby, Winifred (1934), *Women and a Changing Civilization*, Bodley Head, London, p. 191.

68. Stevenson, *British Society*, p. 169; Holcombe, Lee (1983), *Wives and Property*, Martin Robertson, Oxford, pp. 24, 222.

69. PRO HLG 52/846, Provision of accommodation for single business women. The pamphlet was called 'Consider her palaces'. The representative of the National Council of Women later contacted the Ministry with a plan for a cooperative home for single people, which she said had been commended by a working-class audience to which she had shown it; Hilyer, Mrs C. Isabel (1934), *Eventide Homes*, Hilyer, Hampstead.

70. Stevenson,*British Society*, pp. 131–2; Stone and Rowe, *The Measurement*, p. 34.

71. Edwards, Elsie E. (1935), *Report on Electricity in Working-class Homes*, Electrical Association for Women, London, p. 47.

72. Ibid., p. 40.

73. *Architects' Journal* (1943), 'Flats at Clapton', 12 Aug, vol. 98, pp. 111–14.

74. Ravetz, Alison (1974), *Model Estate*, Croom Helm, London, pp. 50, 89; Ravetz, Alison (1974), 'From Working-class Tenement to Modern Flat: Local Authorities and Multi-storey Housing between the Wars', pp. 122–50 in Anthony Sutcliffe (ed.), *Multi-storey Living*, Croom Helm, London, see p. 143.

75. Ravetz, 'From Working-class Tenement', p. 137.

76. Frampton, Kenneth (1980), *Modern Architecture, a Critical History*, Thames and Hudson, London, pp. 155–6.

77. Ibid., pp. 226–7.

78. Willett, John (1978), *The New Sobriety 1917–1933*, Thames and Hudson, London, pp. 124–8.

79. Ibid., pp. 130–1.

80. Ravetz, 'From Working-class Tenement', p. 137; Benton, Charlotte and Tim (1979), 'Architecture, Contrasts of a Decade', pp. 47–61 in *Thirties*, catalogue of exhibition at the Hayward Gallery, Oct 1979–Jan 1980; Arts Council of Great Britain, London, pp. 57–8.

81. Coe, Peter and Reading, Malcolm (1981), *Lubetkin and Tecton*, Arts Council of Great Britain, London, p. 121; Jones, Edward and Woodward, Christopher (1983), *A Guide to the Architecture of London*, Weidenfeld and Nicolson, London, pp. 344–5.

82. *Thirties*, Arts Council of Great Britain, London, p. 267.
83. Benton, 'Architecture', pp. 58, 60.
84. Jones and Woodward, *A Guide*, p. 322; *Architect and Building News*, (1938), 'Dolphin Square, Westminster', 7 Jan, vol. 153, pp. 6–11.
85. Bayley, Stephen (1975), *The Modern Flat*, Open University Press, Milton Keynes, p. 69.
86. Coe and Reading, *Lubetkin*, p. 135.
87. Ravetz, 'From Working-class Tenement', pp. 131, 145; Bayley, *Modern Flat*, pp. 75–6.
88. Oliver, Paul, Davis, Ian and Bentley, Ian (1981), *Dunroamin*, Barrie and Jenkins, London, pp. 13, 50.
89. Calder, Angus (1971), *The People's War*, Panther, London, pp. 309, 382–3.
90. Ibid., pp. 220, 251–2, 446; Burnett, *Plenty*, p. 327.
91. Stevenson, *British Society*, pp. 445, 454; Burnett, *Plenty*, p. 330.
92. Women's Group on Public Welfare (1943), *Our Towns, A Close-up*, OUP, London, p. 3.
93. Ibid., p. 42.
94. Hansard, House of Commons (1947), 5th series, vol. 437, HMSO, London, col 2736.
95. Ibid., col 2746.
96. Burnett, *Plenty*, p. 345; Marwick, Arthur (1982), *British Society since 1945*, Penguin, Harmondsworth, p. 18.
97. Stevenson, *British Society*, pp. 452–3; Central Housing Advisory Committee, Sub-Committee on the design of dwellings (1944), *Design of Dwellings*, HMSO, London, p. 61 (known as the Dudley Report).
98. Beveridge, Sir William (1942), *Report on the Social Insurance and Allied Services*, Cmd. 6404, HMSO, London, pp. 132–3; McDowell, L. (1983), 'Towards an Understanding of the Gender Division of Urban Space', *Environment and Planning D: Society and Space*, March, vol. 1, no. 1, pp. 59–72. See pp. 63–4. See also Burton, Elaine (1944), *Domestic Work*, Frederick Muller, London, p. 12.
99. Craig, F. W. S. (1975), *British General Election Manifestos 1900–1974*, Macmillan, London, pp. 124, 129; Labour Party (1943), *Your Home planned by Labour*, London, p. 2.
100. Foot, Michael (1975), *Aneurin Bevan 1945–1960*, Granada, St Albans, p. 66.
101. Dudley Report, paras 11, 22. For a full account of the Report's impact, see Foot, *Bevan*, pp. 77 ff and Merrett, *State Housing*, pp. 102–3.
102. Dudley Report, pp. 58, 62.
103. Ibid., paras 33–5, 87–90.
104. Wilson, Janet C. (1949), 'An Inquiry into Communal Laundry Facilities', *Ministry of Works National Building Studies Special Report No. 9*, HMSO, London, pp. 21, 32.
105. Gaffin, Jean and Thoms, David (1983), *Caring and Sharing*, Cooperative Union, Manchester, see section on 'Housing 1945–51'.
106. Wilson, Elizabeth (1980), *Only Halfway to Paradise*, Tavistock, London, p. 21; quotation from Ian Mikardo.

107. New Towns Committee (1946), *Final Report*, Cmd. 6876, HMSO, London, para 127 (known as the Reith Report).
108. Wright, Myles (1982), *Lord Leverhulme's Unknown Venture*, Hutchinson Benham, London, pp. 206, 212.
109. Ibid., pp. 52–3, 56–7.
110. Ibid., p. 68; Wolfe, Lawrence (1945), *The Reilly Plan*, Nicholson and Watson, London, pp. 14, 98–103.
111. Wolfe, *Reilly Plan*, p. 25.
112. Ibid., pp 87–8, 98–102.
113. Ibid., pp. 26–7.
114. Wright, *Lord Leverhulme*, p. 204; Allan, Adrian R. and Turner, Sheila M. (1981), 'The Papers of Sir Charles Reilly', *Planning History Bulletin*, vol. 3, no. 3, pp. 18–22, see pp. 20–1.
115. Merrett, *State Housing*, pp. 102–3; Foot, *Bevan*, pp. 82–6.
116. Ravetz, 'From Working-class Tenement', p. 146; Cooney, E. W. (1974), 'High Flats in Local Authority Housing in England and Wales since 1945', pp. 151–80 in Anthony Sutcliffe (ed.), *Multi-storey Living*, Croom Helm, London, p. 152.
117. Anderson, Frances M. D. (1983), 'Multi-storey Council Housing', unpub. M. Soc. Sci. thesis, Faculty of Commerce and Social Science, University of Birmingham, pp. 110–11.
118. Marwick, *British Society*, p. 68; Hole, W. V. and Attenburrow, J. J. (1966), *Houses and People*, HMSO, London, p. 59.
119. Merrett, *State Housing*, p. 103; Ministry of Housing and Local Government (1961), *Homes for Today and Tomorrow*, HMSO, London, known as the Parker Morris Report.
120. Parker Morris Report, p. iv.
121. Merrett, *State Housing*, p. 105.
122. Burnett, John (1980), *A Social History of Housing 1815–1970*, Methuen, London, pp. 295–6.
123. Ibid., p. 273.
124. Ibid., p. 297.

CHAPTER 10

1. Ravetz, Alison (1984), 'The Home of Woman: a View from the Interior', *Built Environment*, vol. 10, no. 1, pp. 8–17. See p. 14 for kitchen as distinct part of house.
2. Daunton, M. J. (1983), 'Experts and the Environment', *Journal of Urban History*, Feb, vol. 9, no. 2, pp. 233–50. See p. 243.
3. Fishman, Robert (1982), *Urban Utopias in the Twentieth Century*, MIT Press, Cambridge, Mass., pp. 197, 298.
4. Hayden, Dolores (1981), *The Grand Domestic Revolution*, MIT Press, Cambridge, Mass., pp. 263–5.
5. Bouchier, David (1983), *The Feminist Challenge*, Macmillan, London, pp. 10–12.
6. See Taylor, Barbara (1983), *Eve and the New Jerusalem*, Virago,

London, pp. 275–9 for a detailed history of Victorian feminism in England.

7. Ibid., p. 277; Bouchier, *Feminist Challenge*, p. 13.

8. Bouchier, *Feminist Challenge*, pp. 10, 13,; Taylor, *Eve*, p. 125.

9. Giedion, Siegfried (1948), *Mechanization takes Command*, OUP, New York, pp. 512–13; Ravetz, Alison (1968), 'The Victorian Coal Kitchen and its Reformers', *Victorian Studies*, June, vol. 11, pp. 435–60, see p. 460.

10. Cowan, Ruth Schwartz (1976), 'Two Washes in the Morning and a Bridge Party at Night: the American Housewife between the Wars', *Women's Studies*, vol. 3, no. 2, pp. 147–71, see p. 164.

11. Panton, Mrs J. E. (1888), *From Kitchen to Garret*, Ward and Downey, London, p. 4.

12. Enid (1911), 'The Lady at the Round Table', *The Referee*, 28 May; FGCM, cuttings 1911, p. 278. See also Peel, Mrs C. S. (1917), *The Labour-saving House*, John Lane, London, pp. 30–1; Meredith, M. (1911), 'Housing of Educated Women Workers', *The Englishwoman*, Feb, vol. 9, no. 26, pp. 159–64, see p. 160.

13. *Englishwoman's Review of Social and Industrial Questions* (1899), 15 Apr, vol. 30, pp. 133–4; Callen, Anthea (1980), *Women in the Arts and Crafts Movement 1870–1914*, Astragal Books, London, p. 171; Schultz, R. Weir (1908), 'Architecture for Women', *Architectural Review*, vol. 24, pp. 153–4, see p. 153; Cohen, M. (1912), 'Man-built houses', *The Standard*, 12 March.

14. Gates, G. Evelyn (ed.) (1923), *The Woman's Year Book 1923–24*, Women Publishers, London, pp. 313, 386, 390.

15. Martineau, Harriet (1983), *Autobiography*, vol. II, Virago, London, first pub. 1877, p. 228. The plans of Martineau's house are held by the University of Birmingham, Harriet Martineau Papers, HM 1302, Plan of the Knoll, Ambleside.

16. Coatts, Margot (1983), *A Weaver's Life, Ethel Mairet 1872–1952*, Crafts Council, London, pp. 37–9, 48–50.

17. Purdom, C. B. (1913), *The Garden City*, Dent, London, p. 162. The Howard Cottage Society did try to obtain a loan from the PWLB for Meadow Way Green North, but it was not considered to be working-class housing; see Chapter 6, p. 111 above.

18. Swenarton, Mark (1981), *Homes Fit for Heroes*, Heinemann Educational Books, London, p. 47.

19. Potter, Philip, E. S. (1983), 'State Housing for General Needs: Policy and Practice in Birmingham 1900–1935', unpub. M Phil thesis, University of Birmingham, p. 38; PRO RECO 1/482, Ministry of Reconstruction, Report by Mr Bryce Leicester on Public Utility Societies and Housing, Dec 1917, p. 39; Ministry of Reconstruction (1918), *Housing in England and Wales*, Memorandum by the advisory housing panel on the emergency problem, Cd. 9087, HMSO, London, para 14.

20. Cd. 9087, para 6.

21. Ibid., para 22; Swenarton, *Homes Fit*, pp. 69, 80.

22. See Swenarton, *Homes Fit*, pp. 80–1, 84, 117–21 for full details of the financial difficulties.
23. Ibid., pp. 46–7; PRO HLG 52/881, Minutes of Housing Committee meeting, 11 May 1920.
24. Ibid., p. 118.
25. Cd. 9087, para 1.
26. Potter, 'State Housing', p. 45; Daunton, M. J. (1983), *House and Home in the Victorian City*, Edward Arnold, London, pp. 294–5.
27. Back, Glen (1984), 'Hard Times Arrive for the Typically British Movement', *Town and Country Planning*, vol. 53, no. 5, pp. 148–50, see p. 148.
28. Ibid.; Report of the Chief Registrar of Friendly Societies for the year 1926 (1927), Part 3, Industrial and Provident Societies, HMSO, London, p. 44 gives numbers of returns made by land and housing societies as follows: 1918, 201; 1919, 235; 1920, 331; 1921, 340.
29. Rowan, Caroline (1982), '"Mothers, vote Labour!" The State, the Labour Movement and Working-class Mothers, 1900–1918', pp. 59–84 in Rosalind Brunt and Caroline Rowan (eds), *Feminism, Culture and Politics*, Lawrence and Wishart, London, pp. 76–7.
30. Ibid., pp. 63–6.
31. Ibid., pp. 69–70.
32. Ibid., p. 76; Jones, Gareth Stedman (1983), *Languages of Class*, CUP, Cambridge, pp. 217–19.
33. Rowan, 'Mothers', p. 82.
34. Phillips, Marion (1918), *The Labour Woman* 'Co-operative House-keeping and Housing Reform', Feb, vol. 5, no. 22, pp. 255–6. See above, Chap. 8, p. 137.
35. Furniss, A. D. Sanderson and Phillips, Marion (1920), *The Working Woman's House*, Swarthmore Press, London, pp. 18–26.
36. Wornum, G. Grey (1931), 'Modern Flats', *RIBA Journal*, 2 May, vol. 38, no. 13, pp. 435–55. See discussion, p. 454.
37. Burnett, John (1980), *A Social History of Housing 1815–1970*, Methuen, London, pp. 138–52.
38. Stamp, Gavin (1981), 'Sources of Traditionalism in British Architecture: the English House 1860–1914', *International Architect*, vol. 1, no. 6 (issue 6), pp. 35–42, see p. 39; Sutcliffe, Anthony (1984), 'Anglo-French Perspectives on the Creation and Experience of the Domestic Environment', *Planning History Bulletin*, vol. 6, no. 1, pp. 18–32, see p. 22.
39. Gaskell, S. Martin (1974), 'A Landscape of Small Houses: the Failure of the Workers' Flat in Lancashire and Yorkshire in the Nineteenth Century', pp. 88–121 in Anthony Sutcliffe (ed.), *Multi-storey Living*, Croom Helm, London, p. 114.
40. Thomas, Keith (1983), *Man and the Natural World*, Allen Lane, London, pp. 243–54; Wiener, Martin J. (1981), *English Culture and the Decline of the Industrial Spirit 1850–1980*, CUP, Cambridge, pp. 46–64.
41 Muthesius, Hermann (1979), *The English House*, Crosby Lockwood Staples, London (first pub. 1904), p. 7.

42. Burnett, *Social History of Housing*, pp. 162–3.
43. Thomas, Percy (1937), 'Presentation to Sir Raymond Unwin of the Royal Gold Medal', *RIBA Journal*, 24 April, vol. 44, no. 12, pp. 581–2, see p. 581.
44. Hardy, Dennis (1979), *Alternative Communities in Nineteenth-century England*, Longman, London, p. 2; see also Armytage, W. H. G. (1961), *Heavens Below*, RKP, London.
45. Hardy, *Alternative Communities*, pp. 9–11; Darley, Gillian (1978), *Villages of Vision*, Granada, St Albans, pp. 122–47.

CHAPTER 11

1. Ramprakash, Deo (ed.), *Social Trends no. 14*, HMSO, London, p. 117.
2. Ibid., pp. 117, 119.
3. Ibid., p. 31.
4. Ibid., p. 31; *Homes for the Future* (1983), Institute of Housing and RIBA, London, pp. 11–12.
5. Ibid., p. 3.
6. Martin, Jean and Roberts, Ceridwen (1984), *Women and Employment: a Lifetime Perspective*, HMSO, London, pp. 11, 191.
7. Ibid., p. 101.
8. Thomas, Graham and Shannon, Christine Zmrockzek (1982), 'Techology and Household Labour: are the Times a-changing?', paper presented at the British Sociological Association Conference, Manchester, 5–8 April, pp. 18–19.
9. Vanek, Joann (1974), *Scientific American*, Nov, vol. 231, no. 5, pp. 116–20, see p. 118; Oakley, Ann (1976), *Housewife*, Penguin, Harmondsworth, pp. 6–7; Thomas and Shannon, 'Technology', p. 17; St John-Brooks, Caroline (1982), 'Must Girls always be Girls?', *New Society*, 1 April, vol. 60, no. 1011, pp. 9–11, see p. 11.
10. Thomas and Shannon, 'Technology', p. 26; Joshi, Heather (1984), 'The New Workers', *Guardian*, 17 Jan, p. 20; Luxton, Meg (1980), *More than a Labour of Love*, Women's Educational Press, Toronto, p. 185.
11. Ramprakash, *Social Trends*, p. 93.
12. Marwick, Arthur (1982), *British Society since 1945*, Penguin, Harmondsworth, p. 118; Segal, Lynne (1983), '"Smash the family?" Recalling the 1960s', pp. 25–64 in Lynne Segal (ed.), *What is to be Done about the Family?*, Penguin, Harmondsworth, see p. 46.
13. Wates, Nick (1980), 'Getting a Place Together', *Vole*, 13 March, vol. 3, no. 6, pp. 9–11, see p. 11.
14. Ibid., pp. 10–11.
15. Wates, Nick and Wolmar, Christian (eds) (1980), *Squatting, The Real Story*, Bay Leaf Books, London, p. 174.
16. Rigby, Andrew (1974), *Communes in Britain*, RKP, London, p. 3; Abrams, Philip and Mcculloch, Andrew (1976), 'Men, Women, and

Communes', pp. 246–75 in Diana Leonard Barker and Sheila Allen (eds), *Sexual Divisions and Society*, Tavistock, London, see p. 248.

17. Rigby, Andrew (1974), *Alternative Realities: a Study of Communes and their Members*, RKP, London, pp. 94, 97, 100, 318.

18. Segal, 'Smash', p. 48; Abrams and Mcculloch, 'Men, Women', p. 250.

19. Abrams and Mcculloch, 'Men, Women', p. 252.

20. Rigby, *Communes*, pp. 142–3.

21. Abrams and Mcculloch, 'Men, Women', pp. 262, 272.

22. Segal, 'Smash', p. 59; Wates, 'Getting a Place', p. 10.

23. On housing single people see, for example: Department of the Environment (1982), *Housing Initiatives for Single People of Working Age*, DOE, London; Grace, Peter W. (1981), 'City Homes for Brummie Singles', *Chartered Quantity Surveyor*, June, vol. 3, no. 11, pp. 359–60.

24. Housing Corporation (1984), *Design and Contract Criteria for Fair Rent Projects*, HC, London, ref 1.1.1, pp. 1, 10–11.

25. Correspondence with all regions of the Housing Corporation, and in particular West Midlands, 5 Dec 1983; North West, 20 Dec 1983.

26. Correspondence with HC, West Region, 29 Dec 1983 and 16 Jan 1984.

27. Sedgwick, Carey (1983), 'Observatory', *The Observer*, 28 August, p. 23; private communication with Keith Lodge, 9 May 1983.

28. Correspondence with the Building Societies Association, 22 Nov 1983.

29. Telephone conversation and private communication with Neville Fay, 24 Jan 1984 and 29 March 1984.

30. 'Gingerbread Houses' (1981), *Architects' Journal*, 23 Sept, vol. 174, no. 38, pp. 588–91, see p. 589.

31. Ibid.

32. 'Bridge over Troubled Water' (1972), *Architects' Journal*, 27 Sept, vol. 156, no. 39, pp. 680–3.

33. Information on Nina West Homes from telephone conversation with Nina West, 25 Jan 1984. See also Collins, Wendy, Friedman, Ellen and Pivot, Agnes (1978), *Women, The Directory of Social Change*, Wildwood House, London, pp. 59–60.

34. Information on Hummingbird Housing Association from interview with Mrs Stella Goldman, 5 June 1984, London. See also Bourne, Richard (1982), 'Hummingbird Brainchild', *New Society*, 22 July, vol. 61, no. 1027, p. 145.

35. Arnold, Denise and McFarlane, Barbara (1979), 'Women's Right to House', *Slate*, no. 13, pp. 17–18, see p. 17.

36. Ibid., pp. 17–18.

37. Greater London Council (1983), *Draft Alterations to the Greater London Development Plan*, GLC, London, paras 6.25, 6.40.

38. Ibid., para 6.40; Rowbotham, Sheila (1984), 'Sharing the Caring', *New Statesman*, 13 Jan, vol. 107, no. 2756, pp. 8–10, see p. 10.

39. Segal, Lynne (1983), 'Lessons out of Feminism', *New Statesman*, 26 August, vol. 106, no. 2736, pp. 12–13, see p. 13.

40. Rowbotham, 'Sharing the Caring', p. 10.

41. Newham Docklands Forum and GLC Popular Planning Unit (1983),

The People's Plan for the Royal Docks, Newham Docklands Forum and GLC Popular Planning Unit, London, p. 13.

42. Carmichael, Kay (1982), 'Saints and Sinners', *New Society*, 11 March, vol. 59, no. 1008, p. 395.

43. Hayden, Dolores (1981), 'What would a Non-sexist City be Like? Speculations on Housing, Urban Design, and Human Work', pp. 167–84 in Catherine R. Stimpson, Elsa Dixler, Martha J. Nelson and Kathryn B. Yatrakis (eds), *Women and the American City*, University of Chicago Press, Chicago, see pp. 175–6.

44. Mackay, David (1977), *Multiple Family Housing*, Thames and Hudson, London, pp. 130–3, see p. 130; see also Merryweather, Nigel and Rayner, Steve (1973), 'Danish Collective Housing', *Architectural Design*, Nov, vol. 43, no. 11, pp. 692–4.

45. See *Deutsche Bauzeitung* (1982), April, vol. 116, no. 4, articles as follows: 'Wohngenossenschaft, "Im Spitz"', pp. 16–21; 'Arbeitersiedlung in Windisch', pp. 22–5; 'Wohnhaus in München-Perlach', pp. 26–9.

46. Warner, Sam Bass Jr (1979), 'The Public Invasion of Private Space and the Private Engrossment of Public Space', pp. 171–7 in Swedish Council for Building Research, *Growth and Transformation of the Modern City*, SCBR, Stockholm, see p. 176.

47. RIBA/PSI (1978), *Women in the Architectural Profession*, RIBA/PSI, London, p. 3; Dwyer, Julia (1984), 'Feminism versus Professionalism', *WEB Quarterly*, Spring no. 1, pp. 5–7, see p. 7; Kellner, Peter (1984), 'Tinker, Tailor, Soldier, Sailor . . . but What if you're a Woman?', *New Statesman*, 27 April, vol. 107, no. 2771, p. 7.

48. New Architecture Movement (1977/1978), *NAM Handbook 1978/1979*, NAM Liaison Group, London.

49. *Slate* (1978), 'Feminism and Architecture', no. 9, p. 18.

50. Boys, Jos (1984), 'Is there a Feminist Analysis of Architecture?', *Built Environment*, vol. 10, no. 1, pp. 25–34, see p. 32.

51. Kjaer, Bodil (1982), 'A Woman's Place', *Architects' Journal*, 15 Sept, vol. 176, no. 37, pp. 86–7.

52. Dwyer, 'Feminism', p. 7.

53. Wates, Nick (1982), 'The Liverpool Breakthrough', *Architects' Journal*, 8 Sept, vol. 176, no. 36, pp. 51–8, see p. 55.

54. Ibid., p. 56; see also Lubbock, Jules (1983), 'Housing for Need', *New Statesman*, 14 Oct, vol. 106, no. 2743, pp. 27–8.

55. Manser, Jose (1983), 'Raising the Roof', *Guardian*, 30 Nov, p. 12.

56. *Architects' Journal* (1983), 'Birth of a Movement', 12 Oct, vol. 178, no. 41, p. 56: See also Wates, Nick (1982), 'Shaping a Service in Manchester', *Architects' Journal*, 4 Aug, pp. 26–8.

57. Wates, Nick (1983), 'ACTAC in Action', *Architects' Journal*, 12 Oct, vol. 178, no. 41, pp. 57–63, see p. 63.

58. Rakoff, Robert, M. (1977), 'Ideology in Everyday Life: the Meaning of the House', *Politics and Society*, vol. 7, pp. 85–104, see p. 103.

59. *Scoop*, The newsletter of the Society of Co-operative Dwellings, no. 6,6/78, p. 16, quoted in Brion, Marion and Tinker, Anthea (1980), *Women in Housing*, Housing Centre Trust, London, p. 8.

60. Forsyth, James Codrington and Andersson, Sten (1983), 'Build for Change, Build for People', *Open House*, vol. 8, no. 1, pp. 26–31, see p. 27.
61. Habraken, N. J. (1972), *Supports*, Architectural Press, London.
62. Ravetz, Alison and Low, Jim (1980), 'PSSHAK 18 Months on', *Architects' Journal*, 27 Feb, vol. 171, no. 9, pp. 425–39.
63. Ibid., p. 437.
64. Sudjic, Deyan (1979), 'Freeing Tenants inside their Homes', *New Society*, 3 May, vol. 48, no. 865, pp. 263–4, see p. 264. See also *Architects' Journal* (1978), 'Brockley Park Adaptable Row Housing, Lewisham, London', 19 July, vol. 168, no. 29, pp. 113–24.
65. Forsyth and Andersson, 'Build for Change', pp. 30–1.
66. White, David (1983), 'DIY Homes', *New Society*, 29 Sept, vol. 65, no. 1089, p. 496; Dineen, Michael (1982), 'Build it Yourself Catches on Fast', *Observer*, 14 Nov, p. 3.
67. *Architects' Journal* (1980), 'Do-it-yourself Vernacular', 17 Dec, vol. 172, no. 51, pp. 1185–205.
68. Ellis, Charlotte (1984), 'Self-build Selection', *Architects' Journal*, 25 Jan, vol. 179, no. 4, pp. 36–9.
69. Dineen, 'Build it Yourself', p. 3.
70. Beer, Anne R. (1982), 'The External Environment of Housing Areas', *Built Environment*, vol. 8, no. 1, pp. 25–9, see p. 26: Jones, Glyn (1983), 'Skeleton in a Top Architect's Closet', *New Scientist*, 30 June, vol. 98, no. 1364, p. 946; *Time Out* (1981), 'What Award-winning Houses are Like to Live in', 16 Jan – 22 Jan, no. 561, p. 6.
71. Hillier, Bill, Hanson, Julienne, Peponis, John, Hudson, John and Burdett, Richard (1983), 'Space Syntax', *Architects' Journal*, 30 Nov, vol. 178, no. 48, pp. 47–63, see p. 49.
72. Girouard, Mark (1973), 'The Outside Story', *Times Literary Supplement*, 23 Feb, no. 3703, pp. 201–2, see p. 202.
73. Rapoport, Amos (1982), *The Meaning of the Built Environment*, Sage, Beverly Hills, California, p. 22.
74. Stamp, Gavin (1981), 'Sources of Traditionalism in British Architecture: the English House 1860–1914', *International Architect*, vol. 1, no. 6 (issue 6), pp. 35–42, see p. 42.
75. Darley, Gillian and Davey, Peter (1983), 'Sense and Sensibility', *Architectural Review*, Sept, vol. 174, no. 1039, pp. 23–5.
76. Gradidge, Roderick (1984), 'Back to Firm Foundations', *The Times*, 30 March, p. 10.
77. Warman, Christopher (1984), 'Homes away from Home in an Ideal Setting', *The Times*, 7 March, p. 3.
78. Hayden, 'What Would', pp. 178–80; Rock, Cynthia, Torre, Susana and Wright, Gwendolyn (1980), 'The Appropriation of the House: Changes in House Design and Concepts of Domesticity', pp. 83–100 in Gerda R. Wekerle, Rebecca Petersen and David Morley (eds), *New Space for Women*, Westview Press, Boulder, Colorado, pp. 95–7.
79. Forsyth, James Codrington and Andersson, Sten (1982), 'Build for People, a Question of Architectural Ideas', *Open House*, vol. 7, no. 4, pp. 23–31, see p. 26; see also Schmertz, Mildred F. (1981), 'Housing

and Community Design for Changing Family Needs', pp. 195–210 in Suzanne Keller (ed.), *Building for Women*, Lexington Books, Lexington, Mass., p. 196.

80. Pahl, R. E. (1983), 'Concepts in Context: Pursuing the Urban of "Urban" Sociology', pp. 371–82 in Derek Fraser and Anthony Sutcliffe (eds), *The Pursuit of Urban History*, Edward Arnold, London, pp. 377–8.
81. Ramprakash, *Social Trends*, p. 186.
82. Huws, Ursula (1984), 'The New Home Workers', *New Society*, 22 March, vol. 67, no. 1113, pp. 454–5, see p. 455.
83. Jordan, Bill (1984), 'The Social Wage: a Right for All', *New Society*, 26 April, vol. 68, no. 1118, pp. 143–4.

Index